Island Voices

ISLAND VOICES

Stories from the West Indies

Selected and Introduced by

ANDREW SALKEY

LIVERIGHT

NEW YORK

SBN 87140-504-0 Clothbound
SBN 87140-024-3 Paperbound
Library of Congress Catalog Card Number 73-114386

Published in the United States of America
by Liveright Publishing Corporation, 1970

Originally published as Stories from the Caribbean
© Elek Books Limited 1965, London, England

Manufactured in the United States of America

To

Eliot, Jason

and

Pat

" . . . islands can only exist
If we have loved in them."

from *Islands* by Derek Walcott

CONTENTS

		Page
Acknowledgments		9
Introduction		11
VILLAGE TRAGEDY	John Hearne (*Jamaica.*)	15
THE LOST COUNTRY	John Hearne	27
MY AUNT GOLD TEETH	V. S. Naipaul (*Trinidad*)	40
THE RAFFLE	V. S. Naipaul	48
A CHRISTMAS STORY	V. S. Naipaul	52
MAN, IN ENGLAND, YOU'VE JUST GOT TO LOVE ANIMALS	Samuel Selvon (*Trinidad*)	70
WHEN GREEK MEETS GREEK	Samuel Selvon	75
GUSSY AND THE BOSS	Samuel Selvon	78
CANE IS BITTER	Samuel Selvon	84
A FREE COUNTRY	R. O. Robinson (*Jamaica*)	95
A SHIRT APIECE	R. O. Robinson	110
SMALL ISLAN' COMPLEX	Donald Hinds (*Jamaica*)	117
BUSMAN'S BLUES	Donald Hinds	123
ANY LAWFUL IMPEDIMENT	Donald Hinds	129
THE VERY FUNNY MAN: A TALE IN TWO MOODS	H. Orlando Patterson (*Jamaica*)	133
ONE FOR A PENNY	H. Orlando Patterson	139
THE VALLEY OF COCOA	Michael Anthony (*Trinidad*)	146
PITA OF THE DEEP SEA	Michael Anthony	152

		Page
TRIUMPH	C. L. R. James (*Trinidad*)	158
LA DIVINA PASTORA	C. L. R. James	174
BIRDS OF A FEATHER	George Lamming (*Barbados*)	178
HUNTERS AND HUNTED	Jan Carew (*British Guiana*)	189
THE STRAGGLERS	Claude Thompson (*Jamaica*)	200
THE HOUSE OF MANY DOORS	Claude Thompson	203
MISS CLARKE IS DYING	Edgar Mittelholzer (*British Guiana*)	211
A LONG LONG PAUSE	Denis Williams (*British Guiana*)	218
THE WINTERING OF MR. KOLAWOLE	O. R. Dathorne (*British Guiana*)	223
THE BLACK ANGEL	Edward Braithwaite (*Barbados*)	227
THE SILK-COTTON TREE	A. N. Forde (*Barbados*)	240
SET DOWN THIS	Cecil Gray (*Trinidad*)	246
Biographical Notes		255

ACKNOWLEDGMENTS

Acknowledgments and thanks are due to the authors for permission to publish their stories in this anthology.

Grateful acknowledgment is also made to the following for permitting stories to be reprinted: the publishers of 'My Aunt Gold Teeth' by V. S. Naipaul, and the editors of *Encounter* for 'A Christmas Story' by V. S. Naipaul; the publishers of *The Evening Standard* for 'Man, in England, you've just got to love animals' by Samuel Selvon, MESSRS. MACGIBBON & KEE LTD. and MESSRS. A. M. HEATH LTD. for 'When Greek meets Greek' by Samuel Selvon, and the editors of *Bim* for 'Gussy and the Boss' and 'Cane is Bitter' by Samuel Selvon; the B.B.C. for 'Small Islan' Complex', 'Busman's Blues', and 'Any Lawful Impediment' by Donald Hinds; the editors of *The New Left Review* for 'The Very Funny Man: A Tale in Two Moods' by H. Orlando Patterson; the editors of *Bim* for 'The Valley of Cocoa' and 'Pita of the Deep Sea' by Michael Anthony; JONATHAN CAPE LTD. and the editors of *Best Stories of 1928* for 'La Divina Pastora' by C. L. R. James; the publishers of *Suspense* for 'Village Tragedy' by John Hearne; the publishers of *The Atlantic Monthly* (U.S.A.) for 'The Lost Country' by John Hearne; and we also thank Mr. Hearne's agents, MESSRS. DAVID HIGHAM ASSOCIATES LTD.; the editors of *Bim* for 'Birds of a Feather' by George Lamming; the editors of *Perspective* (U.S.A.) for 'Hunters and Hunted' by Jan Carew; the editors of *Bim* for 'Miss Clarke is Dying' by Edgar Mittelholzer; the NIGERIAN BROAD-CASTING CORPORATION for 'The Wintering of Mr. Kolawole' by O. R. Dathorne; and the editors of *Bim* for 'The Black Angel' by Edward Braithwaite, 'The Silk-cotton Tree' by A. N. Forde, and 'Set Down This' by Cecil Gray.

INTRODUCTION

There is nothing so risky as trying to define West Indian writing as simply the corporate literary output of a number of regional writers. Moreover, to make the point that these writers from the islands and territories of the West Indies, with no literary tradition, little or no publishing facilities, and no loyal book-buying public, have none the less in the face of all this produced their 'corporate' work in fifteen years is beguiling to say the least.

Yet, the temptation remains: West Indian writing has sprung from regional sources, and it has attracted attention in a short period of time, with very nearly two hundred books from not many more than twenty-five writers.

Many West Indians, being the indefatigable emigrants we were forced to become ever since the economics of British imperialism gave us the taste for wandering, now find it easy to think of the West Indian writer as a 'natural exile', living in America and writing about Jamaica and Harlem as the Jamaican poet and novelist, Claude McKay, did, or living in England and writing equally convincingly about Trinidad and London as V. S. Naipaul has, or for that matter, remaining in Jamaica and setting a novel in Kenya as the distinguished Jamaican novelist, V. S. Reid, risked successfully.

In fact, so far, much of the enthusiasm, energy and direction of West Indian writing has found edge and thrust outside the West Indies, and has continued to develop, perhaps not so dynamically but certainly with great expectations. I think, too, that it is well to remember that most of the West Indian writers, who were first published while they were living abroad and who have since decided to make a name for themselves there, do remain away from home and hope that their facility for 'total recall' will not desert them; and the few, who doubt this 'facility', usually return to the West Indies but are soon off again, to England where they know the literary grass is greener, even to Paris to satisfy their curiosity for *la vie de l'ecrivain expatrie*, and to Africa to take up a university post and to write.

Shortly before he died in 1955, Roger Mais, the Jamaican novelist, described the West Indian writer as ". . . essentially a travelling, 'gambling' man with a manuscript or two in his bag and a big dream of contributing to contemporary English literature."

Few of the 'gamblers' have won through. It is my opinion that those who have are the Trinidadian author and political analyst, C. L. R. James, with his two brilliant works of non-fiction, *Black Jacobins* and *Beyond a Boundary*, V. S. Naipaul also fromTrinidad with his novel, *A House for Mr. Biswas*, and George Lamming from Barbados with his remarkable autobiographical novel, *In the Castle of My Skin;* and so have Samuel Selvon from Trinidad with his first book, *A Brighter Sun*, Edgar Mittelholzer from British Guiana with *A Morning at the Office*, and Wilson Harris also from British Guiana with his 'Guiana Quartet', a series of four short novels.

It is also my opinion that V. S. Reid's *New Day* is a very important historical novel, perhaps more as a contribution to Jamaican and West Indian writing than to contemporary English literature. But this is not to say that it is merely a 'regional' work. Clearly, it is the literary diamond that has cut the farthest along the path towards Jamaica's awareness of a national identity.

Two other outstandingly impressive contributions to West Indian writing are *Voices Under the Window* by the Jamaican novelist, John Hearne, and *Black Midas* by Jan Carew from British Guiana.

Naturally, West Indian writing is still gathering momentum. It is not yet an easily recognizable 'way of writing'. At the moment, it is vitally shapeless. And its 'shapelessness' is spreading and taking in, all at once, not only the gold but also some of the dross of the established literatures of England and America.

How West Indian is West Indian writing? you may well ask. But is it not really another way of asking *How West Indian is the West Indies?*

Both these questions are very nearly impossible to answer. And, alas, the break-up of the Federation of the West Indies, which might have provided a useful clue had it come off, makes any intelligent, positive reply sadly unforthcoming.

But surely, some sort of makeshift response is possible. And I think that, at the centre of the speculation, it would be unwise to ignore the dominating influences of Western civilization, the long-term effects of British cultural and educational standards, the compelling attractiveness of English literature, and the use of English as *the* language in the West Indies.

Of course, this cosy accounting for the phenomenon of West Indian writing leads inevitably to the question: *How English is West Indian writing?* and on to the answer, which is undeniably: *As English as the West Indian usage of the common language will allow.* Such an answer is not so embarrassing as it seems; for the West Indian writer is well aware that he may use the language of the English writer in order to discover the quintessence of his 'West Indianness', the bed-rock of his society, its dreams, and so go on to recognize the meaning and importance of the expression *West Indian writing*.

C. L. R. James said, not so long ago, that ". . . the mass of the West Indian people are not seeking a national identity, they are expressing one."

Indeed, in the West Indies, a general questioning is going on, a search for a 'newness', a *'cool* upheaval of the spirit' as Ellsworth Keane, the poet and jazz musician from St. Vincent, has described it. And I do believe that the West Indian writers are the very root and rhythm of it.

I think that some of the stories in this anthology point to the new West Indian trend towards self-criticism and self-discovery. Don't be misled by the humour and light-heartedness of most of the contributions, particularly when reading the three short pieces by Donald Hinds, "A Free Country" and "A Shirt Apiece" by R. O. Robinson, "Gussy and the Boss" and "Cane is Bitter" by Samuel Selvon, and "The Wintering of Mr. Kolawole" by O. R. Dathorne. And above all, beware V. S. Naipaul's three stories.

Self-critical laughter is certainly one of the key directions of West Indian writing. And for me, it is, perhaps, the West Indian writer's most effective path-finding instrument.

ANDREW SALKEY

John Hearne (*Jamaica.*)

Village Tragedy

THE old boar slashed Ambrose Beckett across the abdomen. It was done between one brazen squeal and another, while Ambrose Beckett still turned on the wet clay of the path and before the echo of his last, useless shot wandered among the big peaks around the valley.

The men with whom Ambrose Beckett had been hunting turned and saw the ridge-backed, red-bristled beast vanish like a cannon ball into a long stretch of fairy bamboo, which can cling like cobwebs and cut like broken glass if you are a man and not a pig who has been hunted for five years, has killed fourteen dogs, and just killed its first man.

Before the men reached him, they saw Ambrose Beckett's wildly unbelieving face, like grey stone, and the dark arches of his spurting blood shining on the wet dull clay under the tree ferns. Then he had fallen like a wet towel among the leaf mould, clutching the clay in his slack fingers, with one distant, protesting scream sounding from the back of his throat.

They bandaged him after stuffing, inexpertly, bits of their shirts and handkerchiefs into his wounds. Nothing they did, however, could stop a fast, thick welling of blood from where he had been torn. And no comfort could stop his strangled, far away screaming. They made some sort of a stretcher from two green branches and a blanket. They covered him with another blanket and began to carry him across the mountains to the village.

The trail was very narrow and the floor of the rain forest was steep and wet. Each time they slipped and recovered balance, they jolted the stretcher. After a while they forced themselves not to shudder as Ambrose Beckett screamed. Soon he began to moan and the slow, dirty blood began to trickle from his mouth, and they knew that he would never reach the village alive.

When they realized this, they decided to send Mass Ken's half-witted son, Joseph, ahead of them to tell the doctor and the parson.

Joseph was the biggest idiot any man could remember being born in the village. He inhabited a world of half-articulate fantasy and ridiculous confusion. He was strong enough to kill a man with his hands, and he wept if a child frowned at him.

In Cayuna the children do not throw stones at their naturals, but they tease them, and Joseph, who loved to wait outside the school and watch the children going home, would be seen crouched between the roots of the cotton tree, weeping disconsolately because the boys had scowled as they passed and said: "Joseph! What you doin' here, man?"

Joseph could learn nothing, and remembered little from one minute to the next unless you gave him a great blow across the head when giving him the simplest instructions. But he was marvellous on the mountains.

Now, with Ambrose Beckett dying on the blanket, the men standing around and thin bands of mist drifting past them to fill the damp, darkening spaces among the trees, they gave Joseph his instructions.

"Doctor!" said Mass Ken, and cuffed Joseph across his slab of a head. "Doctor! You hear?" He hit him again. "Tell doctor an' tell parson dem mus' come quick. Tell dem come quick, you hear! Tell dem Mass Ambrose sick bad. Sick! Sick! You hear!"

Joseph's big, stone head rocked again under a blow, and his odd, disorganized face closed its askew planes into a grin of pure understanding. He went off among the huge trees and thick wet bush and into the mist. When he had gone ten steps they could no longer hear him.

It was twelve miles and four thousand feet down to the village, and Joseph did it in four hours. At ten o'clock that night he started to bang happily on the door of the Manse, and kept it up until the Reverend Mackinnon put his head out of the window. When he heard the shutter slamming against the wall, Joseph ran to the middle of the lawn, capering and shouting.

"What?" called the Reverend Mackinnon. "What is it, Joseph?" He could see nothing but a vague, starlit blur bounding up and down the lawn, but he recognized the manner and the voice.

Joseph jumped higher and shouted again, his voice tight and brazen with self-importance. Finally the Reverend Mackinnon came downstairs and, when Joseph ran to the door, cuffed the boy until he became calm. Then he got the story.

"Doctor!" he said, turning Joseph around and giving him a push.

Leaving the parson, Joseph ran across the damp Bahama grass of the lawn to where he could see the deep yellow of a light in one window of a big house along the road. Doctor Rushie was still up: it was one of the nights that he got drunk, as he did, regularly and alone, twenty times a month.

"Good God!" said Rushie. "How far up did it happen, Joseph?"

Joseph gestured. Distance, except in terms of feet and yards, was not of much importance in his life.

"Have you told Parson?" the doctor asked. He was drunk, but not much. Had the news come a little later, he would have been very drunk and quite incapable. Now he was only a little drunk and knew what to do. He went to the window and bawled for his servant until the man called back sleepily from the outhouse.

"Saddle the mule," Doctor Rushie shouted, "and put on your clothes. Bring a lantern. Hurry up!"

In about five minutes the doctor was riding out of the village, with his manservant trotting ahead, the circle of light from the lantern sliding quickly from side to side across the path. There was a stand of golden cup trees along this stretch of the bridle-path and the dropped fruit broke wetly under the hooves of the mule and a thick, sugary scent came up on the cold air, cutting through the hot, oily smell of the lantern.

They overtook the Reverend Mackinnon, who had no manservant and who was riding his stubby grey gelding alone in the dark.

By the lantern light Doctor Rushie could see the parson's very pale, long face and his lank grey hair fallen across his forehead and full of burrs from the long grass of the steep bank beside the narrow path.

"You've heard?" the Doctor said. It was not really a question and they were riding on in the darkness behind the bob and sway of the lantern while the parson was nodding his head . . .

Back on the road, Joseph sat on a big stone outside the doctor's house. Nobody had told him what to do after delivering his messages and he felt confused and restless.

The doctor's house, and the Reverend Mackinnon's were up the road from the village. Neither man had thought to inform the people down there as to what had happened up on the mountain. Soon Joseph rose from the stone, ran down the road to the village, and began to race about the street from side to side, talking loudly to himself. It was not long before he had awakened every house within sound of his voice.

"Joseph, you bad boy," screeched Mr. Tennant, the schoolmaster, "what are you doing here, at this hour?"

Joseph flapped a big, dirty hand at him excitedly.

"Boy, if I bring a switch out to you . . ." Mr. Tennant said.

Joseph shot away down the street like a dog, but he continued to talk very loudly.

Mr. Tennant, with a tight, moist smile on his plump lips and carrying a long supple-jack cane, came from his house. Joseph bolted for the shoemaker's doorway. Only Elvira, Joseph's smallest sister, could get as much sense from his clogged speech as quickly as Mass Emmanuel, the shoemaker.

"Joseph," said Mass Emmanuel, as the natural found refuge in his doorway, "why you not sleepin', eh? What a bad bwoy. I've a good mind to let teacher flog you."

He put an arm across the boy's trembling shoulders.

Joseph told him about Ambrose Beckett, imitating with great vividness the terrible, ripping twitch of the boar's head; writhing enthusiastically on the ground to show what it had been like with Mass Ambrose. Mass Emmanuel translated as the people began to come from the houses. Then they all looked up to the hill at the other end of the village, to where Ambrose Beckett's house stood. They began to move towards the house.

"Lawd King!" said Miss Vera Brownford. "Fancy! Mass Ambrose! A fine man like dat. Poor Miss Louise!"

She was the centre of the older women of the village as they went up the hill to the house where Ambrose and Louise Beckett had lived for thirty years. Vera Brownford was ninety-eight, or maybe a hundred. Perhaps she was much more. Her first grandchild had been born before anyone now alive in the village, and only a few people could still remember her, dimly, in early middle age. Her intimate participation in every birth, death and wedding was, for the village, an obligatory ritual. She had lived so long and so completely that she had grown to want nothing except freedom from pain. At times the shadow-line between life and death was not very distinct to her expectation, her desire or her feeling, but she understood the terror and confusion that the crossing of the line brought to those younger than herself. And, understanding this, she gave comfort as a tree gives shade, or as a stream gives water to those who fetch it, with a vast, experienced impartiality. It was her occupation.

Among the younger men and women, Joseph was still the centre of interest as they went up the hill. His mime performance of Ambrose Beckett and the boar had begun to acquire the finish of art. In all his life he had never experienced such respect for his ability and knowledge. He was almost gone off his poor mind with happiness.

"Joseph," said Mass Emmanuel suddenly, coming back down the path which was leading them to Louise Beckett's darkened house. "Joseph, I forgot. We gwine to need ice to pack Mass Ambrose. Tell dem to give you ice. Ice, you hear. At Irish Corner."

He gave a five-shilling note to the boy and hugged the huge, smoothly sloping shoulders and smiled at him. Only for two people, Elvira and Emmanuel, would Joseph remember anything unaccompanied by a blow.

Joseph turned and raced down the path. He seemed to weave through the murmurous crowd like a twist of smoke. Before he was out of earshot they heard him singing his own chant, which was a mingle of all the hymns and songs he had ever listened to. He was always adding to it and, though it had no more conscious structure than a roll of thunder, it had a remarkable, pervasive quality, coming to you from a dozen points at once.

The Reverend Mackinnon and Doctor Rushie met the party of return-ing hunters about five miles from the village. They heard the dogs barking and saw the lantern lights jump among the pines on the saddle between the peaks ahead of them. This was on the side of a great valley, on a trail worn through a stretch of ginger-lilies. The night was very cold and mist was coming down from the sharp, fuzzy peaks and piling up into the valley below, and the air was full of a thin, spicy tang as the hooves crushed the long ginger-lily leaves against the stones.

"Ho-yah!" shouted the doctor's manservant when they saw the lights. "Is dat you, Mass Ken? Is dat you, Mass Huntley?"

"Yes." The answer rolled back slowly, thin and lost in the air of the huge valley. "Who dere?"

"Doctor. Doctor and Parson. How Mass Ambrose stay?"

"Him dead!"

He was dead, right enough, when the two parties met. In the glare from the lanterns his skin was the colour of dough and earth mixed, quite drained of blood. The blankets between which he lay were dark and odorous with blood. His mouth had half opened and one eye had closed tightly, twisting his face and leaving the other eye open. It gave him an unbelievably knowing and cynical leer.

"Well I'll be damned," Doctor Rushie said. And then, seeing Mackinnon's face: "Beg your pardon, but look at that."

"Look at what?" the Reverend Mackinnon said stiffly. He had never liked Rushie much, and now he did not like him at all.

"His face. How many dead men have you seen?"

"I don't know. As many as you, I suppose."

"Exactly," Doctor Rushie said. "Probably more. But how many have you seen die with one eye closed? You know it's generally both eyes wide open. Sometimes both closed, but not often. Damned odd, eh?"

"I hardly think it's important, Doctor," the Reverend Mackinnon said. His long, ugly Scots face was tightly ridged with disgust. Only the presence of the villagers kept him polite.

"No," the doctor said, "it's not important. I just noticed it. Well— no point in hanging around here. Let's get him home."

Going down the track, the doctor and the parson rode behind.

"What a dreadful thing to have happened, eh, Doctor?" said the Reverend Mackinnon. "I can hardly believe it."

He always felt guilty about not liking Doctor Rushie; and he constantly asked himself wherein he, as a minister, had failed to contact the drunken, savagely isolated creature who rode behind him.

"I can believe it," the doctor said. "Do you know how many ways the world has of killing you? I was adding up the other night. It comes to thousands. Simply thousands."

The Reverend Mackinnon could find no answer to this. There were answers, he knew, but none that he cared to risk with the lonely, brutal man who, more or less, cared for the health of their village and a score of other villages in the district.

He was not even a very good doctor, the Reverend Mackinnon thought, and felt a cold flush of shame because the thought gave him satisfaction.

"He was such a strong, vital man, too," the Reverend Mackinnon said a little later. He was unable to bear the night with the mist blowing damp and cold across his face, piling up in the valley so that it seemed they were riding across the air, and the bobbing lanterns lighting up the silent men as they scrambled awkwardly with the stretcher on the narrow track.

"He was a strong man," the doctor said dryly.

"The other day I saw him clearing that land of his up by the river, with his two sons. He was doing twice as much as they," Mackinnon continued.

"Oh, he was a good farmer all right," the doctor agreed, in the same dry tone. "He ought to have been, with what he acquired these last few years. He knew what he wanted, all right."

"He was an example to his community," Mackinnon said with solemn emphasis. "God-fearing and responsible. An example. If only he'd had an education. They would have made him a Justice of the Peace. He was an example. A Christian example."

"Well, maybe his sons will become examples, too," the doctor told him. "With such a daddy, I don't see how they can help it."

"The boys," said the Reverend Mackinnon, "have fallen far from the stem. Thomas has his father's sense of duty, but he is weak. And Sidney cares only for himself, his pleasures and his land. He caused Ambrose Beckett a great deal of worry."

"Did he?" said the doctor politely.

"Oh, yes. He was a constant source of concern. Which one of them do you think will get the holding, eh? Thomas or Sidney?"

"Couldn't say," the doctor replied. "I was only Beckett's doctor, not his lawyer. Probably they'll have equal shares. He had enough, God knows, for these parts."

The Reverend Mackinnon frowned and shifted uneasily in the saddle. "*Oh, God*," he said to himself, "*make Thomas get the holding*." He looked sombrely over the nodding head of his beast at the vague blur of the stretcher. The men were moving fast now, because Ambrose Beckett was dead and they could heave the stretcher about quickly.

Twenty years before this, Ambrose Beckett had rented land from the church. It was the first move in a programme which had made him the largest peasant farmer in the parish. It had been good land and he had paid a good rent. But since the war, when everything had gone up, the rent had fallen to a fraction of the land's value, and the Reverend Mackinnon had been looking for some way to increase it. He was essentially a timid man, who only felt courage and confidence on Sundays when he stood unassailable in the pulpit, with God and the Hosts at his back.

His method of attack in the matter of the rent had been to mount a series of hints. Veiled and off-hand at first, they had evolved after three years into frequent references to the difficulties and embarrassments of a priest in the modern world. Pride and timidity had kept him from stating an open claim—these and the reasonable certainty that Ambrose Beckett would, at first, refuse to pay more; would refuse with all the plausibility and righteousness of a man who valued an acre, really, more than he regarded a wife, and who knew his own usefulness as a parishioner. "*I am not covetous,*" the Reverend Mackinnon told himself in the darkness. "*I do not want it for myself. But the Manse is falling to bits, and if I send Jean home next year, she will need clothes. Perhaps two sets within the year? girls grow so fast at her age.*"

Given time, he knew, he could have persuaded Ambrose Beckett. It would have been painful, but it would have come. Now he would have to begin again with the sons. If Thomas were the heir, it would be easy. He was a gentle, almost girlish lad, very devout and proud of his family's influence in the church. But Sidney would be difficult. Difficult and slow. And arrogant.

Sidney always treated the Reverend Mackinnon with a casual politeness more infuriating, more unreachable than hostility, with a bland indifference which only on occasion became genially ferocious.

The afternoon, for instance, when Mackinnon had caught him making love to a little East Indian girl under a huge rock by the river. The lad had raised his head from beside the girl's blind, contorted face and stared at the parson with cool, amused malice. And the next day, Sunday, while Mackinnon was preaching a sermon on the sin of fornication, he had looked down from the pulpit to the front pew where Ambrose Beckett sat in a hot, high-buttoned black suit among his family, and had seen such a sparkle of conspiratorial intimacy in Sidney's eyes that he had floundered in his speech.

While they were bringing the body of Ambrose Beckett down from the mountain, Joseph had reached the market town of Irish Corner. He knocked on the zinc fence around the shop until the Chinese keeper came down and a small crowd had gathered. Then he told the story of Ambrose and the boar again, giving a really practised and gigantic performance. He had great difficulty in making them understand what had happened, or what he wanted, but they finally got it. Then they cut a great block of ice, wrapped it in a crocus bag, hoisted it on to Joseph's head, and set him on the road back to the village.

He had hardly stopped running since the late afternoon and he streamed with sweat as if he had been put under a hose; but he was not tired and he was crazy with excitement. He had never played such a central part in anything, and perhaps he sensed obscurely that he never would again.

Suddenly he slowed his long, effortless jog-trot up the steep road. He stopped. The ice in its wrapping of crocus bag was cool and wet between his hands and on his huge, idol's head. From his great heaving lungs there burst an ecstatic grunt. Ice . . . Ice . . . If he got back quickly, they would chip a white, glittering, jagged lump for him; a piece around which he could curl his tongue; a bit to hold above his bent-back head and opened mouth, so that the cold, unimaginable drops would hit the back of his throat; a bit with edges he could rub across tightly shut eyelids and then feel the cold water drying on his skin!

He danced with happiness, balancing the huge block as if it were a hat. As far up as his village, ice was still a luxury; except for the Doctor, who had a machine which made ice-cubes. . . .

The people at Ambrose Beckett's house heard the dogs as the men came up the hill. Louise Beckett rushed from the house and down the path towards the light from the lanterns. When she saw the stretcher she began to cry and moan wildly, covering her face and clutching her body.

Her two sons came close to her. "Mother . . . Mother," Thomas said. He embraced her tightly and began to cry, too. Sidney put his arm around her shoulders and said softly: "I will take care of you, Mother. I will take care of you. Don't cry. Don't cry."

Inside the house the body was laid out on the kitchen table. The table was too short and the feet hung over the edge. Doctor Rushie shut the people out and, by the light of four lamps, sewed up the hideous openings in Ambrose Beckett's body.

Once during this operation he spoke, as if to the corpse. "You poor devil," he said, "this must have hurt like blazes. But the other thing would have hurt you more and it would have lasted longer."

Outside, in the tiny, stiffly furnished drawing-room, Vera Brownford sat on the old-fashioned horsehair sofa. Louise Beckett sat close up beside her, resting her head on that old, indestructible breast which was as thin and hard as a piece of hose-pipe, and yet as hugely comfortable as a warm ocean.

"Cry good, child," Vera Brownford said. "Cry good. If you don't cry, you will get sick. Oh, Lawd, it hard to lose a man. It hard to lose a good man like Ambrose. Cry good, child. It much easier."

The old, dry voice flowed smoothly, uttering banalities that sheer experience gave the weight of poetry. Louise Beckett cried noisily.

The women of the village stood around the sofa; the men gathered near the door and outside, each group around one of the hunters, who told in whispers what it had been like. The children waited on the fringes of each group, some of them looking with wide stares towards the locked kitchen door.

The Reverend Mackinnon hovered between the men and the women. Finally he went across to Louise Beckett.

"Louise," he said, "you must take comfort. Remember your beloved husband is not gone. He only waits for you in our Master's house. He was a good man, Louise. A true Christian man. Take comfort in that, and in the promise of everlasting life. . . ."

Louise Beckett raised her stunned face and looked at him from red eyes. "Thank you, Parson," she whispered, and burrowed her head against Vera Brownford's breast.

Among the men, Huntley was saying in a hard, unbelieving voice: "Jesus, it happen so quick. I tell you, Mass Emmanuel, it happen before we even see it."

"How things happen so, eh?" Emmanuel said. "Truly, it is like the Bible say: 'In the midst of life we are in death.' "

"That is true, Emmanuel," said the Reverend Mackinnon, joining them. "That is very true." He laid a hand on Sidney's shoulder and gave it a little squeeze. "But remember, as Christians we need not fear death if we live so that death finds us prepared for God. We must remember the life God showed us through his only Son and, in our turn, live so that each day we can say to ourselves: 'Today I did God's will.' "

He looked closely at Sidney as he spoke; but the young man's face was closed, sullen with grief, unreadable.

Mr. Tennant, the schoolmaster, cleared his throat. He thought very highly of the Reverend Mackinnon, but he also felt that in the village he should reinforce the parson, providing the practical epilogues to the more refined utterances of the church.

"It is you and Thomas now, Sidney," Mr. Tennant said. "You must act like men. Work the land as diligently as your father. Look after your good mother. . . ."

They heard a hard, heavy grunting outside in the dark, and then Joseph stepped into the room. He was lathered about the lips, with sweat and water from the ice mingled on his face and staining his clothes.

Everyone stopped talking when they saw the ice. Mass Ken, Joseph's father, took the boy by the arm and led him into the room. Four of the men who had hunted that day with Ambrose Beckett followed him. They stripped the clothes and mattress from the springs and spread old newspapers under the bed. They unwrapped the ice from the course, shaggy crocus and one of the men split it into five great lumps with an ice-pick. Then they spread old newspapers on the bare springs and waited awkwardly in the half-dark of the little bedroom where Ambrose Beckett had lain with his wife for thirty years.

Outside, one of the younger men who had been on the hunt laid his hand shyly on Sidney's arm.

"Sidney," he said, "I sorry, you see. If it was me own Papa, I couldn't sorry more. Lawd, Sidney, don't worry. I will help you. You gwine to need anoder man to help you wid dat lan' you an' Mass Ambrose was clearing? What you gwine put in it, bwoy? It is one nice piece of ground."

Tears shone in Sidney's eyes. He was remembering how powerful and comforting his father had looked in the sunlight as they cleared the land by the river. His friend's words were sweet and warm and made him feel comforted again.

"T'ank you, Zack," he said. "T'ank you. Thomas an' me will need a help. Papa did want to put citrus in dat piece. Dat is de crop pay well now, you know. Since de war over, everybody want orange oil again."

Thomas looked suddenly and with disturbance at his brother. "When Papa say we was gwine put citrus in?" he asked. "You know we only talk about it. Las' time we talk, you remember I say we should plant ginger. I like ginger. It safe."

"Everybody plant ginger, Thomas," Sidney said gently and inflexibly. "Papa did always say too much ginger was gwine to kill de smallholders. Time some of us plant somet'ing else."

The door to the kitchen opened and they saw Doctor Rushie framed in the opening, with the lamplight yellow-white behind him. Sidney and Thomas, Mass Ken and Emmanuel went into the kitchen and brought the body out. The Doctor had been very thorough. He had even washed the stains from Ambrose Beckett's body and wrapped it in the sheet from the sons' bed, which stood in the kitchen.

When the body was brought out, some of the women began to wail. Louise Beckett set up a long howling cry and ran across the room.

She held the dead face between her hands. She was twitching like an exhausted animal.

"Mass Ambrose," she cried, "Mass Ambrose!"

The Reverend Mackinnon led them in prayer around the bed after they had packed the body among the ice lumps. Then the people started to go home. All went except Vera Brownford and three of Louise Beckett's closest friends, who stayed to watch the body.

It was now the blackest part of the morning, before the sun began to touch the mountain tops and make the sky glow with pink and green.

The Reverend Mackinnon went home and tiredly unsaddled his stumpy grey gelding. He went up to bed and thought about the gentle, exhausted wife he had buried two years before; and worried about the plump, soundly sleeping daughter a hundred miles away in boarding school.

Doctor Rushie went home, and his manservant led the mule away while the Doctor sat down to finish the bottle he had been drinking when Joseph came. He thought about the wounds in Ambrose Beckett's body and whether if he had got to him right away he could have saved a life. He thought, also, about the sliver from Ambrose Beckett's rectum which he had sent down to Queenshaven for analysis a week ago and which, he was positive, showed the beginnings of malignant cancer. . . .

Lying in the bed they had shared from childhood, Sidney and Thomas clung to each other and sobbed in the painful, tearing manner of grown men. In between grieving for their father they argued as to the wisdom of planting citrus or ginger.

In the room with the body, the women sat and watched. Once Louise Beckett leaned forward and touched the damp sheet wonderingly.

"Mass Ambrose?" she asked softly. "You gawn? You really gawn. . . .?"

In the kitchen of his home, Joseph snuggled into bed beside Elvira, his little sister, and began to cry bitterly. She woke when she heard him crying and asked him what was the matter. He told her how he had run all the way to Irish Corner and back with the ice, and how no one had thought to give him a little piece.

The ingratitude and thoughtlessness of the mourners shocked the little girl profoundly. She wiped the tears from his big, sweaty face and hugged him, rocking him in her thin arms and kissing him with little quick maternal pecks.

Very soon he was fast asleep.

John Hearne

The Lost Country

Afterwards, when he was strong enough to walk, he used to go in the cool glow of first dusk to the river. Seated on a bollard, the boards of the narrow wharf still warm from the day's sun, he would let the huge sweep of brown water flow without hindrance through a mind which seemed to operate, when it did at all, in anguished, undirected spasms. One night he told himself that thought was trying to struggle free from confusion like a broken snake drowning in the swamp, and with the formation of that image he was suddenly well again. He could remember beyond the surging, white waters of the estuary and the dull scrub on the flat bank opposite, as far as Maraca, Overlook, the Narrows and the bleached rocks of Paramuni Rapids where the real forest began. He sat for a long time and restored the lost country slowly to his tattered mind, going up through the vaults and green-black shadows of the forest to the harsh, lemon light and dry-grass smell of the high savannas, where a line of men on the horizon seemed to walk not over the edge of the world but simply on and on into the secret reaches of the enormous sky.

When his wife called tentatively from the shadow of the warehouse at his back, he answered and heard his own voice for the first time in six months. During this time something not himself, something deeper even than the chaos, had spoken the forgotten simplicities of intercourse; but the words, once in space between him and another, had struck no echo.

"Yes?" he called; then strongly: "Yes, Daphne. I'm here. I was just coming."

He swung around on the bollard and watched her white dress become definite as she drew near in the light of the evening. As she came up beside him, he took her hand and kissed the fingers with tranquil and deliberate intimacy.

"I was worried," she said uncertainly. "It was getting so late. Aren't you hungry?"

He looked up at the handsome, solid-featured face in which a timid intuition of happiness had begun to stir cautiously. Then he smiled, and the desolate, careful discipline of the past half-year collapsed and she flung herself on to his lap, put her arm around his neck and cried easily against his shoulder.

"It's all right," he told her. "I'm all right now. It's all over."

"Oh, Harry," she said, "I thought it would never be over. I thought you'd never come back, Harry. Harry, darling."

"Poor girl," he said. "My poor old girl. Don't cry, honey. It's all over now. I was just sitting here, and I began to remember the interior. You know, everything about it, even the smell." He raised her chin and smiled again. "It's only fair, really. It nearly destroyed me, I guess, so it's only fair for it to give something back."

When he put his hand on the front of her dress and stroked it and the brown swell of her breast, she began to smile sensuously, with indulgent approval, and pressed against him until she realized that he was fondling her as a baby would explore a piece of velvet, with the absorbed innocence of pure learning.

But the next day, when he went to see the doctor to whom he owed his life and reason, he learned that it was not really over.

"You can't work in the bush again, Harry," his doctor told him. "If you try to go back, you'll be dead in two years."

"You're not serious," Harry Hamilton answered. "You don't mean that I have to spend the rest of my days on this stinking coast. That's a death sentence, Marie."

"Life sentence," Marie Rau said, and looked at him with wry, helpless compassion. "Listen, Harry. Listen good. What happened to you down on the Catacuma was simply the last of a lot of things. You're overexposed, Harry, don't you understand? Sometime in the last twenty years you walked too far and too fast one day. Maybe it was on a lot of days. Or maybe you got too much sun. Or too much fever. Or one bush ulcer too many. Take your pick. I think it was all of them together, and sunstroke on the Catacuma just meant that you had reached the end of something."

"I don't believe you," Harry Hamilton told her bleakly. "You've cooked this up with Daphne. It's an excuse to keep me from going inside again. She has wanted that for a long time."

"If it makes you feel any better," Marie Rau said, "you can believe that." She smiled at him and tossed her head in gentle mockery, and he grinned back without much amusement but with complete understanding.

"All right," he said. "Forgive and forget. I didn't mean what I said. I was just getting used to it."

"That's what I'm here for," she said, and rested her elbows on the desk, her long, beautiful hands clasped under her chin, and looked steadily at the big, wasted man before her.

She was an East Indian and had been the first woman of her race in the Colony to defy the past by taking a profession. After she had come back, there had been a lonely, sterile time for her during which she had grown the remote, ironic dignity and sadness that had nothing to do with what she really was. Harry Hamilton had been her first patient, twenty years before, after she had been sitting for three months in an empty office beyond the always empty waiting-room. He had come to her to have his hand dressed where a badly held fishing line upriver had torn through to the bone. Hers was the first name-plate he had seen that morning as he walked up from the wharf, and he had come in because he was dizzy and nauseated with the pain of his swollen, infected flesh, but mainly because he had never been able to feel or think in the terms that an East Indian and a woman would be either less or more of a doctor than any other.

He was seventeen then to her twenty-five, in the first month of his Articles as a Surveyor, and beneath the fresh, Scottish colouring she had seen the profound, antique stamp of his Carib mother as, with stoical detachment, he watched her probe the reeking fissure across the palm of his hand. And sensing in the radiant, vulnerable candour of the boy's face something kindred, visionary and inarticulate, she had spoken out of the silent pride in which she had begun to harbour the nearly exhausted remnants of her own expectation and committed strength. Often, since then, she had wondered what would have happened to her in this colony of mediocre ambitions and insipid nostalgias if Harry Hamilton had not come into her life that morning.

Now she said: "What are you thinking, Harry?"

"I was trying to salvage something from the prospect," he answered, and shook his head slowly. "But there's nothing. We've destroyed the meaning of this country on the coast, Marie. You know that? First the

Dutch. Then the English and the Africans. Masters and slaves both. They were united on that. Your people, too, although they came late. Only my mother's people know that you can't take the earth out of time, squeeze it into endless departments of use like—like the rooms in a house, but they don't have the words to tell us. I was beginning to understand, and maybe if I could have had another twenty years I would have found the words to convince you coast people. But not now. Not now."

When he was working again he still went to the river in the late afternoons before dark, to the same wharf and the same bollard, screened from the murmur of the town by the high, tarred wall of the warehouse. The ships came up the river, lifting as the long Atlantic took them over the bar, discharged their cargoes into the pungent caverns of wood near where he sat, and went back downstream, heavy with a return of copra, sugar, bauxite, hides and timber. Harry Hamilton watched them come and go with interest, without regret; he liked to see the stark light of the arc lamps transfiguring the decks, and the big cranes groping in the holds, and the efficient tumult of shining men. But with the coming of the wide, blunt-bowed river steamer around the bend from upstream, he would become suddenly alert. And when the jangling bell told him that it was about to begin the sluggish crab crawl across to its berth, he would rise and walk slowly down to the landing stage. Often there were men aboard whom he had known, and on those nights his wife learned not to expect him home until she saw him, very often at the breakfast table the next morning, his eyes alive and glittering, his face sallow with stale liquor, and his voice rough with too much talking.

Occasionally, too, he was able to join the Department plane when it took the field officers and supplies up to the district stations. But in those places that he had known, looking out for a few hours over the country in which he had felt happy and meaningful, he understood the extent of his dispossession. He understood this and came back whenever he could, in the way that a man who has irrecoverably lost a woman will wait an hour on a street corner for her to pass with another, she now more remote, for ever untouchable, than if he had never known her, her smile at the other and her hand on his quite unreal actions, revealing the lost love with an appalling, magnified clarity, like an atom of coral sunk in pure, excluding glass. It was on one of these flights to the interior, at Shemarang on the Courenbice River, that he met Bargie.

They had flown up early in the morning as far as the cattle station at Haut Desir on the Venezuelan border, and early in the afternoon had come down the river to Shemarang. When you came in to land at Shemarang, a small Indian boy stood in the bow of a beached wood-skin and threw stones into the water. The plane banked steeply above a high sandstone bluff on the far bank, and you saw a tilted, green-furred bed of forest and a far-away brown shining coil of river against a diagonal horizon; then, as abruptly as the next frame in a lantern-slide show, you were below the level of the tree-tops, with trees blurring into a wall of green-streaked brown and the river unravelling furiously like ribbon tugged from a spool. Then you saw the ripples spreading from the still surface of the landing basin as the little boy threw stones into the water, and the floats of the *Norton* struck just beyond the place where the farthest ripple was captured by the hard rush of the main stream. A leaping sheet of rust-tinged black water blotted the bank from view, and then, wavering and smeared at first, becoming clearer as the water ran from the glass, there appeared the moored corials and woodskins, the white sandy slope of the clearing, the tree stumps scattered on it like stubborn old teeth and, at the top of the slope, the three huts standing high on their great plugs of iron heart. The forest began close behind the huts, and even from the river you could see the tunnels going into the green and the deep shadows.

Now Harry Hamilton sat with Buster McKitterick, the pilot, in the largest of the huts, which was the General Store, drinking beer and watching two Indians unload the supplies for the survey camp thirty miles up Shemarang Creek. The plane was lashed close to the shore, and a black man stood on one of the floats and directed the Indians as one of them handed the sacks of coffee, flour, sugar and tinned goods from the open cabin door to the other standing on the bank. It was cool and dark and restful in the General Store, and the beer washed the engine fumes from the back of the throat.

"Have another?" Buster McKitterick asked.

"Yes," Harry Hamilton said. "Thanks."

The East Indian who owned the store came from behind the zinc-topped bar with two wet bottles and poured for them.

"Have a drink, Stephen," Buster McKitterick said.

"Well, thank you, Captain McKitterick," the East Indian said. "I will have a beer, sir."

He took the money from McKitterick and went back behind the bar and took another bottle from the big water-filled bucket and pried the cap off. He raised the bottle to McKitterick and Hamilton and drank. Then he leaned his elbows on the zinc and gazed through the open door at the men around the plane. He was young and very good-looking; handsome in the ripe, sculptured fashion of many East Indians. His hair looked as if it had been polished, and it was beginning to go grey at the sides and in the widow's peak.

"Niggers," the East Indian, Stephen, said reflectively, almost idly. "They don't wort' nuttin'. That nigger down there, Lloyd, him is the only one I know will do anyt'ing wid him life. An' dat's because him is a small-island man, from Barbados."

"What sort of talk is that, Stephen?" Harry Hamilton said in the same lazy and reflective voice. "How a damn' coolie like you can talk about niggers? If it wasn't for the pork knockers and timbermen buying your stores, how you would make a living?"

"And is hell I catch to get money out of dem sometimes," Stephen told him. "But is true what I say, Mister Hamilton. You must know is true. Niggers worse dan Indians, an' Gawd knows de bucks is bad enough. Lawd, de times I stay here an' see de pork knockers going down to Zuyder, each of dem wid a cartridge case holding, five, six, seven hundred pounds' worth of diamond. But you t'ink dey would put some of dat into anyt'ing? Not dem. Is fine clothes an' women an' spree until de money done, an' den back up de river to look for more diamond. What a people!"

"Stephen," Buster McKitterick said, "I do believe you're a racialist."

"What dat, Captain?" Stephen asked.

"He means that you believe in the master race, Stephen," Harry Hamilton told him. "Do you?"

"I don't know about master race," Stephen said seriously, "but I know say how Gawd give every people a sickness. De white man get greed, de Portugee get swell foot, we East Indian, weak chest, but de black man, him get de worst of all. Laziness."

"Now you see why we're a colony," Harry Hamilton said to McKitterick, who was an American. "The bloody British don't even have

the trouble of divide and rule. We take care of the division for them."
He looked at Stephen and shook his head with as much rueful amusement as despair.

"Go on, Stephen," McKitterick said. "There must be something
good in our black brothers. Tell us something good."

"Yes," Stephen told them. "Dem is good for one t'ing. Spend money.
Nobody can spend money like dem. An' nobody can beg like dem.
Like de one I have living on me back dere now." He jerked his head
over his shoulder at the shut door between the store-room and the bar.

"Who is that?" Harry Hamilton said. "Anybody who can get something for nothing out of you, Stephen, must be worth knowing."

"Is an old pork knocker," Stephen said. "Damn' old madman called
Bargie. Him was prospecting up beyond the falls and get sick. Him
crawl in here one day like an old wild dog looking for a bush to die
under. Well, I couldn't turn him away, no, an' I know him a few year,
so I give him a corner until him get better. Damn it! I don't t'ink him
is ever goin' to get better. All him do is lie dere an' drink my condensed milk."

"What's wrong with him?" Harry Hamilton asked.

"I dun'no," Stephen answered. "It sound like T.B. Boy, him have a
cough, you see. But like I did tell you, Mister Hamilton, Captain, him is
de real nigger. You know how many time in his life Bargie strike it rich?
Seven!" He held up his small, neat brown hands and showed them
seven fingers. His vitally good-looking face held contempt and astonishment. "Seven times Bargie find good stones. One time, dem tell me,
de assay office in Zuyder give him five thousand dollar. An' him don't
have ten cents leave. If him had been one of my people, now, him
would have a big store and a thousand acre of rice."

"And he's really bad sick?" Harry Hamilton asked.

"Lawd, yes, Mister Hamilton. Sick near to death."

Harry Hamilton got up from the long Berbice chair and went to
the bar.

"Let me see him," he said, and raised the flap in counter.

"Sure." There was faint surprise in Stephen's voice, and then he
looked at Harry Hamilton with a sudden calculating sparkle in his
fine eyes. "Sure t'ing, Mister Hamilton. You ought to see him." He
opened the door leading into the store-room.

In the store-room it was cool and light, strongly scented with the odours of cheese, brown soap, coffee and salt fish. At the back there was an open window, and the man lay under it in a low-slung hammock. He was dressed in torn, khaki shorts and a roughly darned bush jacket; the red 'good luck' sash around his waist was stained and faded. On the floor beside him was a pair of rubber-soled canvas boots, with the canvas of both torn where the swell of the big toe joints had stretched it. The plaited *wareshi* leaning in the corner by his head was empty except for a rolled-up string hammock, a bush knife and a filthy old felt hat. There was a big enamel mug at his side, with most of the enamel flaked off, showing the dark metal; a wasp had drowned in the dregs of thinly mixed condensed milk at the bottom of the mug. He rested his head on a folded blanket so old that the nap had worn to a greasy smoothness, and he gazed up at Harry Hamilton with hard, appraising and incorrigible eyes.

"Bargie," Stephen said, and the affection in his tone was curious and touching after the sentiments he had voiced outside. "I bring someone to see you. Mister Hamilton from Survey."

"I hear of you, Mister Hamilton," Bargie said, "but we never meet up, eh? How you do, sir?"

"Stephen tells me your chest gone bad on you," Harry Hamilton said. "You sick long?"

"Some little. De rains catch me bad dis trip an' I tek a fever." The weak, panting voice was dry, nearly bored, as if seeking to convey in that laconic assessment the measure of a suave disdain—not bravado nor insensible fatalism, but simply a serene detachment from and contempt for the expected and accessory impotence of what was mere flesh born to distress and treason.

"You got more than the fever, man," Harry Hamilton told him, and as he said this Bargie began to cough, and after a little Buster McKitterick came to the door and gravely watched the writhing, drawn-together body in the hammock. Harry Hamilton took his eyes from Bargie and looked at McKitterick, pulling the corners of his mouth in a downward grimace and shaking his head.

"Man," Stephen said as the last crashing rasp expired, leaving a silence that still seemed to throb with a pulse of terrible sound. "Man, Bargie, you don't have cough; you have devil inside you."

"Bargie," Harry Hamilton said, "you better come with us when we fly back to Zuyder this afternoon. We'll be leaving as soon as the survey boat comes down for the supplies."

"Hospital?" The assured and contemplative gaze was suddenly bleak with caution.

Harry Hamilton nodded.

"How long?"

"How the hell would I know?" Harry Hamilton said. "I'm not a doctor."

"All right," Bargie told him. "I better come wid you. I need a little feeding before I go into de bush again."

"Yes," Harry Hamilton said, "you get some good feeding inside you. I think that's a good idea. You want a beer?"

"By Christ, Mister Hamilton, a beer would go good now. T'ank you. Stephen, you don't hear de boss say bring a beer for me?" The long, heavy-jawed death's head was suddenly bright with inspiring and outrageous gaiety as he winked at Harry Hamilton. "All I have been getting from dis damn' coolie is a few crackers an' a little milk so thin you could see de bottom of de mug."

Stephen sniffed, grinned and reached for the mug beside Bargie. "Black people," he said, fondly. "You know, Bargie, if Gawd tek you black people to heaven in a Cadillac, you gwine complain say it not a Rolls-Royce."

Bargie watched the East Indian go from the room with the dirty mug and smiled again at Harry Hamilton, his sunken face burnished with that same shocking and incorruptible gaiety.

"Dat's a good bwoy, you know, Mister Hamilton," he said. "I like tease him a little, but him is a real good bwoy."

Later in the afternoon, when the survey boat had come and gone, the two Indians carried Bargie down from the store. He didn't weigh much, and holding the two ends of his hammock they took him easily down the slope. At the plane Harry Hamilton and McKitterick helped the Indians to ease the hammock into the cabin and on to the floor behind the two pilot seats. Stephen followed with the old *wareshi* and the torn canvas boots. He looked sad and lost, and kept rearranging the *wareshi* and the boots and asking Bargie if he wanted another blanket under his head or another one as cover.

"It can get cold up there, you know, Bargie," he said. "It all right, man; you can have anoder blanket. Captain will bring it back to me nex' time him come."

When the engines turned over he squeezed quickly between McKitterick and Hamilton and jumped from the cabin to the float and on to the bank. McKitterick taxied the plane out of the basin and swung into the current. He opened the throttle, and they went down river very fast and lifted above the forest before they had reached the bluff. The plane banked steeply to follow the river course down to Zuyder Town, and Harry Hamilton could see the clearing and the forest closing around it and Stephen on the bank standing a little way from the others and lifting his hand. Then they were flying north by east down the river and the country was tidy, formal and miniature, like a garden, with a thin blue mist beginning to form among the tree-tops and close to the banks, and with loops of shining water beyond, as far as they could see.

They reached Zuyder Town just before dark, and McKitterick brought them in low over the line of lights along the water front and on to the basin. Bargie was sleeping, and he didn't wake even when McKitterick taxied the plane in from the middle of the basin and ran the floats up the wooden slipway that led down from the jetty.

Harry Hamilton opened the cabin door and jumped down on to the wet, smooth boards of the slip as the mechanics came running to make the plane fast for the night. He went quickly up the slip along the jetty to the telephone in the landing office and called the number of his home.

"We've just got in," he said to his wife. "Can you come for me now?"

"Yes, darling," she said. "I'll be there in a few minutes."

"Is Marie with you?"

"Yes."

"Good. I thought she might be. Ask her to come, too. I want her to have a look at a man we brought down."

Two of the mechanics were carrying Bargie up the jetty from the plane. He was awake now, and as they laid him on the bench along the wall of the office he raised his hand in greeting to Harry Hamilton.

"Man," he said, "dat's de best sleep I catch in a long time. I must buy me an aeroplane."

"How're you feeling?" Harry Hamilton asked him.

"Great, Mister Hamilton. A little more rest like I just have an' I'll be back on de old form."

"Good," Harry Hamilton said. "I've asked a doctor to come down and have a look at you. She'll see about getting you into the hospital."

"Doctor is a woman?"

"Yes. She's very good. She's my doctor."

"Oh. Well, if you say so, Mister Hamilton, I'll tek it dat she good."

Harry Hamilton's wife and Marie Rau arrived in Marie's car a few minutes later, and Harry Hamilton, his wife and McKitterick sat in a corner of the office while Bargie was being examined. Then Marie Rau joined them.

"What's the verdict?" McKitterick asked her.

"What do you think?" Marie Rau said. "Galloping consumption is only the most obvious. There's a lot else, including a rheumatic heart. I'll get the hospital to send down for him now."

She picked up the telephone, and Harry Hamilton went back to Bargie.

"She says you're pretty sick," Harry Hamilton said.

"I did guess so, Mister Hamilton."

"You have anybody you want me to tell about you?"

"No. I is alone now."

"If you go back to the interior," Harry Hamilton said, "it's going to kill you."

"What place don't kill you?" Bargie asked him.

"No, listen," Harry Hamilton said. "I can get you a job in Zuyder when you come out. Come and see me down at Survey, and I'll find you something there."

"I will keep you in mind, Mister Hamilton."

"That's about all you will do," Harry Hamilton said. "Keep me in mind. Well, remember that I warned you, eh? Remember that I gave you good advice."

"I'll remember, Mister Hamilton," Bargie said. "I know dat you have to do it. As duty."

From the yard beyond the office they heard the soft clanging of the ambulance bell.

"I'll come and look for you," Harry Hamilton told him.

"Yes, Mister Hamilton, you do dat. I sorry we never meet up before."

When the attendants came into the office with the stretcher, Bargie began to cough; by the time they had taken him to the door he was contorted with his furious search for breath. Harry Hamilton was very sorry to see him reduced like that before the women, and to see the passive and aloof self-sufficiency of that battered face now broken by a mindless struggle. He knew that the genial arrogance of that face had been earned without illusions or self-pity, but with a prodigal, debonair commitment of all endurance and all resources; and listening to the sad, racked sounds as the attendants dispassionately closed the doors of the ambulance, he felt warm with anger and shame.

That night after dinner he sat with his wife and Marie Rau on the veranda above the garden in which, since he could no longer go to the interior, he had begun to spend a great deal of time. His house was on the edge of town, by the sea wall, and they could hear the sighing of the tide as it rolled across the mud flats and the soft crash of waves against the stone; the voices from the road by the wall were filtered into murmurs by the hedge of Barbados Pride which he had planted along the fence and which had grown high during the last year.

"But, Harry," Marie Rau said, "he can't go back to prospecting. I don't think he'll ever leave the hospital, myself, but even if he does, he could never survive another month in the bush. Doesn't he know how sick he is? Didn't you tell him?"

"I told him, all right," Harry Hamilton said. "At least, we exchanged formal advice and polite acknowledgment. Neither of us was taking it very seriously."

"You ought to be ashamed. You ought to know better. Do try to do something. I think you actually want that poor old ruin to go back and kill himself, Harry."

"I don't want him to. I simply know that if he can walk, he will."

"But why, Harry? For what? For a few diamonds he knows he'll never find now, and will never live to sell if he does find them."

"Oh, no, Marie," Harry Hamilton said quickly. "It's not like that at all. The diamonds are important, but they're only a part of it. Only a sort of means, really. A justification."

But how to tell it? he thought then, as he looked at the doubtful faces of the two people he loved most in the world. Is there any way of communicating it to those who have never experienced it? Who never, from the shabby confines of this coast, will understand that it is there to be experienced. Will never understand that we are lost without something like the interior. They see only the gains. Bargie's diamonds, the gold dust and manganese, the cattle from the savanna. The least part of it. A reminder merely. Necessary tokens, because we forget easily, of what has been endured, contemplated, promised: the reassurance that immemorable nostalgias of the spirit will be made real finally. The ancestral heritage greater and more precious than any one race or one history or one hope. Too intense and too real to be encountered directly. Only to be seen from the corner of the eye in the way that the Indians are born knowing, that Bargie learned, that I was learning. How to tell it, my God? And how to tell that it will be perceptible in our later isolation as the elusive, half-remembered fragment of some enormous, receding and unpossessable dream?

V. S. Naipaul (*Trinidad*)

My Aunt Gold Teeth

I NEVER knew her real name and it is quite likely that she did have one, though I never heard her called anything but Gold Teeth. She did, indeed, have gold teeth. She had sixteen of them. She had married early and she had married well, and shortly after her marriage she exchanged her perfectly sound teeth for gold ones, to announce to the world that her husband was a man of substance.

Even without her gold teeth my aunt would have been noticeable. She was short, scarcely five foot, and she was fat, horribly, monstrously fat. If you saw her in silhouette you would have found it difficult to know whether she was facing you or whether she was looking sideways.

She ate little and prayed much. Her family being Hindu, and her husband being a pundit, she, too, was an orthodox Hindu. Of Hinduism she knew little apart from the ceremonies and the taboos, and this was enough for her. Gold Teeth saw God as a Power, and religious ritual as a means of harnessing that Power for great practical good, her good.

I fear I may have given the impression that Gold Teeth prayed because she wanted to be less fat. The fact was that Gold Teeth had no children and she was almost forty. It was her childlessness, not her fat, that oppressed her, and she prayed for the curse to be removed. She was willing to try any means—any ritual, any prayer—in order to trap and channel the supernatural Power.

And so it was that she began to indulge in surreptitious Christian practices.

She was living at the time in a country village called Cunupia, in County Caroni. Here the Canadian Mission had long waged war against the Indian heathen, and saved many. But Gold Teeth stood firm. The Minister of Cunupia expended his Presbyterian piety on her; so did the headmaster of the Mission school. But all in vain. At no time was Gold Teeth persuaded even to think about being converted. The idea horrified her. Her father had been in his day one of the best-known Hindu pundits,

40

and even now her husband's fame as a pundit, as a man who could read and write Sanskrit, had spread far beyond Cunupia. She was in no doubt whatsoever that Hindus were the best people in the world, and that Hinduism was a superior religion. She was willing to select, modify and incorporate alien eccentricities into her worship; but to abjure her own Faith—never!

Presbyterianism was not the only danger the good Hindu had to face in Cunupia. Besides, of course, the ever-present threat of open Muslim aggression, the Catholics were to be reckoned with. Their pamphlets were everywhere and it was hard to avoid them. In them Gold Teeth read of novenas and rosaries, of squads of saints and angels. These were things she understood and could even sympathize with, and they encouraged her to seek further. She read of the mysteries and the miracles, of penances and indulgences. Her scepticism sagged, and yielded to a quickening, if reluctant, enthusiasm.

One morning she took the train for the County town of Chaguanas, three miles, two stations and twenty minutes away. The Church of St. Philip and St. James in Chaguanas stands imposingly at the end of the Caroni Savannah Road, and although Gold Teeth knew Chaguanas well, all she knew of the church was that it had a clock, at which she had glanced on her way to the Railway Station nearby. She had hitherto been far more interested in the drab ochre-washed edifice opposite, which was the Police Station.

She carried herself into the churchyard, awed by her own temerity, feeling like an explorer in a land of cannibals. To her relief, the church was empty. It was not as terrifying as she had expected. In the gilt and images and the resplendent cloths she found much that reminded her of her Hindu temple. Her eyes caught a discreet sign: CANDLES TWO CENTS EACH. She undid the knot in the end of her veil, where she kept her money, took out three cents, popped them into the box, picked up a candle and muttered a prayer in Hindustani. A brief moment of elation gave way to a sense of guilt, and she was suddenly anxious to get away from the church as fast as her weight would let her.

She took a bus home, and hid the candle in her chest of drawers. She had half feared that her husband's Brahminical flair for clairvoyance would have uncovered the reason for her trip to Chaguanas. When after four days, which she spent in an ecstasy of prayer, her husband had mentioned nothing, Gold Teeth thought it safe to burn the candle.

She burned it secretly at night, before her Hindu images and sent up, as she thought, prayers of double efficacy.

Every day her religious schizophrenia grew, and presently she began wearing a crucifix. Neither her husband nor her neighbours knew she did so. The chain was lost in the billows of fat around her neck, and the crucifix was itself buried in the valley of her gargantuan breasts. Later she acquired two holy pictures, one of the Virgin Mary, the other of the crucifixion, and took care to conceal them from her husband. The prayers she offered to these Christian things filled her with new hope and buoyancy. She became an addict of Christianity.

Then her husband, Ramprasad, fell ill.

Ramprasad's sudden unaccountable illness alarmed Gold Teeth. It was, she knew, no ordinary illness, and she knew, too, that her religious transgression was the cause. The District Medical Officer at Chaguanas said it was diabetes, but Gold Teeth knew better. To be on the safe side, though, she used the insulin he prescribed and, to be even safer, she consulted Ganesh Pundit, the masseur with mystic leanings, celebrated as a faith-healer.

Ganesh came all the way from Feunte Grove to Cunupia. He came in great humility, anxious to serve Gold Teeth's husband, for Gold Teeth's husband was a Brahmin among Brahmins, a *Panday*, a man who knew all five Vedas; while he, Ganesh, was a mere *Chaubay* and knew only four.

With spotless white *koortah*, his dhoti cannily tied, and a tasselled green scarf as a concession to elegance, Ganesh exuded the confidence of the professional mystic. He looked at the sick man, observed his pallor, sniffed the air inquiringly. "This man," he said slowly, "is bewitched. Seven spirits are upon him."

He was telling Gold Teeth nothing she didn't know. She had known from the first that there were spirits in the affair, but she was glad that Ganesh had ascertained their number.

"But you mustn't worry," Ganesh added. "We will 'tie' the house— in spiritual bonds—and no spirit will be able to come in."

Then, without being asked, Gold Teeth brought out a blanket, folded it, placed it on the floor and invited Ganesh to sit on it. Next she brought him a brass jar of fresh water, a mango leaf and a plate full of burning charcoal.

"Bring me some ghee," Ganesh said, and after Gold Teeth had done so, he set to work. Muttering continuously in Hindustani he sprinkled the water from the brass jar around him with the mango leaf. Then he melted the ghee in the fire and the charcoal hissed so sharply that Gold Teeth could not make out his words. Presently he rose and said, "You must put some of the ash of this fire on your husband's forehead, but if he doesn't want you to do that, mix it with his food. You must keep the water in this jar and place it every night before your front door."

Gold Teeth pulled her veil over her forehead.

Ganesh coughed. "That," he said, rearranging his scarf, "is all. There is nothing more I can do. God will do the rest."

He refused payment for his services. It was enough honour, he said, for a man as humble as he was to serve Pundit Ramprasad, and she, Gold Teeth, had been singled out by fate to be the spouse of such a worthy man. Gold Teeth received the impression that Ganesh spoke from a first-hand knowledge of fate and its designs, and her heart, buried deep down under inches of mortal, flabby flesh, sank a little.

"Baba," she said hesitantly, "revered Father, I have something to say to you." But she couldn't say anything more and Ganesh, seeing this, filled his eyes with charity and love.

"What is it, my child?"

"I have done a great wrong, Baba."

"What sort of wrong?" he asked, and his tone indicated that Gold Teeth could do no wrong.

"I have prayed to Christian things."

And to Gold Teeth's surprise, Ganesh chuckled benevolently. "And do you think God minds, daughter? There is only one God and different people pray to Him in different ways. It doesn't matter how you pray, but God is pleased if you pray at all."

"So it is not because of me that my husband has fallen ill?"

"No, to be sure, daughter."

In his professional capacity Ganesh was consulted by people of many faiths, and with the licence of the mystic he had exploited the commodiousness of Hinduism, and made room for all beliefs. In this way he had many clients, as he called them, many satisfied clients.

Henceforward Gold Teeth not only pasted Ramprasad's pale forehead with the sacred ash Ganesh had prescribed, but mixed substantial amounts with his food. Ramprasad's appetite, enormous even in sickness, diminished; and he shortly entered into a visible and alarming decline that mystified his wife.

She fed him more ash than before, and when it was exhausted and Ramprasad perilously macerated, she fell back on the Hindu wife's last resort. She took her husband home to her mother. That venerable lady, my grandmother, lived with us in Port-of-Spain, in Woodbrook.

Ramprasad was tall and skeletal, and his face was grey. The virile voice that had expounded a thousand theological points and recited a hundred *puranas* was now a wavering whisper. We cooped him up in a room called, oddly, 'the pantry'. It had never been used as a pantry and one can only assume that the architect, in the idealistic manner of his tribe, had so designated it some forty years before. It was a tiny room. If you wished to enter the pantry you were compelled, as soon as you opened the door, to climb on to the bed: it fitted the room to a miracle. The lower half of the walls were concrete, the upper close lattice-work; there were no windows.

My grandmother had her doubts about the suitability of the room for a sick man. She was worried about the lattice-work. It let in air and light, and Ramprasad was not going to die from these things if she could help it. With cardboard, oil-cloth and canvas she made the lattice-work air-proof and light-proof.

And, sure enough, within a week Ramprasad's appetite returned, insatiable and insistent as before. My grandmother claimed all the credit for this, though Gold Teeth knew that the ash she had fed him had not been without effect. Then she realized with horror that she had ignored a very important thing. The house in Cunupia had been tied and no spirits could enter, but the house in Woodbrook had been given no such protection and any spirit could come and go as it chose. The problem was pressing.

Ganesh was out of the question. By giving his services free he had made it impossible for Gold Teeth to call him in again. But thinking in this way of Ganesh, she remembered his words: "It doesn't matter how you pray, but God is pleased if you pray at all."

Why not, then, bring Christianity into play again?

She didn't want to take any chances this time. She decided to tell Ramprasad.

He was propped up in bed, and eating. When Gold Teeth opened the door he stopped eating and blinked at the unwonted light. Gold

Teeth, stepping into the doorway and filling it, shadowed the room once more and he went on eating. She placed the palms of her hands on the bed. It creaked.

"Man," she said.

Ramprasad continued to eat.

"Man," she said in English, "I thinking about going to the chu'ch to pray. You never know, and it better to be on the safe side. After all, the house ain't tied——"

"I don't want to pray in no chu'ch," he whispered in English, too.

Gold Teeth did the only thing she could do. She began to cry.

Three days in succession she asked his permission to go to church, and his opposition weakened in the face of her tears. He was now, besides, too weak to oppose anything. Although his appetite had returned, he was still very ill and very weak, and every day his condition became worse.

On the fourth day he said to Gold Teeth, "Well, pray to Jesus and go to chu'ch, if it will put your mind at rest."

And Gold Teeth straight away set about putting her mind at rest. Every morning she took the trolley-bus to the Holy Rosary Church, to offer worship in her private way. Then she was emboldened to bring a crucifix and pictures of the Virgin and the Messiah into the house. We were all somewhat worried by this, but Gold Teeth's religious nature was well known to us; her husband was a learned pundit and when all was said and done this was an emergency, a matter of life and death. So we could do nothing but look on. Incense and camphor and ghee burned now before the likeness of Krishna and Shiva as well as Mary and Jesus. Gold Teeth revealed an appetite for prayer that equalled her husband's for food, and we marvelled at both, if only because neither prayer nor food seemed to be of any use to Ramprasad.

One evening, shortly after bell and gong and conchshell had announced that Gold Teeth's official devotions were almost over, a sudden chorus of lamentation burst over the house, and I was summoned to the room reserved for prayer. "Come quickly, something dreadful has happened to your aunt."

The prayer-room, still heavy with fumes of incense, presented an extraordinary sight. Before the Hindu shrine, flat on her face, Gold Teeth lay prostrate, rigid as a sack of flour, a large amorphous mass. I had only seen Gold Teeth standing or sitting, and the aspect of Gold Teeth prostrate, so novel and so grotesque, was disturbing.

My grandmother, an alarmist by nature, bent down and put her ear to the upper half of the body on the floor. "I don't seem to hear her heart," she said.

We were all somewhat terrified. We tried to lift Gold Teeth but she seemed as heavy as lead. Then, slowly, the body quivered. The flesh beneath the clothes rippled, then billowed, and the children in the room sharpened their shrieks. Instinctively we all stood back from the body and waited to see what was going to happen. Gold Teeth's hand began to pound the floor and at the same time she began to gurgle.

My grandmother had grasped the situation. "She's got the spirit," she said.

At the word 'spirit', the children shrieked louder, and my grandmother slapped them into silence.

The gurgling resolved itself into words pronounced with a lingering ghastly quaver. "Hail Mary, Hara Ram," Gold Teeth said, "the snakes are after me. Everywhere snakes. Seven snakes. Rama! Rama! Full of grace. Seven spirits leaving Cunupia by the four-o'clock train for Port-of-Spain."

My grandmother and my mother listened eagerly, their faces lit up with pride. I was rather ashamed at the exhibition, and annoyed with Gold Teeth for putting me into a fright. I moved towards the door.

"Who is that going away? Who is the young *daffar*, the unbeliever?" the voice asked abruptly.

"Come back quickly, boy," my grandmother whispered. "Come back and ask her pardon."

I did as I was told.

"It is all right, son," Gold Teeth replied, "you don't know. You are young."

Then the spirit appeared to leave her. She wrenched herself up to a sitting position and wondered why we were all there. For the rest of that evening she behaved as if nothing had happened, and she pretended she didn't notice that everyone was looking at her and treating her with unusual respect.

"I have always said it, and I will say it again," my grandmother said, "that these Christians are very religious people. That is why I encouraged Gold Teeth to pray to Christian things."

Ramprasad died early next morning and we had the announcement on the radio after the local news at one o'clock. Ramprasad's death was the only one announced and so, although it came between commercials, it made some impression. We buried him that afternoon in Mucurapo Cemetery.

As soon as we got back my grandmother said, "I have always said it, and I will say it again: I don't like these Christian things. Ramprasad would have got better if only you, Gold Teeth, had listened to me and not gone running after these Christian things."

Gold Teeth sobbed her assent; and her body squabbered and shook as she confessed the whole story of her trafficking with Christianity. We listened in astonishment and shame. We didn't know that a good Hindu, and a member of our family, could sink so low. Gold Teeth beat her breast and pulled ineffectually at her long hair and begged to be forgiven. "It is all my fault," she cried. "My own fault, Ma. I fell in a moment of weakness. Then I just couldn't stop."

My grandmother's shame turned to pity. "It's all right, Gold Teeth. Perhaps it was this you needed to bring you back to your senses."

That evening Gold Teeth ritually destroyed every reminder of Christianity in the house.

"You have only yourself to blame," my grandmother said, "if you have no children now to look after you."

V. S. Naipaul

The Raffle

They don't pay Primary School teachers a lot in Trinidad, but they allow them to beat their pupils as much as they want.

Mr. Hinds, my teacher, was a big beater. On the shelf below *The Last of England* he kept four or five tamarind rods. They are good for beating. They are limber, they sting and they last. There was a tamarind tree in the schoolyard. In his locker Mr. Hinds also kept a leather strap soaking in the bucket of water every class had in case of fire.

It wouldn't have been so bad if Mr. Hinds hadn't been so young and athletic. At the one school sports I went to, I saw him slip off his shining shoes, roll up his trousers neatly to mid-shin and win the Teachers' Hundred Yards, a cigarette between his lips, his tie flapping smartly over his shoulder. It was a wine-coloured tie: Mr. Hinds was careful about his dress. That was something else that somehow added to the terror. He wore a brown suit, a cream shirt and the wine-coloured tie.

It was also rumoured that he drank heavily at week-ends.

But Mr. Hinds had a weak spot. He was poor. We knew he gave those 'private lessons' because he needed the extra money. He gave us private lessons in the ten-minute morning recess. Every boy paid fifty cents for that. If a boy didn't pay, he was kept in all the same and flogged until he paid.

We also knew that Mr. Hinds had an allotment in Morvant where he kept some poultry and a few animals.

The other boys sympathized with us—needlessly. Mr. Hinds beat us, but I believe we were all a little proud of him.

I say he beat us, but I don't really mean that. For some reason which I could never understand then and can't now, Mr. Hinds never beat me. He never made me clean the blackboard. He never made me shine his shoes with the duster. He even called me by my first name, Vidiadhar.

This didn't do me any good with the other boys. At cricket I wasn't allowed to bowl or keep wicket and I always went in at number eleven.

48

My consolation was that I was spending only two terms at the school before going on to Queen's Royal College. I didn't want to go to Q.R.C. so much as I wanted to get away from Tranquillity (that was the name of the school). Mr. Hinds's favour made me feel insecure.

At private lessons one morning Mr. Hinds announced that he was going to raffle a goat—a shilling a chance.

He spoke with a straight face and nobody laughed. He made me write out the names of all the boys in the class on two foolscap sheets. Boys who wanted to risk a shilling had to put a tick after their names. Before private lessons ended there was a tick after every name.

I became very unpopular. Some boys didn't believe there was a goat. They all said that if there was a goat, they knew who was going to get it. I hoped they were right. I had long wanted an animal of my own, and the idea of getting milk from my own goat attracted me. I had heard that Mannie Ramjohn, Trinidad's champion miler, trained on goat's milk and nuts.

Next morning I wrote out the names of the boys on slips of paper. Mr. Hinds borrowed my cap, put the slips in, took one out, said, "Vidiadhar, is your goat", and immediately threw all the slips into the wastepaper-basket.

At lunch I told my mother, "I win a goat today."

"What sort of goat?"

"I don't know. I ain't see it."

She laughed. She didn't believe in the goat, either. But when she finished laughing she said: "It would be nice, though."

I was getting not to believe in the goat, too. I was afraid to ask Mr. Hinds, but a day or two later he said, "Vidiadhar, you coming or you ain't coming to get your goat?"

He lived in a tumbledown wooden house in Woodbrook and when I got there I saw him in khaki shorts, vest and blue canvas shoes. He was cleaning his bicycle with a yellow flannel. I was overwhelmed. I had never associated him with such dress and such a menial labour. But his manner was more ironic and dismissing than in the classroom.

He led me to the back of the yard. There *was* a goat. A white one with big horns, tied to a plum tree. The ground around the tree was filthy. The goat looked sullen and sleepy-eyed, as if a little stunned by the smell it had made. Mr. Hinds invited me to stroke the goat. I stroked it. He closed his eyes and went on chewing. When I stopped stroking him, he opened his eyes.

Every afternoon at about five an old man drove a donkey-cart through Miguel Street where we lived. The cart was piled with fresh grass tied into neat little bundles, so neat you felt grass wasn't a thing that grew but was made in a factory somewhere. That donkey-cart became important to my mother and me. We were buying five, sometimes six bundles a day, and every bundle cost six cents. The goat didn't change. He still looked sullen and bored. From time to time Mr Hinds asked me with a smile how the goat was getting on, and I said it was getting on fine. But when I asked my mother when we were going to get milk from the goat, she told me to stop aggravating her. Then one day she put up a sign:

RAM FOR SERVICE
Apply Within For Terms

and got very angry when I asked her to explain it.

The sign made no difference. We bought the neat bundles of grass, the goat ate, and I saw no milk.

And when I got home one lunch-time I saw no goat.

"Somebody borrow it," my mother said. She looked happy.

"When it coming back?"

She shrugged her shoulders.

It came back that afternoon. When I turned the corner into Miguel Street I saw it on the pavement outside our house. A man I didn't know was holding it by a rope and making a big row, gesticulating like anything with his free hand. I knew that sort of man. He wasn't going to let hold of the rope until he had said his piece. A lot of people were looking on through curtains.

"But why all-you want to rob poor people so?" he was shouting. He turned to his audience behind the curtains. "Look, all-you, just look at this goat!"

The goat, limitlessly impassive, chewed slowly, its eyes half-closed.

"But how all you people so advantageous? My brother stupid and he ain't know this goat, but I know this goat. Everybody in Trinidad who know about goat know this goat, from Icacos to Mayaro to Toco to Chaguaramas," he said, naming the four corners of Trinidad. "Is the most useless-est goat in the whole world. And you charge my brother for this goat? Look, you better give me back my brother money, you hear."

My mother looked hurt and upset. She went inside and came out with some dollar notes. The man took them and handed over the goat.

That evening my mother said, "Go and tell your Mr. Hinds that I don't want this goat here."

Mr. Hinds didn't look surprised. "Don't want it, eh?" He thought, and passed a well-trimmed thumb-nail over his moustache. "Look, tell you. Going to buy him back. Five dollars."

I said, "He eat more than that in grass alone."

That didn't surprise him, either. "Say six, then."

I sold. That, I thought, was the end of that.

One Monday afternoon about a month before the end of my last term I announced to my mother, "That goat raffling again."

She became alarmed.

At tea on Friday I said casually, "I win the goat."

She was expecting it. Before the sun set a man had brought the goat from Mr. Hinds, given my mother some money and taken the goat away.

I hoped Mr. Hinds would never ask about the goat. He did, though. Not the next week, but the week after that, just before school broke up.

I didn't know what to say.

But a boy called Knolly, a fast bowler and a favourite victim of Mr. Hinds, answered for me. "What goat?" he whispered loudly. "That goat kill and eat long time."

Mr. Hinds was suddenly furious. "Is true, Vidiadhar?"

I didn't nod or say anything. The bell rang and saved me.

At lunch I told my mother, "I don't want to go back to that school."

She said, "You must be brave."

I didn't like the argument, but I went.

We had Geography the first period.

"Naipaul," Mr. Hinds said right away, forgetting my first name, "define a peninsula."

"Peninsula," I said, "a piece of land entirely surrounded by water."

"Good. Come up here." He went to the locker and took out the soaking leather strap. Then he fell on me. "You sell my goat?" Cut. "You kill my goat?" Cut. "How you so damn' ungrateful?" Cut, cut, cut. "Is the last time you win anything I raffle."

It was the last day I went to that school.

V. S. Naipaul

A Christmas Story

Though it is Christmas Eve my mind is not on Christmas. I look forward instead to the day after Boxing Day, for on that day the inspectors from the Audit Department in Port-of-Spain will be coming down to the village where the new school has been built. I await their coming with calm. There is still time, of course, to do all that is necessary. But I shall not do it, though my family, from whom the spirit of Christmas has, alas, also fled, have been begging me to lay aside my scruples, my new-found faith, and to rescue us all from disgrace and ruin. It is in my power to do so, but there comes a time in every man's life when he has to take a stand. This time, I must confess, has come very late for me.

It seems that everything has come late to me. I continued a Hindu, though of that religion I saw and knew little save meaningless and shameful rites, until I was nearly eighteen. Why I so continued I cannot explain. Perhaps it was the inertia with which that religion deadens its devotees. It did not, after all, require much intelligence to see that Hinduism, with its animistic rites, its idolatry, its emphasis on mango leaf, banana leaf and—the truth is the truth—cowdung, was a religion little fitted for the modern world. I had only to contrast the position of the Hindus with that of the Christians. I had only to consider the differing standards of dress, houses, food. Such differences have today more or less disappeared, and the younger generation will scarcely understand what I mean. I might even be reproached with laying too great a stress on the superficial. What can I say? Will I be believed if I say that to me the superficial has always symbolized the profound? But it is enough, I feel, to state that at eighteen my eyes were opened. I did not have to be 'converted' by the Presbyterians of the Canadian Mission. I had only to look at the work they were doing among the backward Hindus and Moslems of my district. I had only to look at their schools, to look at the houses of the converted.

My Presbyterianism, then, though late in coming, affected me deeply. I was interested in teaching—there was no other thing a man of my limited means and limited education could do—and my Presbyterianism was a distinct advantage. It gave me a grace in the eyes of my superiors. It also enabled me to be a good teacher, for between what I taught and what I felt there was no discordance. How different the position of those who, still unconverted, attempted to teach in Presbyterian schools!

And now that the time for frankness has come, I must also remark on the pleasure my new religion gave me. It was a pleasure to hear myself called Randolph, a name of rich historical associations, a name, I feel, thoroughly attuned to the times in which we live and to the society in which I found myself, and to forget that once—I still remember it with shame—I answered, with simple instinct, to the name of—Choonilal. That, however, is so much in the past. I have buried it. Yet I remember it now, not only because the time for frankness has come, but because only two weeks ago my son Winston, going through some family papers—clearly the boy had no right to be going through my private papers, but he shares his mother's curiosity—came upon the name. He teased, indeed reproached, me with it, and in a fit of anger, for which I am now grievously sorry and for which I must make time, while time there still is, to apologize to him, in a fit of anger I gave him a sound thrashing, such as I often gave in my school-teaching days to those pupils whose persistent shortcomings were matched by the stupidity and backwardness of their parents. Backwardness has always roused me to anger.

As much as by the name Randolph, pleasure was given me by the stately and *clean*—there is no other word for it—rituals sanctioned by my new religion. How agreeable, for instance, to rise early on a Sunday morning, to bathe and breakfast and then, in the most spotless of garments, to walk along the still quiet and cool roads to our place of worship, and there to see the most respectable and respected, all dressed with a similar purity, addressing themselves to the devotions in which I myself could participate, after for long being an outsider, someone to whom the words *Christ* and *Father* meant no more than *winter* or *autumn* or *daffodil*. Such of the unconverted village folk who were energetic enough to be awake and alert at that hour gaped at us as we walked in white procession to our church. And though their admiration was sweet, I must confess that at the same time it filled me with shame to reflect that not long before I too formed part of the gaping crowd. To walk past their gaze was peculiarly painful to me, for I, more perhaps than anyone

54

in that slow and stately procession, *knew*—and by my silence had for nearly eighteeen years condoned—the practices those people indulged in in the name of religion. My attitude towards them was therefore somewhat stern, and it gave me some little consolation to know that though we were in some ways alike, we were distinguished from them not only by our names, which after all no man carries pinned to his lapel, but also by our dress. On these Sundays of which I speak the men wore trousers and jackets of white drill, quite unlike the leg-revealing dhoti which it still pleased those others to wear, a garment which I have always felt makes the wearer ridiculous. I even sported a white solar topee. The girls and ladies wore the short frocks which the others held in abhorrence; they wore hats; in every respect, I am pleased to say, they resembled their sisters who had come all the way from Canada and other countries to work among our people. I might be accused of laying too much stress on superficial things. But I ought to say in my own defence that it is my deeply held conviction that progress is not a matter of outward show, but an attitude of mind; and it was this that my religion gave me.

It might seem from what I have so far said that the embracing of Presbyterianism conferred only benefits and pleasure. I wish to make no great fuss of the trials I had to endure, but it is sufficient to state that, while at school and in other associations my fervent adherence to my new faith was viewed with favour, I had elsewhere to put up with the constant ridicule of those of my relations who continued, in spite of my example, in the ways of darkness. They spoke my name, Randolph, with accents of the purest mockery. I bore this with fortitude. It was what I expected, and I was greatly strengthened by my faith, as a miser is by the thought of his gold. In time, when they saw that their ridiculing of my name had not the slightest effect on me—on the contrary, whereas before I had had in my signature suppressed my first name behind the black initial C, now I spelt out Randolph in full—in time they desisted.

But that was not the end of my trials. I had up to that time eaten with my fingers, a manner of eating which is now so repulsive to me, so ugly, so unhygienic, that I wonder how I managed to do it until my eighteenth year. Yet I must now confess that at that time food never tasted as sweet as when eaten with the fingers, and that my first attempts to eat with the proper implements of knife and fork and spoon were almost in

55

the nature of shameful experiments, furtively carried out; and even when I was by myself I could not get rid of the feeling of self-consciousness. It was easier to get used to the name of Randolph than to knife and fork.

Eating, then, in my determined manner one Sunday lunchtime, I heard that I had a visitor. It was a man; he didn't knock, but came straight into my room, and I knew at once that he was a relation. These people have never learned to knock or to close doors behind them.

I must confess I felt somewhat foolish, to be caught with those implements in my hand.

"Hello, Randolph," the boy, Hori, said, pronouncing the name in a most offensive manner.

"Good afternoon, *Hori*."

He remained impervious to my irony. This boy, Hori, was the greatest of my tormentors. He was also the grossest. He strained charity. He was a great lump of a man and he gloried in his brutishness. He fancied himself a debater as well, and many were the discussions and arguments we had had, this lout—he strained charity, as I have said—insisting that to squat on the ground and eat off banana leaves was hygienic and proper, that knives and forks were dirty because used again and again by various persons, whereas the fingers were personal and could always be made thoroughly clean by washing. But he never had *his* fingers clean, that I knew.

"Eating, Randolph?"

"I am having my lunch, *Hori*."

"Beef, Randolph. You are progressing, Randolph."

"I am glad you note it, *Hori*."

I cannot understand why these people should persist in this admiration for the cow, which has always seemed to me a filthy animal, far filthier than the pig, which they abhor. Yet it must be stated that this eating of beef was the most strenuous of my tests. If I persevered it was only because I was strengthened by my faith. But to be found at this juncture —I was in my Sunday suit of white drill, my prayer book was on the table, my white solar topee on the wall, and I was eating beef with knife and fork—to be found thus by Hori was a trifle embarrassing. I must have looked the picture of the over-zealous convert.

My instinct was to ask him to leave. But it occurred to me that that would have been too easy, too cowardly a way out. Instead, I plied my knife and fork with as much skill as I could command at that time.

He sat, not on a chair, but on the table, just next to my plate, the lout, and gazed at me while I ate. Ignoring his smile, I ate, as one might eat of sacrificial food. He crossed his fat legs, leaned back on his palms and examined me. I paid no attention. Then he took one of the forks that were about and began picking his teeth with it. I was angry and revolted. Tears sprang to my eyes. I rose, pushed away my plate, pushed back my chair, and asked him to leave. The violence of my reaction surprised him, and he did as I asked. As soon as he had gone I took the fork he had handled and bent it and stamped on it and then threw it out of the window.

Progress, as I have said, is an attitude of mind. And if I relate this trifling incident with such feeling, it is because it demonstrates how difficult that attitude of mind is to acquire, for there are hundreds who are ready to despise and ridicule those who they think are getting above themselves. And let people say what they will, the contempt even of the foolish is hard to bear. Let no one think, therefore, that my new religion did not bring its share of trials and tribulations. But I was sufficiently strengthened by my faith to bear them all with fortitude.

My life thereafter was a lonely one. I had cut myself off from my family, and from those large family gatherings which had hitherto given me so much pleasure and comfort, for always, I must own, at the back of my mind there had been the thought that in the event of real trouble there would be people to whom I could turn. Now I was deprived of this solace. I stuck to my vocation with a dedication which surprised even myself. To be a teacher it is necessary to be taught; and after much difficulty I managed to have myself sent to the Training College in Port-of-Spain. The competition for these places was fierce, and for many years I was passed over, because there were many others who were more fitting. Some indeed had been born of Presbyterian parents. But my zeal, which ever mounted as the failures multiplied, eventually was rewarded. I was twenty-eight when I was sent to the Training College, considerably older than most of the trainees.

It was no pleasure to me to note that during those ten years the boy Hori had been prospering. He had gone into the trucking business and he had done remarkably well. He had bought a second truck, then a third, and it seemed that to his success there could be no limit, while my own was always restricted to the predictable contents of the brown-paper pay-packet at the end of the month. The clothes in which I had

57

taken such pride at first became less resplendent, until I felt it as a disgrace to go to church in them. But it became clear to me that this was yet another of the trials I was called upon to undergo, and I endured it, until I almost took pleasure in the darns on my sleeves and elbows.

At this time I was invited to the wedding of Hori's son, Kedar. They marry young, these people! It was an occasion which surmounted religious differences, and it was a distinct pleasure to me to be again with the family, for their attitude had changed. They had become reconciled to my Presbyterianism and indeed treated me with respect for my profession, a respect which, I fear, was sometimes missing in the attitude of my superiors and even my pupils. The marriage rites distressed me. The make-shift though beautiful tent, the coconut-palm arches hung with clusters of fruit, the use of things like mango leaves and grass and saffron, the sacrificial fire, all these things filled me with shame rather than delight. But the rites were only a small part of the celebrations. There was much good food, strictly vegetarian but somehow extremely tempting; and after a period of distate for Indian food, I had come back to it again. The food, I say, was rich. The music and the dances were thrilling. The tent and the illuminations had a charm which not even our school hall had on concert nights, though the marriage ceremony did not of course have the grace and dignity of those conducted, as proper marriages should be, in a church.

Kedar received a fabulous dowry, and his bride, of whose face I had just a glimpse when her silk veil was parted, was indeed beautiful. But such beauty has always appeared to me skin deep. Beauty in women is a disturbing thing. But beyond the beauty it is always necessary to look for the greater qualities of manners and—a thing I always remind Winston of—no one is too young or too old to learn—manners and *ways*. She was beautiful. It was sad to think of her joined to Kedar for life, but she was perhaps fitted for nothing else. No need to speak of the resplendent regalia of Kedar himself: his turban, the crown with tassels and pendant glass, his richly embroidered silk jacket, and all those other adornments which for that night concealed so well the truck-driver that he was.

I left the wedding profoundly saddened. I could not help reflecting on my own position and contrasting it with Hori's or even Kedar's. I was now over forty, and marriage, which in the normal way would have come to me at the age of twenty or thereabouts, was still far from me. This was my own fault. Arranged marriages like Kedar's had no part in my scheme of things. I wished to marry, as the person says in *The Vicar of Wakefield*, someone who had qualities that would wear well. My choice was severely restricted. I wished to marry a Presbyterian lady who was intelligent, well brought up and educated, and wished to marry me. This last condition, alas, I could find few willing to fulfil. And indeed I had little to offer. Among Hindus it would have been otherwise. There might have been men of substance who would have been willing to marry their daughters to a teacher, to acquire respectability and the glamour of a learned profession. Such a position has its strains, of course, for it means that the daughter remains, as it were, subject to her family; but the position is not without its charms.

You might imagine—and you would be correct—that at this time my faith was undergoing its severest strain. How often I was on the point of reneging I shudder to tell. I felt myself about to yield; I stiffened in my devotions and prayers. I reflected on the worthlessness of worldly things, but this was a reflection I found few to share. I might add here, in parenthesis and without vanity, that I had had several offers from the fathers of unconverted daughters, whose only condition was the one, about my religion, which I could not accept; for my previous caste had made me acceptable to many.

In this situation of doubt, of nightly wrestling with God, an expression whose meaning I came only then fully to understand, my fortune changed. I was appointed a headmaster. Now I can speak! How many people know of the tribulations, the pettiness, the intrigue which schoolteachers have to undergo to obtain such promotion? Such jockeying, such jealousy, such ill-will comes into play. What can I say of the advances one has to make, the rebuffs one has to suffer in silence, the waiting, the undoing of the unworthy who seek to push themselves forward for positions which they are ill-qualified to fill but which, by glibness and all the outward shows of respectability and efficiency and piety, they manage to persuade our superiors that they alone can fill? I too had my adversaries. My chief rival—but let him rest in peace! I am, I trust, a Christian, and will do no man the injustice of imagining him to persist in error even after we have left this vale of tears.

In my fortune, so opportune, I saw the hand of God. I speak in all earnestness. For without this I would surely have lapsed into the ways of darkness, for who among us can so steel himself as to resist temptation for all time? In my gratitude I applied myself with renewed dedication to my task. And it was this that doubtless evoked the gratification of my superiors which was to lead to my later elevation. For at a time when most men, worn out by the struggle, are content to relax, I showed myself more eager than before. I instituted prayers four times a day. I insisted on attendance at Sunday School. I taught Sunday School myself, and with the weight of my influence persuaded the other teachers to do likewise, so that Sunday became another day for us, a day of rest which we consumed with work for the Lord.

And I did not neglect the educational side. The blackboards all now sparkled with diagrams in chalks of various colours, projects which we had in hand. Oh, the school was such a pretty sight then! I instituted a rigid system of discipline, and forbade indiscriminate flogging by pupil teachers. All flogging I did myself on Friday afternoons, sitting in impartial judgment, as it were, on the school, on pupils as well as teachers. It is surely a better system, and I am glad to say that it has now been adopted throughout the island. The most apt pupils I kept after school, and for some trifling extra fee gave them private lessons. And the school became so involved with work as an ideal that had to be joyously pursued and not as something that had to be endured, that the usefulness of these private lessons was widely appreciated, and soon larger numbers than I could cope with were staying after school for what they affectionately termed their 'private'.

And I married. It was now in my power to marry virtually anyone I pleased, and there were among the Sunday School staff not a few who made their attachment to me plain. I am not such a bad looking fellow! But I wished to marry someone who had qualities that would wear well. I was nearly fifty. I did not wish to marry someone who was much younger than myself. And it was my good fortune at this juncture to receive an offer—I hesitate to use this word, which sounds so much like the Hindu custom and reminds one of the real estate business, but here I must be frank—from no less a person than a schools inspector, who had an unmarried daughter of thirty-five, a woman neglected by the men of the island because of her attainments—yes, you read right—which were considerable, but not of the sort that proclaims itself to the world. In our attitude to women much remains to be changed! I have often, during these past days, reflected on marriage. Such a turning, a point in time whence so many consequences flow. I wonder what Winston, poor boy, will do when his time comes.

My establishment could not rival Hori's or Kedar's for splendour, but within it there was peace and culture such as I had long dreamed of. It was a plain wooden house, but well built, built to last, unlike so many of these modern monstrosities which I see arising these days; and it was well ordered. We had simple bentwood chairs with cane bottoms. No marble-topped tables with ball-fringed lace! No glass cabinets! I hung my treasured framed teaching diploma on the wall, with my religious pictures and some scenes of the English countryside. It was also my good fortune at this time to get an old autographed photograph of one of our first missionaries. In the decoration of our humble home my wife appeared to release all the energy and experience of her thirty-five years which had so far been denied expression.

To her, as to myself, everything came late. It was our fear, confirmed by the views of many friends who behind their expressions of goodwill concealed as we presently saw much uncharitableness, that we would be unable to have children, considering our advanced years. But they, and we, underestimated the power of prayer, for within a year of our marriage Winston was born.

The birth of Winston came to us as a grace and a blessing. Yet it also filled me with anxiety, for I could not refrain from assessing the difference between our ages. It occurred to me, for instance, that he would be thirty when I was eighty. It was a disturbing thought, for the companionship of children is something which, perhaps because of my profession, I hold especially dear. My anxiety had another reason. It was that Winston, in his most formative years, would be without not only my guidance—for what guidance can a man of seventy give to a lusty youngster of twenty?—but also without my financial support.

The problem of money, strange as it might appear, considering my unexpected elevation and all its accruing benefits, was occupying the minds of both my wife and myself. For my retirement was drawing near, and my pension would scarcely be more than what I subsisted on as a simple pupil teacher. It seemed then that like those pilgrims, whose enthusiasm I admire but cannot share, I was advancing towards my goal by taking two steps forward and one step back, though in my case a likelier simile might be that I was taking one step forward and one step back. So success always turns to ashes in the mouth of those who seek it as ardently as I had! And if I had the vision and the depth of faith which I now have, I might have seen even then how completely false are the things of this world, how much they flatter only to deceive.

We were both, as I say, made restless. And now the contemplation of baby Winston was a source of much pain to both of us, for the poor innocent creature could scarcely know what anguish awaited him when we would both be withdrawn from this vale of tears. His helplessness, his dependence tortured me. I was past the age when the taking out of an insurance policy was a practicable proposition; and during my days as a simple teacher I never had the resources to do so. It seemed, then, that I was being destroyed by my own good fortune, by the fruits of all my endeavour. Yet I did not heed this sign.

I continued while I could giving private lessons. I instituted a morning session as well, in addition to the afternoon one. But I did so with a heavy heart, tormented by the thought that in a few years this privilege and its small reward would be denied me, for private lessons, it must be understood, are considered the prerogative of a headmaster: in this way he stamps his character on the school. My results in the exhibition examinations for boys under twelve continued to be heartening; they far surpassed those of many other country schools. My religious zeal continued unabated; and it was this zeal which, burning in those years when most men in my position would have relaxed—they, fortunate souls, having their children fully grown—it was this surprising zeal, I say, which also contributed, I feel, to my later elevation which, as you will see from the plain narration of these events, I did not seek.

My retirement drew nearer. I became fiercer at school. I wished all the boys under me could grow up at once. I was merciless towards the backward. My wife, poor creature, could not control her anxiety with as much success as myself. She had no occupation, no distracting vocation, in which her anxiety might have been consumed. She had only Winston, and this dear infant continually roused her to fears about his future. For his sake she would, I believe, have sacrificed her own life! It was not easy for her. And it required but the exercise of the mildest Christian charity to see that the reproaches she flung with increased acerbity and frequency at my head were but expressions of her anxiety. Sometimes,

I must confess, I failed! And then my own unworthiness would torment me, as it torments me now.

We confided our problems to my wife's father, the schools inspector. Though we felt it unfair to let another partake of our troubles, it is none the less a recognized means of lightening any load which the individual finds too heavy to bear. But he, poor man, though as worried on his daughter's behalf as she was on Winston's, could offer only sympathy and little practical help. He reported that the authorities were unwilling to give me an extension of my tenure as headmaster. My despondency found expression in a display of temper, which he charitably forgave; for though he left the house, promising not to do another thing for us, he presently returned, and counselled patience.

So patient we were. I retired. I could hardly bear to remain at home, so used had I been to the daily round, the daily trials. I went out visiting, for no other reason than that I was afraid to be alone at home. My zeal, I believe, was remarked upon, though I took care to avoid the school, the scene of my late labours. I sought to take in for private lessons two or three pupils whose progress had deeply interested me. But my methods were no longer the methods that found favour! The parents of these children reported that the new headmaster had expressed himself strongly, and to my great disfavour, on the subject, to such a degree, in fact, that the progress of their children at school was being hampered. So I desisted; or rather, since the time has come for frankness, they left me.

The schools inspector, a regular visitor now at our humble, sad home, continued to counsel patience. I have so far refrained in this narrative from permitting my wife to speak directly; for I wish to do nothing that might increase the load she will surely have to bear, for my wife, though of considerable attainments, has not had the advantages of a formal education on which so much stress is nowadays laid. So I will refrain from chronicling the remark with which she greeted this advice of her father's. Suffice it to say that she spoke a children's rhyme without any great care for its metre or rhyme, the last of which indeed she destroyed by accidentally, in her haste, pulling down a vase from the centre-table on to the floor, where the water ran like one of the puddles which our baby Winston so lately made. After this incident relations between my wife and her father underwent a perceptible strain; and I took care to be out of the house as often as possible, and indeed it was pleasant to forget one's domestic troubles and walk abroad and be greeted as 'Headmaster' by the simple village folk.

Then, as it appears has happened so regularly throughout my life, the clouds rolled away and the sky brightened. I was appointed a School Manager. The announcement was made in the most heart-warming way possible, by the schools inspector himself, anticipating the official notification by a week or so. And the occasion became a family reunion. It was truly good to see the harassed schools inspector relaxing at last, and to see father and daughter reasonably happy with one another. My delight in this was almost as great as the delight in my new dignity.

For a school managership is a good thing to come to a man in the evening of his days. It permits an exercise of the most benign power imaginable. It permits a man at a speech day function to ask for a holiday for the pupils; and nothing is as warming as the lusty and sincere cheering that follows such a request. It gives power even over headmasters, for one can make surprise visits and it is in one's power to make reports to the authorities. It is a position of considerable responsibility as well, for a school manager manages a school as much as a managing director manages a company. It is in his power to decide whether the drains, say, need to be remade entirely or need simply be plastered over to look as new; whether one coat of paint or two are needed; whether a ceiling can be partially renovated and painted over or taken out altogether and replaced. He orders the number of desks and blackboards which he considers necessary, and the chalks and the stationery. It is, in short, a dignity ideally suited to one who has led an active life and is dismayed by the prospect of retirement. It brings honour as well as reward. It has the other advantage that school managers are like civil servants; they are seldom dismissed; and their honours tend to increase rather than diminish.

I entered on my new tasks with zeal, and once again all was well at our home. My wife's father visited us regularly, as though, poor man, anxious to share the good fortune for which he was to a large measure responsible. I looked after the school, the staff, the pupils. I visited all the parents of the pupils under my charge and spoke to them of the benefits of education, the dangers of absenteeism, and so on. I know I will be forgiven if I add that from time to time, whenever the ground appeared ripe, I sowed the seed of Presbyterianism or at any rate doubt among those who continued in the ways of darkness. Such zeal was unknown among school managers. I cannot account for it myself. It might be that my early austerity and ambition had given me something of the crusading zeal. But it was inevitable that such zeal should have been too much for some people to stomach.

For all his honour, for all the sweet cheers that greet his request for a holiday for the pupils, the school manager's position is one that sometimes attracts adverse and malicious comment. It is the fate of anyone who finds himself in a position of power and financial responsibility. The rumours persisted; and though they did not diminish the esteem in which I was so clearly held by the community—at the elections, for example, I was approached by all five candidates and asked to lend my voice to their cause, a situation of peculiar difficulty, which I resolved by promising all five to remain neutral, for which they were effusively grateful—it is no good thing for a man to walk among people who every day listen eagerly—for flesh is frail, and nothing attracts our simple villagers as much as scurrilous gossip—to slanders against himself. It was beneath my dignity, or rather, the dignity of my position, to reply to such attacks; and in this situation I turned, as I was turning with growing frequency, to my wife's father for advice. He suggested that I should relinquish one of my managerships, to indicate my disapproval of the gossip and the little esteem in which I held wordly honour. For I had so far succeeded in my new functions that I was now the manager of three schools, which was the maximum number permitted.

I followed his advice. I relinquished the managership of a school which was in a condition so derelict that not even repeated renovations could efface the original gimcrackery of its construction. This school had been the cause of most of the rumours, and my relinquishing of it attracted widespread comment and was even mentioned in the newspapers. It remained dear to me, but I was willing for it to go into other hands. This action of mine had the effect of stilling rumours and gossip. And the action proved to have its own reward, for some months later my wife's father, ever the bearer of good tidings, intimated that there was a possibility of a new school being put up in the area. I was thoroughly suited for its management; and he, the honest broker between the authorities and myself, said that my name was being mentioned in this connection. I was at that time manager of only two schools; I was entitled to a third. He warmly urged me to accept. I hesitated, and my hesitations were later proved to be justified. But the thought of a new school fashioned entirely according to my ideas and principles was too heady. I succumbed to temptation. If now I could only go back and withdraw that acceptance! The good man hurried back with the news; and within a fortnight I received the official notification.

I must confess that during the next few months I lost sight of my doubts in my zeal and enthusiasm for the new project. My two other schools suffered somewhat. For if there is a thing to delight the heart of the school manager, it is the management of a school not yet built. But, alas! We are at every step reminded of the vanity of wordly things. How often does it happen that a person, placed in the position he craves, a position which he is in every way suited to fill, suddenly loses his grip! Given the opportunity for which he longs, he is unable to make use of it. The effort goes all into the striving.

So now it happened with me. Nearly everything I touched failed to go as it should. I, so careful and correct in assessments and estimates, was now found repeatedly in error. None of my calculations were right. There were repeated shortages and stoppages. The school progressed far more slowly than I would have liked. And it was no consolation to me to find that in this moment I was alone, in this long moment of agony! Neither to my wife nor to her father could I turn for comfort. They savoured the joy of my managership of a new school without reference to me. I had my great opportunity; they had no doubt I would make use of it; and I could not bear disillusioning them or breaking into their happiness with my worries.

My errors attracted other errors. My errors multiplied, I tell you! To cover up one error I had to commit twenty acts of concealment, and these twenty had to be concealed. I felt myself caught in a curious inefficiency that seemed entirely beyond my control, something malignant, powered by forces hostile to myself. Until at length it seemed that failure was staring me in the face, and that my entire career would be forgotten in this crowning failure. The building went up, it is true. It had a respectable appearance. It looked a building. But it was far from what I had visualized. I had miscalculated badly, and it was too late to remedy the errors. Its faults, its weaknesses would be at once apparent even to the scantily trained eye. And now night after night I was tormented by this failure of mine. With the exercise of only a little judgment it could so easily have been made right. Yet now the time for that was past! Day after day I was drawn to the building, and every day I hoped that by some miracle it would have been effaced during the night. But there it always stood, a bitter reproach.

Matters were not made easier for me by the reproaches of my wife and her father. They both rounded on me and said with justice that my failure would involve them all. And the days went by! I could not—I have never liked bickering, the answering of insult with insult—I could not reproach them with having burdened me with such an enterprise at the end of my days. I did it for their glory, for I had acquired sufficient to last me until the end of my days. I did it for my wife and her father, and for my son Winston. But who will believe me? Who will believe that a man works for the glory of others, except he work for the glory of God? They reproached me. They stood aside from me. In this moment of need they deserted me.

They were bitter days. I went for long walks through our villages in the cool of the evening. The children ran out to greet me. Mothers looked up from their cooking, fathers from their perches on the roadside culverts, and greeted me, "Headmaster!" And soon my failure would be apparent even to the humblest among them. I had to act quickly. Failures should be destroyed. The burning down of a school is an unforgiveable thing, but there are surely occasions when it can be condoned, when it is the only way out. Surely this was such an occasion! It is a drastic step. But it is one that has been taken more than once in this island. So I argued with myself. And always the answer was there: my failure had to be destroyed, not only for my own sake, but for the sake of all those, villagers included, whose fates were involved with mine.

Once I had made up my mind, I acted with decision. It was that time of year, mid-November, when people are beginning to think of Christmas to the exclusion of nearly everything else. This served my purpose well. I required—with what shame I now confess it—certain assistants, for it was necessary for me to be seen elsewhere on the day of the accident. Much money, much of what we had set aside for the future of our son Winston had to go on this. And already it had been necessary to seal the lips of certain officials who had rejoiced in my failure and were willing to proclaim it to the world. But at last it was ready. On Boxing Day we would go to Port-of-Spain, to the races. When we returned the following day, the school would be no more. I say 'we', though my wife had not been apprised of my intentions.

With what fear, self-reproach, and self-disgust I waited for the days to pass! When I heard the Christmas carols, ever associated for me with the indefinable sweetness of Christmas Eve—which I now once more feel, thanks to my decision, though underneath there is a sense of doom and destruction, deserved, but with their own inevitable reward—when I heard carols and Christmas commercials on the radio, my heart sank; for it seemed that I had cut myself off from all about me, that once more I had become a stranger to the faith which I profess. So these days passed in sorrow, in nightly frenzies of prayer and self-castigation. Regret assailed me. Regret for what might have been, regret for what was to come. I was sinking, I felt, into a pit of defilement whence I could never emerge.

Of all this my wife knew nothing. But then she asked one day, "What have you decided to do?" and, without waiting for my reply, at once drew up such a detailed plan, which corresponded so closely to what I had myself devised, that my heart quailed. For if, in this moment of my need, when the deepest resource was needed, I could devise a plan which might have been devised by anyone else, then discovery was certain. And to my shame, Winston, who only two or three days before had been teasing me with my previous unbaptised name, Winston took part in this discussion, with no appearance of shame on his face, only thrill and—sad am I to say it—a pride in me greater than I had ever seen the boy display.

How can one tell of the workings of the human heart? How can one speak of the urge to evil—an urge of which Christians more than anyone else are so aware—and of the countervailing urge to good? You must remember that this is the season of goodwill. And goodwill it was. For goodwill was what I was feeling towards all. At every carol my heart melted. Whenever a child rushed towards me and cried, "Headmaster"! I was tormented by grief. For the sight of the unwashed creatures, deprived so many of them of schooling, which matters so much in those early years, and the absence of which ever afterwards makes itself felt, condemning a human being to an animal-like existence, the sight of these creatures, grateful towards me who had on so many evenings gone among them propagating the creed with what energy I could, unmanned me. They were proud of their new school. They were even prouder of their association with the man who had built it.

Everywhere I felt rejected. I went to church as often as I could, but even there I found rejection. And as the time drew nearer the enormity of what I proposed grew clearer to me. It was useless to tell myself that what I was proposing had been often done. The carols, the religious services, the talk of birth and life, they all unmanned me.

I walked among the children as one who had it in his power to provide or withhold blessing, and I thought of that other Walker, who said of those among whom I walked that they were the blessed, and that theirs was the kingdom of heaven. And as I walked it seemed that at last I had seized the true essence of the religion I had adopted, and whose wordly success I had with such energy promoted. So that it seemed that these trials I was undergoing had been reserved to the end of my days, so that only then I could have a taste of the ecstasy about which I had so far only read. With this ecstasy I walked. It was Christmas Eve. It is Christmas Eve. My head felt drawn out of my body. I had difficulty in assessing the size and distance of objects. I felt myself tall. I felt myself part of the earth and yet removed.

And: "No!" I said to my wife at teatime. "No, I will not disgrace myself by this action of cowardice. Rather, I will proclaim my failure to the world and ask for my due punishment."

She behaved as I expected. She had been busy putting up all sorts of Christmas decorations, expensive ones from the United States, which are all the rage now, so unlike the simple decorations I used to see in the homes of our early missionaries before the war. But how changed is the house to which we moved! How far has simplicity vanished and been replaced by show! And I gloried in it!

She begged me to change my mind. She summoned Winston to her help. They both wept and implored me to go through with our plan. But I was firm. I do believe that if the schools inspector were alive, he would also have been summoned to plead with me. But he, fortunate man, passed away some three weeks ago, entrusting his daughter and grandson to my care; and this alone is my fear, that by gaining glory for myself I might be injuring them. But I was firm. And then there started another of those scenes with which I had become only too familiar, and the house which that morning was filled with the enthusiasm of Winston was changed into one of mourning. Winston sobbed, tears running down his plump cheeks and down his well-shaped nose to his firm top lip, pleading with me to burn the school down, and generally behaving as though I had deprived him of a bonfire. And then a number of things were destroyed by his mother, and she left the house with Winston, vowing never to see me again, never to be involved in the disgrace which was sure to come.

And so here I sit, waiting not for Christmas, but in this house where the autographed photograph of one of our earliest missionaries gazes down at me through his rich beard and luxuriant eyebrows, and where the walls carry so many reminders of my past life of endeavour and hardship and struggle and triumph and also, alas, final failure, I wait for the day after Boxing Day, after the races to which we were to have gone, for the visit of the inspectors of the Audit Department. The house is lonely and dark. The radios play the Christmas songs. I am very lonely. But I am strong. And here I lay down my pen. My hand tires; the beautiful letters we were taught to fashion at the mission school have begun to weaken and to straggle untidily over the ruled paper; and someone is knocking.

December 27. How can one speak of the ways of the world, how can one speak of the tribulations that come one's way? Even expiation is denied me. For even as I wrote the last sentence of the above account, there came a knocking at my door, and I went to open unto him who knocked. And lo, there was a boy, bearing tidings. And behold, towards the west the sky had reddened, and the boy informed me that the school was ablaze. What could I do? My world fell about my ears. Even final expiation, final triumph, it seemed, was denied me. Certain things are not for me. In this moment of anguish and despair my first thought was for my wife. Where had she gone? I went out to seek her. When I returned, after a fruitless errand, I discovered that she and Winston had come back to seek me. Smiling through our tears, we embraced. So it was Christmas after all for us. And, with lightened heart, made heavy only by my wrestling with the Lord, we went to the races on Boxing Day, yesterday. We did not gamble. It is against our principles. The inspectors from the Audit Department sent word today that they would not, after all come.

Samuel Selvon (*Trinidad*)

Man, in England, You've Just Got to Love Animals

Back home in the West Indies it have a kind of dog we does call them pot-hounds, because the only time they around the place is when a pot on the fire and food cooking. Another kind, we call them hat-racks because they so thin and cadaverous you could hang a hat on any one of the protruding bones.

But you mustn't feel them is the only two canine specimens it have. And you mustn't feel that the people down here don't like animals. The only thing is, dog is dog and man is man, and never the twain shall meet in them islands, as they meet in Brit'n.

You give a dog a bone and that is that, and if food left over after Man eat, Dog get it. None of this fancy steak lark, or taking the dog to a shop where they trim it and manicure the nails and put on a pants to keep it warm in the winter.

The topic is man's best friend, because in Bayswater Jackson landlady had a bitch what make one set of pups, and she come to Jackson room one morning to give him one.

"Mr. Jackson," the landlady say, "here is a pup for you. I know how fond you are of Bessy, and I'm sure you'll take good care of it."

Now Jackson had a habit, every time he see Bessy, he patting her on the head and remarking what a wonderful animal. And he even went so far as to take Bessy for a walk in the Park one day when the landlady was busy.

But the reason why Jackson getting on like that is only because he want to keep on good terms with her. You know the old saying 'Love me, love my dog'. It so hard for the boys to get a place to live, that when they do get one, they have to make sure that they keep the landlords and landladies in friendly mood.

So Jackson shake his head sadly, cogitate for a few seconds, and say, "Mrs. Feltin, if Bessy make that pup, he deserve a real good master who could bring him up like a stalwart."

"It is a bitch," Mrs. Feltin say.

"That make it worse," Jackson say. "I mean, she have to be brought up like a lady. I can't keep her here in this one room where I have to live."

"Nonsense," Mrs. Feltin say. "She can sleep under the stairs in the basement. You always said you wanted a dog."

That was true. Knowing that words don't cost nothing, one day Jackson did went so far as to say:

"Mrs. Feltin, don't forget, wherever I am, the day that Bessy have young ones you must give one to me."

Jackson watch the puppy wrap up in a white cloth, and Mrs. Feltin holding it like a new-born baby.

"You ain't have a male one?" he asked hopefully.

"No," the landlady say, "I have given them all away. Don't you want it?"

Well, Jackson know that in this country dogs and cats does live real high, and the people does treat them as if they believe in reincarnation. And he know, too, that if he say 'No' he might as well start looking for another place to live.

But he still hedging. "How about if you keep it for me, Mrs. Feltin, and give me when it get big?"

"It's big enough now," Mrs. Feltin say, "and, besides, it won't know you for its master then."

"Yes, I didn't think about that." Jackson stay quiet for a minute. "But how about feeding, and so on?"

"Oh, just a little piece of steak. I'm sure she hasn't a big appetite yet."

Jackson wince when he hear that: stewing meat is the highest he ever treat himself with, except for an occasional 'boiler' on a Sunday. Then he say quickly, noticing the suspicion on Mrs. Feltin face. "All right, thank you very much."

And he take the pup from her and close the door.

"Look what hell I put myself in for," he say to himself. "What to do now? Give it away? Take a ride on the Tube and leave it by High Barnet or Roding Valley, or one of them far-away places with strange-sounding names?"

In the end he put some milk in a saucer and leave it in the corner for the pup and went to work.

In the evening some of the boys drop around to see him and when they see the pup they start to give Jackson hell.

"You keeping a managery now, old man?"

"You could train it for the tracks, boy, and make a lot of money."

"What you going to call it?"

"I ain't keeping it long enough to give it a name," Jackson say. "**Any-body want it?**"

This time so the puppy looking at all of them as if they is criminals, and it only going by the door and sniffing as if it want to get away from this evil company.

"Why you don't dump it in the Serpentine?"

"Or send it for vivisection and get a few bob?"

"You fellars too malicious," Jackson say, though in truth them is ideas that already occur to him and he dismiss them as being too drastic.

"You really want to get rid of it?" one of the boys asked. "Put it in a paper bag and give me when I going, and I go dump it somewhere far from here."

Jackson did that, and the friend take the puppy away and leave it up by Finsbury Park Tube station.

Seven o'clock next morning when Jackson turning to catch a last fifteen minutes' sleep before getting up to dress for work, he hear a yelping and a scratching at the basement door. When he go, he see the puppy.

Jackson haul it inside and put some bread and milk in a saucer, thinking all kinds of ways to get rid of the puppy.

When he was leaving the house to go to work he meet Mrs. Feltin.

"Good morning," she say, "how is the puppy? What do you call her?"

"Am—er—Flossie," Jackson say.

"It's a nice name," Mrs. Feltin say. "If you leave the money with me, I could get some nice steak for her lunch while you're at work."

Poor Jackson had to fork out three-and-six for steak for Flossie, while he himself was studying to get a piece of neck-of-lamb for his own dinner.

Well, the day he get the puppy was a Monday, and the whole week gone by and Jackson low in pocket buying steak for Flossie, and he getting real tired looking after the bitch.

On the Friday he was moaning at work about the situation, when one of his English mates say:

"My missus is looking for a bitch. I'll take Flossie off you."

Now that a solution was at hand, Jackson do some rapid thinking. "That bitch is from good stock," he say. "The mother is a pure Alsatian and the father is a full-blooded fox-terrier. I wasn't thinking so much of giving away as selling."

"Give you ten bob," the Englisher say.

"What about a pound?" Jackson say, and as soon as he see the Englisher was about to agree he add: "Or a guinea. Make it a guinea and call it a deal."

"That's a lot of money," the Englisher say.

"Think of the dog that you getting," Jackson say.

"All right," the Englisher say, "I'll come with you after work."

Jackson make the fellar wait by the station in the evening, and he went home and collect Flossie. But just as he was going out, who he should meet but Mrs. Feltin!

"Where are you taking Flossie?" she ask.

"To the vet," Jackson say, thinking fast. "It look as if she ailing, and I want to make sure is nothing serious."

"Quite right," Mrs. Feltin say.

Jackson hurry off to the Tube station, and hand Flossie over to the Englisher.

"Looks like a mongrel to me," the Englisher observed.

"No, it is a little Hennessy," Jackson say.

"Ten bob," the Englisher say.

"All right," Jackson say, "you have a real bargain there."

The Englisher give Jackson ten bob and went away with Flossie. Jackson had a mild-and-bitter in the pub and start to cogitate on what he would tell Mrs. Feltin when he see her.

When he went back home, he knock at her door.

"What is it, Jackson?" Mrs. Feltin say, alarmed by the look on his face.

"Mrs. Feltin," Jackson say, shaking his head like a man in a daze, "fate has struck me a cruel blow. Something terrible happen."

Mrs. Feltin held her breath. "Not Flossie?" she whisper hoarsely.

"Yes. She pass away during the operation at the vet."

"What was wrong with her?"

"I not so sure. The vet call a big name for the sickness. And I only had she for a few days."

"What a tragic thing to happen," Mrs. Feltin say, and it look as if she want to cry.

Jackson began to warm up. "All my friends admire that little bitch, and she and me was coming good friends. If I had some land in England, I bury her on it myself. I was just thinking how that dog would of gone in the films, like another Lassie. Poor Flossie. She gone to rest in the Happy Hunting Ground, for sure."

"Don't take it so hard," Mrs. Feltin say.

"I can't tell you how I feel," Jackson say.

"I wish there was something I could do," Mrs. Feltin say. And then she brighten up. "Wait a minute. There is something. I am getting back one of the pups from my brother—his landlady doesn't like to have animals in the house. You shall have it. No, no, it's quite all right, don't thank me! I know an animal-lover when I see one."

Samuel Selvon

When Greek meets Greek

ONE morning Ramkilawansingh (after this, we calling this man Ram) was making a study of the notice-boards along Westbourne Grove what does advertise rooms to let. Every now and then he writing down an address or a telephone number, though most of the time his eyes colliding up with *No Colours, Please,* or *Sorry, No Kolors.*

"Red, white and blue, all out but you," Ram was humming a little ditty what children say when they playing whoop. Just as he get down by Bradley's Corner he met Fraser.

"You look like a man who looking for a place to live," Fraser say.

"You look like a man who could tell me the right place to go," Ram say.

"You try down by Ladbroke Grove?" Fraser ask.

"I don't want to go down in that criminal area," Ram say, "at least, not until they find the man who kill Kelso."

"Then you will never live in the Grove," Fraser say.

"You are a contact man," Ram say, "which part you think I could get a room, boy?"

Fraser scratch his head. "I know of a landlord up the road who vow that he ain't ever taking anybody who come from the West Indies. But he don't mind taking Indians. He wouldn't know the difference when he see you is a Indian ... them English people so foolish they believe every Indian come from India."

"You think I stand a chance?" Ram ask.

"Sure, you stand a chance. All you have to do is put on a turban."

"I never wear a turban in my life; I am a born Trinidadian, a real Creole. All the same, you best hads give me the address, I will pass around there later."

So Fraser give him the address, and Ram went on reading a few more boards, but he got discourage after a while and went to see the landlord.

The first thing the landlord ask him was: "What part of the world do you come from?"

"I am an Untouchable from the heart of India," Ram say. "I am looking for a single room. I dwelt on the banks of the Ganges. Not too expensive."

"But you are not in your national garments," the landlord say.

"When you are in Rome," Ram say, making it sound like an original statement, "do as the Romans do."

While the landlord sizing up Ram, an Indian tenant come up the steps to go inside. This fellow was Chandrilaboodoo (after this, we calling this man Chan) and he had a big beard with a hair-net over it, and he was wearing a turban. When he see Ram, he clasp his hands with the palms touching across his chest by way of greeting.

The old Ram catch on quick and do the same thing.

"*Acha, Hindustani,*" Chan say.

"*Acha, pilau, papadom, chickenvindaloo,*" Ram say desperately, hoping for the best.

Chan nod his head, say good morning to the landlord and went inside.

"That was a narrow shave," Ram thought, "I have to watch out for that man."

"That was Mr. Chan," the landlord say, "he is the only other Indian tenant I have at the moment. I have a single room for two pounds. Are you a student?"

"Who is not a student?" Ram say, getting into the mood of the thing. "Man is for ever studying ways and means until he passes into the hands of Allah."

Well, to cut a long story short, Ram get a room on the first floor, right next door to Chan, and he move in that same evening.

But as the days going by, Ram had to live like cat-and-mouse with Chan. Every time he see Chan, he have to hide in case this man start up this Hindustani talk again, or start to ask him questions about Mother India. In fact, it begin to get on Ram nerves, and he decide that he had to do something.

"This house too small for the two of we," Ram say to himself, "one will have to go."

So Ram went down in the basement to see the landlord.

"I have the powers of the Occult," Ram say, "and I have come to warn you of this man Chan. He is not a good tenant. He keeps the bathroom dirty, he does not tidy up his room at all, and he is always chanting and saying his prayers loudly and disturbing the other tenants."

"I have had no complaints," the landlord say.

"But I am living next door to him," Ram say, "and if I concentrate my powers I can see through the wall. That man is a menace, and the best thing you can do is to give him notice. You have a good house here and it would be a pity to let one man spoil it for the other tenants."

"I will have a word with him about it," the landlord say.

Well, the next evening Ram was in his room when he hear a knock at the door. He run in the corner quick and stand upon his head, and say, "Come in."

The landlord come in.

"I am just practising my yoghourt," Ram say.

"I have had a word with Mr. Chan," the landlord say, "and I have reason to suspect that you have deceived me. You are not from India, you are from the West Indies."

Ram turn right-side up. "I am a citizen of the world," he say.

"You are flying false colours," the landlord say. "You do not burn incense like Mr. Chan, you do not dress like Mr. Chan, and you do not talk like Mr. Chan."

"Give me a break, old man," Ram say, falling back on the good old West Indian dialect.

"It is too late. You have already started to make trouble. You must go."

Well, the very next week find Ram out scouting again, giving the boards a perusal, and who he should chance to meet but Fraser.

He start to tell Fraser how life hard, how he had to keep dodging from this Chan fellar all the time, and it was pure torture.

"Listen," Fraser say, "you don't mean a big fellar with a beard, and he always wearing a turban?"

"That sound like him," Ram say. "You know him?"

"Know him!" Fraser say. "Man, that is a fellar from Jamaica who I send to that house to get a room!"

Samuel Selvon

Gussy and the Boss

THE organization known as Industrial Corporation was taken over shortly after the war by a group of European businessmen with interest in the West Indies and renamed the New Enterprises Company, with a financial backing of $50,000, The new owners had the buildings renovated where they stood on the southern outskirts of Port-of-Spain, a short distance from the railway station.

While the buildings were being painted and the old office furniture replaced, none of the employees knew that the company had changed hands. They commented that it was high time the dilapidated offices were given a complete overhauling, and they tried out the new chairs and desks and came to words over who should have the mahogany table and this cabinet and that typewriter.

When the buildings had a new face and they were just settling down with renewed ambitions and resolutions to keep the rooms as tidy as possible, Mr. Jones, the boss, called a staff meeting one evening and told them.

He said he was sorry he couldn't tell them before—some arrangement with the new owners—but that Industrial Corporation was going out of business. He said he had been hoping that at least some of the staff would be able to remain, but he was sorry, they all had to go.

There were ten natives working in the offices at the time, and there was a middle-aged caretaker called Gussy. Gussy had one leg. A shark had bitten off the other in the Gulf of Paria while he was out fishing with some friends.

The ten employees—four girl typists and six clerks—had never thought of joining a trade union, partly because they felt that trade unions were for the poor struggling labourers and they were not of that class. As it was, they could do nothing but make vain threats and grumble; one chap went to one of the newspapers and told the editor the whole story and asked him to do something about it. The editor promised and next day a reporter interviewed Mr. Jones, and the following morning a small news

78

item appeared saying that Industrial Corporation had been taken over by a group of wealthy Europeans, and that there was no doubt the colony would benefit as a result, because new industries would be opened.

After two weeks the ten workers cleared out, leaving Mr. Jones and Gussy. Gussy spoke to Mr. Jones.

He said: "Boss, you know how long I here with the business. I is a poor man, boss, and I have a mother to support, and I sure I can't get a work no way else. Please, chief, you can't talk to the new bosses and them, and put in a word for this poor one-legged man, and ask them to keep me? I ain't have a big work; is just to stay in the back of the place and see that nobody interfere with anything. Make a try for me please, pusher, I would appreciate it very much."

Mr. Jones heard Gussy fumble through this long speech and he promised to see what he could do.

A week later the new staff arrived. Gussy hid behind a door in the storeroom and peeped between a crack, because he was afraid to face all the new people at once. His agitation increased as he saw that they were all white people. Were they all bosses, then? The women too?

Later in the morning, while he was sweeping out the store-room as noiselessly as possible, one of the new employees came to him.

"You're Gussy, the caretaker?" he asked in a kind voice.

Gussy dropped the broom and shoved his crutch under his arm quickly, standing up like a soldier at attention.

"Yes, boss, I is the caretaker."

"Mr. Blade would like a word with you. He is the new manager, as you probably know."

"What about, sir? My job is the caretaker job. My name is Gussy. I lives in Belmont. Age forty-five. No children. I lives with my mother. I gets pay every Friday . . ."

"I know all that," the young man smiled a little. "I am in charge of the staff we have here now. But Mr. Blade wants to see you. Just for a little chat. He likes to be acquainted with everyone who works for him."

Gussy's eyes opened wide and showed white. "So I still have the job, chief? You all not going to fire me?"

"Of course not! Come along, Mr. Blade is a busy man."

When he returned to his post at the back of the building a few minutes later Gussy was full of praise for the new boss, mumbling to himself because there was no one to talk with. When he went home in the evening he told his mother:

"You can't imagine! He is a nice man, he even nicer than Mr. Jones! He tell me is all right, that I could stay on the job as caretaker, being as I was here so long already. When I tell you the man nice!"

But as the days went by Gussy wasn't happy at his job any more. He couldn't get accustomed to the idea that white people were working all around him. He treated them as he treated Mr. Blade, stumping along as swiftly as he could to open the garage door or fill the water cooler or whatever odd chore he was called upon to perform. And whereas formerly he had popped in and out of the outer office sharing a word here and a joke there with the native workers, he now kept himself strictly to the back of the building, turning out an hour earlier in the morning to clean out the offices before any of the staff arrived. True, they treated him friendly, but Gussy couldn't get rid of the idea that they were all bosses.

After a week he began to feel lonely and gathered up enough courage to venture near the office door and peep inside to see how the white people were working.

The young man who had spoken to him the first day, Mr. Garry, saw him and called him inside.

Gussy stumped over to his desk with excuses.

"I was only looking to see if everything all right, boss, to see if anybody want anything. The weather hot, I could go and get some ice outside for you right now——"

Garry said: "It's all right, Gussy, and I don't mind you coming to the office now and then." He lowered his voice. "But you watch out for the boss's wife. Sometimes she drops in unexpectedly to see him, and it wouldn't do for her to see you out here, because—well, because here is not the place you're supposed to be, you understand?"

"But sure, boss, Mr. Garry, I won't come back again here, not at all at all, unless you send for me, I promise you that, boss, sure, sure——"

As for Mr. Blade, the moment he drove up in his Buick Eight, Gussy was there with a rag to wipe the car.

"You know, Gussy," Mr. Blade told him one morning, "you manage to do more with that one leg of yours than many a normal man I know."

"Thank you very much respectfully and gratefully, boss, sir, all the offices clean, the water cooler full up, all the ink pots full up, the

store-room pack away just as Mr. Garry say he want it——" Gussy
rambled on even as Mr. Blade walked inside.

One evening when he had opened the garage door for the boss and he
was reversing out—with Gussy standing at the back and giving all sorts of
superfluous directions with his crutch which Mr. Blade ignored—the
boss looked out of the car window and said: "By the way, Gussy, how
much do you work for?"

"Ten dollars a week, chief, sir, respectfully; it not very much, with me
minding my poor mother, but is enough, sir, I can even manage on less
than that if you feel that it too much——"

"I was thinking of giving you more, what with the rising cost of living.
Let me see, today is Wednesday. Come to see me on Friday morning and
we'll talk about it."

Mr. Blade drove off with Gussy's thanksgiving effusion just warming
up.

The next afternoon was hot, and Gussy was feeling drowsy as he sat on
a soapbox in the storeroom. He felt a strong temptation to go and stand
near the office door. The knowledge that he was soon going to earn a
bigger salary gave him courage. He got up and went and positioned
himself just outside the door. He was in time to hear Mr. Garry telling
the others about how his plane was shot down during the war.

Gussy heard a step behind him and turned around. He didn't know it
was the boss's wife, but it wouldn't have made any difference; he would
have behaved the same way with any white person.

"Just looking in to see if the bosses and them want anything at all, no
offence, madam, indeed——"

This time he dropped the crutch in his consternation.

The woman gave him a look and swept past the outer office.

Mr. Blade was sitting in his swivel chair facing the sea. It was a hot afternoon and he had the window open, but the wind that came in was heavy,
as if the heat had taken all the spirit out of it.

Mr. Blade was a kindly man newly arrived in the colony from England.
He was also a weak man, and he knew it. Sometimes Blade was afraid of
life because he was weak and couldn't make decisions or face up to facts
and circumstances. The palms of his hands were always wet when he was
excited or couldn't find the answer to a problem.

As he sat and watched the sea, he was thinking in a general sort of way
about his life, and when his wife burst into the office, he started.

"Oh hello, dear, didn't expect to see you today."

"Herbert," his wife had a most disquieting habit of getting to the point right away, "I thought you had dismissed all the natives who were here before we came?"

"Of course, dear. As you can see, we only have Europeans and one or two who were born in the island."

"I met a one-legged man outside the office just as I was coming in—who's he?"

"Oh heavens, he's only the caretaker. Surely you didn't think he was on the staff?" Blade shifted his eyes and looked at an almanac on the wall above his wife's head.

"You'll have to get rid of him, you know."

"Look, let's not argue now, please. I don't feel very well in this damn heat."

And the next morning Blade sat down in the swivel chair and he faced the sea again. He knew he was going to fire the caretaker, but he tried to think that he wasn't. He wiped the palms of his hands with a white handkerchief. All his life it had been like that; he felt the old fear of uncertainty and instability which had driven him from England return, and he licked his lips nervously.

He swung the chair and looked at the almanac on the wall. He addressed it as if it were his wife.

"That's a silly attitude to adopt," he said to the almanac in a firm voice, "you can't do that sort of thing. On the contrary, it is good for the prestige of the place that we have a coloured worker. I think we should have more—after all, they do the work just as well."

He sneered at the almanac, then looked for some other object in the room to represent Gussy. He fixed his eyes on the out-basket on his desk.

"The way things are at present," he told the basket, "I'm afraid you'll have to go. We don't really need a caretaker any more, and we can always get a woman to come in and clean the offices. I personally didn't have anything to do with it, mind you, it was—er, the directors' decision. I am very sorry to lose you, Gussy, you are a hard, honest worker."

For a minute Blade wondered if there wasn't something he could do—post money secretly to the man every week, or maybe give him a tidy sum to tide him over for a few months.

The next minute he was laughing mirthlessly—once the handkerchief fell and he unconsciously rubbed his hands together and he heard the squelching sound made by the perspiration. And he talked and reasoned with all the objects in the room, as if they were companions, and some objects agreed with him and others didn't.

The pencil and the inkpot said it was all right, he was a fool to worry, and the almanac told him to get it over with quickly for Christ's sake, but the window and the wall and the telephone said Gussy was a poor harmless creature, and he Blade was a spineless, unprincipled dog, who didn't know his own mind and wasn't fit to live.

With an impatient, indecisive gesture Blade jabbed the button on his desk. One of the girls opened the door.

"That caretaker we have—what is his name—Gusher or Gully or something like that——" the lie in his deliberate lapse of memory stabbed him—"send him in to see me, will you, please."

Gussy was waiting to be called. He had told Mr. Garry how the boss would be wanting to see him, and that was why he was keeping so near the office, so they wouldn't have any trouble finding him. Gussy didn't have an idea how much more money he was going to get, but whatever it was, first thing he was going to do was buy a bottle of polish and shine down the boss's car to surprise him. After that, anything could happen.

He stood in a corner, quietly calculating on his fingers how much he would have to pay if he wanted to put down three months' rent in advance.

"Oh, there you are, Gussy," the girl caught sight of him as she came out, "Mr. Blade wants to see you. You'd better go in right away."

"Thank you, madam, I am right here, going in to see the boss right away, with all due respects, no delay at all."

Gussy shoved his crutch under his armpit and stumped as softly as he could to the boss's door.

Samuel Selvon

Cane is Bitter

IN February they began to reap the cane in the undulating fields at La Romain estate in the southern part of Trinidad. "Crop-time coming boy, plenty of work for everybody," men in the village told one another. They set about sharpening their cutlasses on grinding stones, ceasing only when they tested the blades with their thumb-nails and a faint ping! quivered in the air. Or they swung the cutlass at a drooping leaf and cleaved it. But the best test was when it could shave the hairs off your leg.

Everyone in La Romain was happy as work loomed up in the way of their idleness. They laughed and chatted and the children were given more liberty than usual, so they ran about the barracks and played hoop in those canefields which had not as yet been burnt. In the evening, when the fields were on fire, they ran about catching the black straw which rose on the wind as the flames burnt away the dead trash. They smeared one another on the face and laughed to see the black streaks on the skin. It wouldn't matter now if their exertions made them hungry; there would be money to buy flour and rice when the men worked in the fields, cutting and carting the cane to the weighing-bridge.

In the muddy pond about two hundred yards east of the settlement, under the shade of spreading *laginette* trees, women washed clothes and men bathed mules and donkeys and hog cattle. Naked children splashed about in the pond, hitting the water with their hands and laughing loudly when the water shot up in the air at different angles. For them, laughter was a game to be played, and they liked games. Rays of the morning sun came slantways from half-way up in the sky, casting the shadow of trees on the pond, and playing on the brown bodies of the children, who didn't mind the heat. The women dipped the clothes in the water and beat them on rocks which were already bleached white by this constant usage.

Ramlal came to the pond and sat on the western bank, so that he squinted into the sunlight. He dipped his cutlass in the water and began to sharpen it on the end of a rock on which his wife was beating clothes. He was a big man, and in earlier days was reckoned handsome. But work in the fields had not only tanned his skin to a deep brown but actually changed his features. His nose had a slight hump just above the nostrils, and the squint in his eyes was there even in the night. His teeth were stained brown with tobacco, so brown that when he laughed it blended with the colour of his face, and you only saw the lips stretched wide and heard the rumble in his throat.

Rookmin, his wife, was frail but strong as most East Indian women. She was not beautiful, but it was difficult to take any one feature of her face and say it was ugly. Though she was only thirty-six, hard work and the bearing of five children had taken their toll. Her eyes were black and deceptive, in them the indifferent light of a Hindu. A stranger would have looked at her eyes and said: "A faithless woman, she probably deceives her husband." But only a stranger; not a fellow-Indian. Rookmin was so indifferent to faithlessness that the idea never occurred to her; like most poor Indians in the country districts, half her desires and emotions were never given a chance to live, her life dedicated to wresting an existence for herself and her family. Her breasts sagged from years of suckling. Her hands were wrinkled and callous. The toes of her feet were spread out wide from walking barefooted; Rookmin never had need for a pair of shoes as she never left the village.

Now as she washed the clothes she watched the movement of her husband's hands as the blade slid to and fro on the rock.

"Well, Romesh coming tomorrow, is six months since last he come home," Ramlal spoke. "This time, he not going back. But how town life really change the boy! When you study how we save up we money to send him to college in Port-ah-Spain, when you think how mingy we live so he could get books and clothes. And hear what he had to say when he did come home last time."

"But you think he will agree to what we going to do?" Rookmin asked. "He must be learning all kinds of new things now, and this time might be worse than last time. Suppose he say he want to take creole wife?"

"But you mad or what? That could never happen, he bound to married Drusilla already. And we make arrangements with Sampath already, and he say he glad for Romesh to married she? The boy coming tomorrow, he will help with the crop. We done spend too much money on him already; you forget we have other children."

"He different from the other children," Rookmin said. "Since he learning things in the city, he get different. I don't know what will happen. Anyway, we go see when he come."

After some time Ramlal passed the cutlass on his hairy leg and left a clean path. "*Achchha*," he mumbled to himself. Then he got up and called to his two sons, "All you finish washing the mules?"

"Yes, *bap*," Harin the elder shouted. "We will put them in the sun to dry just now."

Ramlal went off muttering to himself. His wife always put doubts in his mind, forcing him to worry when his wont was to let things happen as the gods decreed. The last time Romesh was home he was nearly frightened at how he spoke, but this time, when he married, all that foolishness would go. Ramlal went by his neighbour to smoke and discuss the work that would start the next day, and to borrow a leather strap for the harness of his mules.

Romesh came home the next day. He had four magazines and three books under his arm, and a suitcase in his hand. There was no reception for him; everyone who could work was out in the fields. Romesh was as tall as the canes on either side of the path on which he walked. He sniffed the smell of burning cane trash, but he wasn't nostalgic. He had prepared for this, prepared for the land on which he had toiled as a boy, the thatched huts, the children running naked in the sun. But he saw how waves of wind rippled over the seas of cane and he wondered vaguely about big things like happiness and love and poetry, and how they could fit into the poor, toiling lives the villagers led.

Romesh met his sisters at home. They greeted him shyly, as if he was a stranger. But he held them in his arms and cried, "*Beti*, do you not know your own brother?" And they laughed and hung their heads on his shoulder. "Everybody gone to work," Seta, the elder said, "an' we cooking food to carry. Pa and Ma was looking out early this morning, they say if you come to tell you to come in the field."

Romesh looked around the hut in which he had grown up. It seemed to him that if he had come back home after ten years, there would still be the old table in the centre of the room, its feet sunk in the earthen floor, the black pots and pans hanging on nails near the window. Nothing would change. They would plant the cane, and when it grew and filled with sweet juice cut it down for the factory. The children would waste away their lives working with their parents. No schooling, no education, no widening of experience. It was the same thing the man had lectured about in Public Library three nights before he came home. The most they would learn would be to wield a cutlass expertly, or drive the mule cart to the railway line swiftly so that before the sun went down they would have worked sufficiently to earn more than their neighbours.

With a sigh like an aged man Romesh opened his suitcase and took out a pair of shorts and polo shirt. He donned these and put the suitcase away in the corner. He wondered where would be a safe place to put his books. He opened the suitcase again and put them in.

Then he talked with his sisters while they prepared the meal. Romesh listened how they stumbled with words, how they found it difficult to express themselves. He thought how regretful it was that they couldn't go to school. He widened his thought and embraced all the children in the village, growing up with such little care, running naked in the mud with a piece of roti in their hands, missing out on the joys of life. It was not a holiday he had come home for. It was to waken the sleeping spirits in his brothers and show them how much happier they and their children could be with education. The last time he was in the village he had tried, but his ideas found no reception, even with his own father and mother.

When the food was ready the three of them set off for the field, and the sun in their eyes making them blind. Romesh held one of his sisters on either hand. Other girls joined them, all carrying food. When they saw Romesh they blushed and tittered, and he wondered what they were laughing at among themselves.

He had a vague feeling that they knew something about him of which he was not aware. But he shook his mind.

There were no effusive greetings when Romesh saw his parents. Sweating as they were, their clothes black with the soot of burnt canes, their bodies caught in the motions of their work, they just shouted out, and he shouted back. Then Ramlal dropped the reins and jumped down from his cart. He curved his hand like a boomerang and swept it across his face. The soot from his shirt sleeve smeared his face as the boomerang wiped away the perspiration.

Rookmin came up and opened her tired arms to receive her son. "*Beta*," she cried as she felt his strong head on her breast. She held him thus, drawing his strength and vitality into her weakened body, and closing her eyes so her emotions wouldn't show.

"*Beta*," his father said, "yuh getting big, yuh looking strong."

They sat down to eat lunch on the grass.

"How things going *Bap*?" Romesh asked. "A good crop this year?"

They fell into conversation about the mules, the canes, work at the factory. No one asked Romesh about how he was getting on, no one seemed anxious to find out what he had learned, or how affairs were going on with the Legislative Council, or if the Government had made any decisions affecting the sugar industry. One watching them as they sat on the ground munching roti, the men with legs drawn under their buttocks, the women squatting with their skirts spread tightly across their legs, the rice and curried *bodi* on the grass in enamel plates, would have thought it was just a family picnic. Romesh was the only one whose blood was not hot; the exertions of the others had their faces flushed, the veins standing out on their foreheads.

Ramlal said: "Yes, *Beta*, good crop, and plenty work for everybody. But this year harder than last year, because rain begin to fall early, and if we don't hurry up wid de work, it will be too much trouble for all of us. The overseer come yesterday, and he say a big bonus for de man who do de most wok. So everybody woking hard for dat bonus. Two of my mules sick, but I have to wok dem, I can't help. And all of us woking hard to get de bonus."

It was only his brothers and sisters, all younger than himself, who looked at Romesh with wonder, wanting to ask him questions about the world outside of their canefields and the village. Their eyes expressed their thoughts, but out of some curious embarrassment they said nothing. In a way, this brother was a stranger, someone who lived far away in the city, coming home once or twice a year to visit them. The last time they had noticed a change, a distant look in his eyes. Silently, they drew apart from this big brother, forming a group in which they were united by their lack of understanding. Almost, they became antagonistic; though Romesh never spoke of the great things he knew, or tried to show off his knowledge, the very way he bore himself, the way he watched the wind in the cane was alien to their feelings. He had had books the last time, but when they opened them eagerly, there were no pictures, just pages and pages of words. And they couldn't read. They watched him in the night crouching in the corner, the book on the floor near to the candle, reading. That alone made him different, set him apart. Once his sister had asked: "What do you read so much about, *Bhai*?" And Romesh looked at her with a strange look and said, "To tell you would only burden you with what you cannot understand. But have patience, little sister. A time will come soon I hope, when all of you will learn to read and write." Then Hari had said: "Why do you feel we will not understand? What is wrong with our brains? Do you think because you go to school you are better than us? Because you get the best clothes to wear, and shoes to put on you feet, because you are favoured by *Bap* and *Mai*?" "Oh *Bhai*, it is not that," Romesh said quickly. "It is only that I have left our village, and have learnt many things which you do not know about. The whole world goes ahead in all fields, in politics, in science, in art. Even now the Governments in the West Indies are talking about federating the islands, and then what will happen to our Indian brothers and sisters? But soon all of us will have a chance. We are brothers, we must not quarrel." But Hari was not impressed. He had turned to his father and mother and said: "See how he has changed. He no longer wants to play our games. He will do no more work in the fields, it is below him to wield a cutlass and lead a mule. His sisters and brothers are all fools, they not good enough for him. I saw him at breakfast time, he hardly touched the *baghi*. No, we have to get chicken for him, we must get the cream from all the cows' milk in the village. Yes, that is what. And who it is does sweat for him to get pretty shirt to wear in Port-ah-Spain?" He held up one of the girls' arms and spanned it with his fingers. "Look how thin she is. All that is for you to be a big man, and now you scorning your own family!"

Romesh had got up from the floor and faced them. He looked now more of a stranger than ever, his eyes burnt with a fierce light, like an Indian god. "How wrong you all are!" He cried out in a ringing voice, "Surely *Bap*, *Mai*, the years must have taught you that you must make a different life for your children, that you must free them from ignorance and the wasting away of their lives? Do you want them to suffer as you have?"

Ramlal had said: "Hush boy! we don't suffer, we bring children in the world and we happy."

"And what will the children do? Grow up in the village here, without learning to read and write? There are schools in San Fernando, surely you can send them there to learn about different things besides driving a mule and using a cutlass? Oh *Bap*, we are such a backward people; all the others move forward to better lives, and we lag behind believing that what is to be, will be. All over Trinidad, in the country districts, our people toil on the land and reap the canes. For years it has been so, years in the same place, learning nothing new, accepting our fate like animals. Political men come from India and give speeches to the Indians in the city. They speak of better things, they tell us to unite and strive for a greater goal. And what does it mean to you? Nothing. You are content to go hungry, to see your children run about naked, emaciated, grow up dull and stupid, slaves to your own indifference. You do not even pretend an interest in the Legislative Council; I remember why you voted for Pragsingh last year; it was because he had given you ten dollars—did I not see it for myself? It were better that we returned to India than stay in the West Indies and live such a low form of existence."

Romesh paused and the family watched wide-eyed. Ramlal sucked his clay pipe noisily. Rookmin held her youngest daughter in her lap, picking her head for lice, and now and then shutting her eyes so the others wouldn't see what she was thinking.

"There is only one solution," he went on. "We must educate the children, open up new worlds in their minds, stretch the horizon of their thoughts——" Suddenly he stopped. He realized that there was no reception. They listened, but his words didn't make sense to them. Doubt assailed his mind. Had he made a wrong approach? And was he sufficiently equipped in himself to propose vast changes in the lives of the people? It seemed to him then how small he was, how there were so many things he didn't know. All the books he'd read, the knowledge he had lapped up greedily in the city, listening to the big shots making speeches in the square—all these he mustered to his assistance. But it was as if his brain was too small, it was like putting your mouth in the sea and trying to drink all the water. Wearily, like an old man who had tried to prove his point merely by repeating—'I am old, I should know,' Romesh sat down on the floor, and there was silence in the hut, a great silence, as if the words he'd spoken had fled the place and gone outside with the wind and the cane.

And so after he had gone back to the city his parents discussed the boy, and concluded that the only thing to save his senses was to marry him off. "You know he like Sampath daughter from long time, and she is a hard-working girl, she go make good wife for him," Rookmin had said. And Ramlal had seen Sampath and made arrangements. Everybody in the village knew of the impending wedding except Romesh.

After lunch Ramlal fished a cigarette zoot from his pocket. Romesh had an idea. He said, "Hari, I bet you I could cut more canes than you."

Hari laughed. "Even though I work the whole morning, is a good bet. You forget to use *poya*, you hands soft and white."

That is the way it should be, Ramlal thought. Education, schools, chut! It was only work put a roti in your belly, only work for which the overseer paid. The marriage would change Romesh, all right. And he felt a pride in his heart as Romesh took up his cutlass and spat on the blade.

The young man went to a patch of the burnt canes. The girls came too, standing by to pile the fallen stalks of sweet juice into heaps, so that they could be loaded quickly on to the carts and raced to the weighing-bridge. The brothers worked a little apart, silently, swiftly. Burnt cane fell as if a machine were at work. The blades swung in the air, glistened for a moment in the sunlight, and descended on the soft stalks near to the roots. Though the work had been started to see who would be the faster, neither of them moved ahead of the other. Sometimes Romesh paused until Hari came abreast, and sometimes Hari waited a few canes for Romesh. Once they looked at each other and laughed together, sweat on their faces getting into their mouths. It was the closest the brothers had ever been since they were children, and to them it was as sweet as the cane they cut. For though in earlier days it was these two who bathed the mules in the pond, played 'pound hand' in the house, there had never been enmity to cause a separation in their relationship, to make them aware of the joy of a return to love and understanding. Now, though no words were spoken, they were once again brother and brother, at least while the work lasted.

Everybody turned to in the field striving to outwork the others, for they all needed the bonus the overseer had promised. Sometimes the women and girls laughed or made jokes to one another, but the men worked silently. And the crane on the weighing-bridge creaked and took the loads. The man who manipulated it grumbled: there was no bonus for him, and he didn't care to work himself to death for a miserly wage.

When darkness fell everybody stopped work as if by signal, and they wended down the path to the village, a good day's work done. Most of the girls, however, had left earlier to prepare supper.

And in Ramlal's hut there was laughter and song that night. Romesh's sisters and younger brother had never really held anything against him, and now that Hari seemed pleased, they dropped all pretence of being embarrassed and made fun. "See *Bhai*, I make *meetai* especially for you," his sister said.

"He works hard, he deserve it," Hari agreed, and he looked at his brother almost with admiration.

After the humble meal, when Ramlal was smoking and Rookmin was searching in the youngest girl's head for lice ("put pitch oil, that will kill them," Ramlal used to advise) Romesh said he was going to visit Drusilla's family.

"Well, what is wrong with that?" He was forced to ask, noticing the look on their faces.

"Well *Beta*, you know," Ramlal began uneasily, "it is not right to go visiting at your *doolahine*——"

"What!" The boy looked from face to face. His mother shut her eyes; the children shuffled their bare feet and began to be embarrassed at the stranger's presence once more.

Ramlal spoke angrily. "Remember this is your father house! Remember the small ones! Careful what you say, you must give respect! You not expect to get married one day, eh? Is a good match we make, boy, she will get a good dowry, and you could live here with we."

"So it has all been arranged," Romesh said slowly, with pain in his voice. "That is why everybody looked at me that way in the fields." His voice dropped lower, as if he were speaking to himself. "My life already planned for me, my path pointed out—cane, labour, boy children, and the familiar village." Then his voice rose again. "And you, *Mai*? You have helped them do this thing to me?"

Rookmin shut her eyes and spoke. "Is the way of our people, is we custom since long time. And you is Indian? The city fool your brains, but you will get back accustom after you married and have children."

Ramlal got up and faced his son. "You have to do what we say," he said with a newly-acquired authority. "Ever since you in the city, we notice how you change. You forgetting custom and how we Indian people does live. And too besides, money getting short. We want help on the estate. The garden want attention, and nobody here to see about the cattle and them. And no work after crop, too besides."

"Then I can go to school in San Fernando," Romesh said. "If there is no money to pay the bus, I will walk. The Government schools are free, you do not have to pay to learn."

"You will married and have boy children," his father said, "and you will stop backanswering your *Bap* . . ."

"*Hai! Hai!*" Drivers urged their carts in the morning sun, and whips cracked crisply on the air. Dew still clung to the grass, to cane leaves which had escaped the fire. Workers were swinging their cutlasses before the heat of the sun began to tell.

That morning Romesh was still asleep when the others left. No one woke him; they moved about the hut in silence. No one spoke; it seemed the children had formed an alliance with their big brother, they avoided their parents and did their duties efficiently and quickly. The boys went to harness the mules, one of the girls to milk the cow, and the other stayed to cook the roti.

About an hour after they left Romesh stirred on the bags on which he slept in the corner. He opened his eyes in full awareness, not mistaking the hut for his dormitory in Port-of-Spain. He could have started the argument again as if no time had elapsed; the night had made no difference. He got up quickly and went into the kitchen to wash his face. He gargled noisily, scraped his tongue with his teeth. Then he remembered his toothbrush and toothpaste in the suitcase. He got them smiling grimly to himself.

While he was eating his sister said: "You going to go away, *Bhai?*" He nodded, his mouth filled with roti.

"If you stay you could teach us the things you know," the girl said. Romesh stopped chewing. He hadn't thought of that. Then he said: "*Baihin*, there are many things I have yet to learn."

"But what will happen to us?"

"Do not put doubts in my mind, little sister," he said crossly. But the girl, as if she had suddenly grown up, pressed him with questions, pleaded with him. It was pitiful, her pleading. She said the same things over and over again, because they were all she knew. She harped on one or two points, with the passion in her making up for a better argument. But the very sameness of her argument irritated the boy, in his mind he thought how stupid she was.

He left the hut and sulked about the village, walking slowly with his hands in his pocket. To think that this thing could happen to him! The smell of the burnt cane was strong in his nostrils. Suddenly he turned and went home. He got his cutlass—it was sharp and clean, even though unused for such a long time. He joined the rest of the family in the fields. Hari said: "Is time you come. Other people start work long time, we have to work extra to catch up with them."

Romesh said nothing, but he hacked savagely at the canes, as if he were cutting his way out of the problem.

Ramlal came up in the mule cart and called out: "Work faster! We a whole cartload behind!" Then he saw Romesh and he came down from the cart and walked rapidly across. "So you come! Is a good thing you make up you mind!"

Romesh wiped sweat from his face. "I am not going to stay, *Bap*. I will help with the crop; you shall get the bonus if I have to work alone in the night. But I am not going to get married. I am going away after the crop."

"You are mad, you will do as I say," Ramlal said loudly, so that other workers lifted their bent backs for a moment to watch.

But Romesh thought deep thoughts and in his mind he said: "To hell with everything! If they are happy so, I am not." And he swung the cutlass tirelessly and knew that when all the canes were cut, it would be time to leave his family and the village. His mind got that far, and he didn't worry about after that . . .

As the wind whispered in the cane, it carried the news of Romesh's revolt against his parents' wishes, against tradition and custom. The girl Drusilla, working a short distance away, turned her brown face from the wind. Women and girls working with her whispered among themselves and laughed. Then one of the bolder women, already married, said: "Well girl, is a good thing. Some of these men too bad. They does beat their wife too much; look at Dulcie husband, he does be drunk all the time, and she does catch hell with him."

But Drusilla bundled the canes together and kept silent. "She too young yet," another said, "look, she breasts not even form yet!" They laughed.

Drusilla did not have any memories to share with Romesh, and her mind was young enough to bend under any weight. But the way her friends were laughing made her angry.

"All you too stupid!" she said, lifting her head with childish pride, so that her sari fell on her shoulder, "you wouldn't say Romesh is the only boy in the village? And too besides, I was not going to married him, if he think he too great for me."

The wind rustled through the cane and went on, and the sun bored into their bodies.

R. O. Robinson (*Jamaica*)

A Free Country

I

STEP lively, boy. Look sharp. You're in my town. You're in the town of Manteca Bay. Take a look around, boy. Look out at the blue Caribbean Ocean. Then swing your head around, boy, and take a look at that shapely filly prancing down the sidewalk.

But don't strain your neck, boy—don't strain your neck. Before you go rushing around my town, listen to me. Listen to Boysie Thomas. I know this town inside out.

Ask me any question you like, boy. Any question at all. See that down-handle Raleigh parked over by the sidewalk? That's my Raleigh. Boysie Thomas goes cruising all over the place on his Raleigh; and Boysie Thomas knows this town inside out. Look sharp! Or else that Mount Coley bus is going to throw a pile of muck on your shirt.

So you want to know who is the biggest fool in Manteca Bay? Easy. Eustace Brown. The biggest fool in this town is Eustace Brown; and if anybody wants me to say that again, I'll just come right out and say it again.

Short, black fellow. Comes from somewhere over by Mount Coley. Waiter at the Casa Verde Hotel, which is about six miles out of town—half-way out to the Rose Hall Estate.

God's love! What a pile of money that boy is making out at Casa Verde! Eustace Brown comes from over by Mount Coley and is making a big pile of money over at Casa Verde.

Mean, though. Hardly ever see him in town. Eustace doesn't pal around. On a Sunday you might bounce into him emerging from the Baptist Church on Duke Street; but apart from that you'll hardly ever come across him at all.

To show what a mean boy this Eustace is, one Saturday morning I was cruising down Barnett Street—on the Raleigh—and as I was manoeuvring the big corner over by the bus station, who should greet my eye but

Eustace Brown—waiting for the Mount Coley bus. So I hopped off the Raleigh sort of cute-like—you know the style, backways—and parked her on the sidewalk and signalled him to come over to the fence.

"Long time no see," I said. "Eustace, boy, what you know?"

"Mornin', Boysie," says Eustace.

"Let's hop over to Ling Pow and kill a quarter quart," I said, bending down to snap off my bicycle clips.

"No, Boysie. De bus soon come."

"How you mean 'no'? We could go up to the top veranda. From Ling Pow's top veranda you can see the whole town, man."

"No, Boysie," says Eustace again. "Suppose de bus come in, an' de man look an' look, an' don't see me an' den gone 'bout him business?"

Mean fellow.

And then there was the First of August Teachers' Dance at Casa Verde. You know the style: Off-Season, so the place is open cheap to any bunch of people that have a title.

That's one dance where you will always find Boysie Thomas, even though I can never lay my hands on a lawful ticket, and this means having to wriggle my way past the doorman. Anyway, when I was through manoeuvring this great official and got myself established in the Ballroom, who should I bounce into but Eustace—toting drinks and bowing and scraping, and saying 'Yes, sir' and 'No, sir' to everybody. Look here, man, I had to laugh: Eustace bowing and scraping to a bunch of cocohead teacher people when he had more money than the pack of them put together. And that ghoulish uniform!

Anyway, I took a seat over by the wall and there was a sweet little brown thing sitting beside me; about twenty-one or twenty-two. You know the style—bright eyes, clean and ripe. She was wearing a sort of dress that I just love to brush my chest against, so I asked her for a dance.

During the first number she held herself stiff. Then, in the second, I asked her her name. Name was Thorpe—Sybil Thorpe, pupil teacher at the Elementary School. Then her address: lived on Barracks Road, close by Posy Williams.

"You know Posy Williams?" I asked her.

"Posy?" she says. "Who don't know Posy Williams?"

And right away I nuzzled her head on to my shoulder. Then I told her my name and she asked me where I worked and I told her "with McGrath".

"Which McGrath? The contractor?"

"Yes."

"You mean it? The big electrical contractor?"

"Yes."

And she moved her eyes as if to say that I must be some sort of a big shot.

Then a big country teacher fellow cut in on me and I hopped over to Eustace and flashed him a smile and said:

"Eustace, you useless millionaire, start living, boy. Take off that ghoulish uniform and catch a dance, boy."

And all Eustace did was to look shy.

Just in case you mistake me for a big shot, let me tell you about Mr. McGrath. Mr. McGrath is the smartest man in Manteca Bay. The very day that the tourist business started up—look here, man, the very day—McGrath jumped into the electrical contracting business. If you know Manteca Bay any at all, or if you live anywhere between Port Antonio and Sav-la-mar, you're sure to know the light blue McGrath station wagon. Buick. Only light blue Buick station wagon on the North Coast.

In my book McGrath is a sort of genius when it comes to the field of electricity. McGrath is what I call a genius operator. But let me tell you something else about McGrath. McGrath is also another kind of genius. He's a genius with women of every race and creed. His name is a name that you'll bounce into in every hole and corner of the Parish of St. James.

Took me on as apprentice at five bobs a week, and then he noticed that I was cutting through the work like an auger-bit and raised me to seven, and then in two twos raised me again to ten.

Then one day he called me into the office.

"Boysie," he said.

"Yes, Mr. McGrath."

"Boysie, yuh can read?"

"Yes, Mr. McGrath."

"Well, read dese," and he handed me three books about wiring big buildings. That was all.

"Thank you, Mr. McGrath."

Right now I am pulling in 'way over a pound a day, and I plan to stick with McGrath.

Anyway, to get back to Miss Sybil Thorpe: right away I was nuzzling in on that dress. At the end of the number I suggested a stroll. The place was getting steamy, I said; too many country people, I said. And she said O.K. So we squeezed through the crush and strolled down by the beach. I spread my jacket on the sand. Cool.

The first half-hour was strictly neutral. Then I tried to nuzzle her head on to my shoulder again, and she held herself stiff and said: "Behave yourself, Boysie. Don't you see that worthless Eustace Brown spying out on us from the veranda?"

God's love! What a wicked fool!

So I had to suppress the voltage. The thing burnt my heart.

"Don't give me that," I said. "This is a free country."

She looked at me as if I was a shark—and a dangerous species of shark.

"All right, where you know Eustace from?"

"Church." Then she said how Eustace might go and tell her father and that would mean a big blow-out.

Listen to me, man. If you ever find yourself in a situation like that, the best thing to do is switch off the voltage altogether.

But not Boysie Thomas. "This is a free country," I said again. And right off the bat she got up and started back towards the Hotel.

"All right, all right. But you don't have to walk away and leave me like that." I called out to her. "Sybil! You're walking away and leaving me." But she wouldn't even slow down.

Back inside the Hotel I hustled over to Eustace with a big grin and said: "Eustace, you rich dog, don't do that to me, man—don't do that to me. She is only my cousin, man. Do you mean to tell me that nowadays a man can't give a little cousin a few minutes of advice without everybody tuning in?"

But all Eustace did was to show me a gold tooth and look shy.

Then I signalled the big country teacher fellow to join me in the bar for half a quart of Appleton's. It was this brainy-boy that brought Sybil to the dance.

"Teacher," I said, pouring him a stiff shot, "teacher, you're a man that knows a lot. Tell me something about Miss Sybil Thorpe."

"Well," he says, "you know the shoemaker shop on Duke Street?"

"Yes," I said, "man named Normie . . ."

"Correct. That's her father—Normie Thorpe, staunch Baptist."

"In that case," I said, "Mr. Thorpe must run soft and deep as a river!"

"Correct again. She is what is known in vulgar circles as a bastard."

"As soft as a river!"

"I have no idea who the mother is," he says, "but Sybil lives with her father and is the apple of his eye."

Then Sybil walks into the bar, looking for her dancing partner. He wasn't in the mood. "You young people go out and dance," he says, adjusting his spectacles and pouring another shot.

He was a friend of mine.

But don't jump to any hasty conclusions, boy. Don't go hopping off to any hasty conclusions. Listen to me. I'm telling you this thing. Right now I'm telling you about bastards.

Boysie Thomas don't claim to be no expert on this subject: for Boysie Thomas is not a bastard himself and so cannot claim to know that subject inside out. But if a girl is a bastard, that's none of her fault, boy. None of her fault at all.

So I can tell you this, boy. Don't jump to hasty conclusions. Don't go hopping off to any conclusions at all. And I can also tell you that in a whole hour of jiving and tripping around I could manage to squeeze nothing from that God-fearing doll—nothing at all.

II

I say to myself: "To hell with Sybil Thorpe; if Sybil Thorpe thinks I'm going to drool around and start losing weight just because she thinks I'm a hundred and seventy-five pounds of dirt, then Sybil Thorpe is not altogether correct in the head. Don't watch that, man. A pack of foolishness."

A Saturday night in October. Boysie Thomas is stepping forth through his gate, complete with down-handle Raleigh. The air is clean with tropical moonlight. There's a pretty humming reaching my ears from downtown. Firecrackers. Noise. Excitement. There's a shower of multicoloured rockets over the Harbour, over by the Henderson wharf. Excitement.

Manteca Bay is celebrating a great football victory over the great town of Sav-la-mar, and Posy Williams is the great goal-getter on the

Manteca Bay side. So I'm cruising over to Posy to join in the merry-making.

Furthermore, Posy Williams scored nothing—not a single goal, man—in that great match. The thing burnt his heart, man. And Posy Williams owes me a penny. Every time there's going to be a great match, I go up to Posy and say:

"Posy, you genius between the goal-post, I bet you a penny that you don't score a single goal in this match."

And Posy says: "Boysie, you bad-mouthed boy, I'll take that bet."

So he forks out a penny and I fork out a penny, and Ling Pow takes the money and puts it up careful in a little safe.

O.K. I'm cruising over to Posy and I turn into Barracks Road. And who is that lovely child wearing shorts—and riding a nifty lady's wheel—about a chain ahead of me? I rise up out of the saddle and advance to investigate. I get abreast of the doll, wrap my left hand around the handle of the lady's wheel and cruise alongside. It is Sybil Thorpe.

"Boysie Thomas," she says, "leave me alone."

But I did this thing cool, man, cool. So the lady cannot be razzled with me.

"Boysie Thomas," she says. "H'mph. Leave me alone, I tell you."

"Sybil, my love," I says, "take a look at that big round moon. There's a big round moon over the Harbour of Manteca Bay tonight, my love. And Boysie Thomas is as free and happy as a bird." Sybil is smiling, so I carry on. "And there are multi-coloured rockets spitting a pretty noise all over the place. Sybil, my love, I would give anything in the world to take you out in a canoe and show you the view out on the Caribbean Ocean."

She slows down to a stop: "True?"

"Sure," I says.

"You mean it?"

"Yes, sure."

"When? Now?"

"Any time. I could pick up a canoe over by the John's Hall Crossing."

"All right, then—" she says, "—all right. But don't let anybody see us going over there, for I don't want to get into any fuss."

"You will come, then?"

"Yes. You go on. Go on, Boysie. Wait for me at the Crossing."

"Sure?"

"Yes. Yes, Boysie—" she pause, "—Boysie," she says, "I wouldn't do you a thing like that. Sure, I'm coming. Wait for me at the John's Hall Crossing."

Boy, I was off! Listen to me, man. I was off! And she came, man. Came cruising over on that nifty lady's wheel: hair up in a bun; wearing white shorts.

"Boysie, I'll race you over to the next corner."

And Boysie rises up slowly in his saddle. But what you mean, man? When Boysie Thomas gets a challenge from a frisky filly to race her over to the next corner, Boysie Thomas does not hackle up himself and ride too fast.

So I took her out in a canoe to show her the nice view from the sea. Then a little nuzzling on the beach. Nice. Then she held my hand and looked at the luminous dial and said:

"Lord have mercy, Boysie! It's almost eleven o'clock and I have almost two miles to ride!"

"All right," I said, "let's go."

Back at the John's Hall Crossing she refused to step off the lady's wheel to tell me a proper good night. So I said: "O.K., if that's the way you feel about it!" Thing burnt my heart, man. And she knew that I was hurt and that hurt her heart.

"Boysie, don't carry on like that."

"Carry on how?"

"Like you don't have any sense."

"To hell with it! This is a free country!"

And that made her lose her temper altogether. She kissed her teeth and rode away and left me.

Next day—Sunday—I was out early for a sea bath and a few body-building exercises, then back to bed for a spell. Then got up and dressed—remembering to clean all the country dirt off the Raleigh before putting on the white shirt—and set out on a cruise. Not a soul in the streets; sun hot and sweet on my back. I was cruising over to Ling Pow to slap a few dominoes with Posy Williams.

Posy is the nicest boy in Manteca Bay. Floor-walker at the Bata Store on Market Street. Nice tall fellow; walks slow with hands flapping even slower. Talks slow, too. Great swimmer, weight-lifter, centre-forward, everything. Rides a Rudge with cable-brakes.

Ling Pow pays me my twopence and Posy starts to talk.

"So, Boysie," says Posy, slow-like, "you were out of town last night."

"That's right, boy," I says.

"Nice girl," he says, shuffling the dominoes on the table. You know the style—slow-like. "You shouldn't have done that."

God's love! What is Posy razzling me about?

I threw down my dominoes, jumped up off the bench and told Posy two big bad words. Right away Ling Pow is razzling me, too, bawling out my name and telling me to stop making noise in his shop.

Let me tell you something about Ling Pow. Ling Pow is a man I like and respect. Ling Pow is the sharpest shopkeeper in Manteca Bay. You'll never find him spreading a rumour, true or false. You'll never catch him spying on innocent young fellows on cool beaches. He never tunes in on a soul; and it would be a waste of time tuning in on Ling Pow, since he is emitting nothing.

But Ling Pow keeps a revolver under his pillow. And if a burglar slides into his shop at dead of night, this will set off a little alarm over Ling Pow's bed, and Ling Pow will wake up and reach for his revolver and step right out and shoot that burglar in the leg.

So Ling Pow is not a man that Boysie Thomas likes to cross; and when Ling Pow tells me to stop making a lot of noise, I stop.

"All right, Ling Pow," I says. "You're a man that I like and respect. I'll settle down again." Ling Pow laughs, so I razzle him a little. Ling Pow is a fellow that you can razzle when he is laughing. Ling Pow is all right, man. "O.K., Ling Pow," I says, "I'll take it easy. I'll take it easy, man. But I don't like how your place smells. Your place smells of too much salt fish and flour and sugar, and a whole swarm of bees that are after biting off my neck. Clean up the place—clean up the place, Ling Pow!"

And Ling Pow is still laughing.

As I take my seat again Posy says:

"Sybil Thorpe is Eustace Brown's woman. You hearing me, Boysie?"

"Lie," I said, shuffling the dominoes.

"I'm not asking you," says Posy, "I'm telling you, man. I'm as sure as fate. What the hell you think Eustace Brown is doing in the house every Sunday?"

"What? Eustace Brown? Eustace Brown cruising around Barracks Road every Sunday? Foolishness!"

"I'm not asking you," says Posy, "I'm telling you! Every Sunday morning Eustace Brown hops over from Casa Verde and establishes himself for the day at a certain address on Barracks Road. Takes over the place. Man-o'-yard!"

"Don't give me that," I says, "Eustace is a clown."

"All right," says Posy, "but anyway, Boysie, you caused her a lot of trouble last night. Listen to me. Her father beat her. Was waiting up for her with a strap."

"Posy, you mad!" I says.

"How you mean, mad? How you mean, mad? You don't know Mass' Normie! Mass' Normie keeps a cowskin strap under his pillow and any time he feels that Sybil is getting too far out of hand he gives her a hell of a beating with it, yes."

"All you people," says Ling Pow, "all you people always beating up one another. Nowadays, anywhere you see a little boy he has a giant of a rock stone in his pocket!"

III

Listen to me, boy. When Mr. McGrath called me into the office a few weeks later and told me about the job over by New Port, I was so glad, boy, that I could jump up in the air. McGrath pays me double time for working out of Manteca Bay, so Boysie Thomas is going to hop back to town on Christmas Eve Night with pounds and shillings bulging from his inside-pocket.

"Big new American hotel," says McGrath. "Gibraltar Cove. An' I don't want to hear that you carryin' on and sky-larkin' all over the place."

"Yes, Mr. McGrath."

"An' I want dat job finish before Christmas."

"All right, Mr. McGrath."

"You know New Port?"

"No, Mr. McGrath."

"Well, let me tell you dis den, Boysie. I know a lot of people in New Port, so watch yourself."

"Yes, Mr. McGrath."

"An' another thing. New Port full of dirty women. So watch you'self in dat connection, too."

"Yes, Mr. McGrath. Thank you, Mr. McGrath."

I had to laugh: McGrath telling me to watch myself, after the exhibition he has been performing for the past umpteen years all up and down the North Coast.

Anyway, boy, I slung the Raleigh on top of the light blue Buick station wagon and headed out for the Parish of St. Mary with nothing but joy in my heart. Mr. McGrath fixed me up in a nice little place at Spring Head and left me as happy as a high-flying kite. Sweet little place: you could strain your neck just looking around to survey all the coconut-trees within range. The Raleigh is parked in a cool outhouse and I am established way up on the top floor, looking out at the blue Caribbean Ocean and surveying coconut-trees.

The first three weeks it was night and day, night and day, with the American people fussing and cussing about getting a certain section of the place finished by the First of December, and Mr. McGrath dropping in on the job every now and again. Work was tearing my clothes, man.

Then one night I cruised over to a noisy bush dance over on the Isabella Banana Estate. People like ants. Curried goat smelling up the place like a wicked incense. So what? So Boysie Thomas is under a spell: Boysie Thomas finds himself nuzzling behind a lignum vitae post. You know the style—meaty thing, half-Indian. All of a sudden there is a fat hand holding me on my shoulder.

"God Almighty, Boysie! What yuh doin' up here?"

It is Joe Hendricks, the giant that drives the Royal Mail, one hand holding me on my shoulder and the other holding a forty-ounce bottle of Two Dagger Rum.

"Sybil send a message," says Joe.

"Lie," I says, releasing the meaty thing. How could Sybil ever talk to a dirty boy like Joe?

"Sure as fate," says Joe, "Sybil ask me to tell yuh that she love yuh."

"True?"

"As there is a God in heaven," says Joe, "Sybil ask me to tell yuh that she dyin' to see yuh."

God's truth! Joe Hendricks is a friend of mine!

"Tell Sybil and Posy to look out for me on Christmas Eve," I said.

"Poor girl can't sleep," says Joe, "can't sleep at all," winking at the half-Indian thing as if I was a wicked two-timing species of barracuda.

Right away this woman boxes me all over my face and I have to back out and leave the rest of the nuzzling to Joe.

That night at Isabella caused me a wicked heartburn. No, not the girl. Look, old man, there is a wall between nuzzling and sin that you are too damned likely to jump over when it's a case of leaning against a lignum vitae post in the bushes of the Parish of St. Mary, with wonder drugs and incense smelling up the place. No, not the girl.

It started with my dynamo. On the way home from Isabella the dynamo on the Raleigh gave out on me, and I had to make it into New Port the following Monday to pick up a new coil. Downed tools at half past three and hustled across to the Pringle Hardware Store, close by the Market. I had the Raleigh parked on the piazza, went in and bought the coil, then came out and stood up on the piazza winding it on. Two chains down the street I could see a station wagon with a lovely brown-skinned creature in American dark glasses relaxing in the front seat. "Boysie Thomas," I says to myself, "make haste, boy. Make haste and adjust that dynamo back on to the wheel. And then, boy, cruise over and parade yourself and your worthy vehicle before the admiring eyes of that rustic Beauty Queen." Beauty Queen? What the hell! Christ!

Foolishness. It was a Buick, light blue, and who was that chivalrous lady-killer stepping forth from the Puerto Nuevo Bar? McGrath!

I doubled back to the Cove and hunted out the watchman and asked him if McGrath had been snooping around.

"Yes, Missa Thomas," he says, "an' he raise a pile o' noise! Say yuh mus' be gettin' slack and how he hear dat yuh rushin' all de women up at Isabella, an' a whole heap o' noise."

So I say: "To hell with McGrath. This is a free country, and if McGrath thinks . . ."

"Missa Thomas," he says, pointing a finger in my face, "watch yuh'self wid me, Missa Thomas. Missa McGrath is a man dat I know from long time, an' Missa McGrath is my frien'."

God's truth! Even the watchman is tuning in on me!

Now let me tell you something about Boysie Thomas. I am five foot eight and weigh a hundred and seventy-five pounds. I live clean, do a little body-building and I am stocky around the chest and shoulders. I wear a brown pair of shoes, brown khaki trousers, a nice white shirt and no hat. I'm an electrician from Manteca Bay and I work with McGrath and I plan to stick with McGrath.

Boysie Thomas likes to cruise around this town and sometimes park over by Ling Pow and associate with wise fellows, such as Messrs. Pow and Williams. I also like to be left alone. Don't tune in on me, man. Just leave me alone like hell, man, and everything will hop along fine between you and me.

I do not like country buses, since country buses have a habit of spitting ugly muck either over my clothes or over my Raleigh. Generally speaking I do not like country people; but I have nothing against them provided they don't come at me with a machete, don't bawl out my name, and don't keep studying every move I make.

The watchman was a little old man named Mass Charlie: around fifty-five. Sort of old joker, in a way. Used to tell me a lot of funny stories about strutting across the horizon in a ten-foot canoe and hammering great sharks with his paddle. Used to be a friend of mine.

But now Mass Charlie is tuning in on me. So I take him by the waist and slap him up like a baby and say:

"Mass Charlie, you are a worthless dog!"

"A beg yuh, Missa Thomas! A beg yuh, sah!"

"Mass Charlie," I says, "you're a worthless dog. Leave me alone, man —don't tune in on me. Don't like hell tune in on me."

"Missa Thomas, as there's a God in heaven, I wouldn't do a thing like that, sah."

"All right, Mass Charlie. All right. But you tell me this one thing. Tell me this little thing. Tell me the name of the woman that was in McGrath's station wagon."

"Jesus Christ, sah! Ah don't know."

"Mass Charlie, as there is a God in heaven, I'll reach for a piece of stick and hammer you all over your body."

"Jesus Christ, sah! A beg yuh, sah! Gal name Thorpe, sah. Come from Manteca Bay. Sybil Thorpe, sah."

Sunday afternoon. Mr. McGrath is definitely at home in Manteca Bay with his faithful wife and playful children. So I venture in through the back gate of the Puerto Nuevo Bar to drown my little sorrows in an easy stream of Appleton.

"B-u-u-o-o-i-i-e-e-s-e-e!"

It's Joe Hendricks. Beside him sits the woman who delivered me a spiteful blow. Joe has a big, ugly paw around her waist.

"Don't bawl out my name," I says. I well know he's broadcasting all my movements on McGrath's frequency; but I wouldn't dare smash him on his sweaty face even though he's only half sober—because he's way over my weight and horsepower.

Joe says: "Missa McGrath mash up yuh life, man." And she, the woman, is laughing a big grin, too. "Mash yuh up all over de place, man. Mash yuh up. But come an' have a drink, Boysie boy."

How could anybody expect me to drink from the same bottle as Joe Hendricks?

I backed out of the place, beat a slow retreat to the coconut-trees and parked my friend—the down-handle Raleigh with the new dynamo—in the cool, waterproof outhouse.

IV

It would have taken a genius operator to finish that job at Gibraltar Cove before Christmas; and I don't claim to be no genius. So on the morning of Christmas Eve, I hopped on to a steamy Diamond T bus and went in to the office to report the situation to Mr. McGrath. O.K. I don't claim to be no genius, but Mr. McGrath knows—not just claims he knows—that he, McGrath, J. J. McGrath, Electrical Contractor of the town of Manteca Bay, is a genius operator; and so he was only after tearing off what was left of my clothes.

"Look 'ere, Boysie," he says, "I told you I wanted you back 'ere by Christmas. Christmas, Boysie! How come de job don't finish?"

Man, I was hardly through the door when McGrath started off on me like that.

"Sorry, Mr. McGrath," I said, "but it's a big hotel, Mr. McGrath, and the job only needs another three or four days to finish."

"No, Boysie. Boysie, I know you, an' I know you can work. You could'a finish dat job long time if it wasn't for sky-larkin'."

"Me, Mr. McGrath? Me, Boysie Thomas? Whoever tell you that, Mr. McGrath, is a liar."

"Look 'ere, Boysie Thomas, don't ask me no question 'bout who telling' me nutten! Don't be damn' fast." McGrath getting vex now.

"Don't fool aroun' wid me, Boysie Thomas. Don't fool aroun' wid me."

"But, Mr. McGrath, I've been bursting my clothes with work. Night and day. Night . . ."

"Don't ask me no question. I hear all what you carryin' on. One day I came through an' you wasn't even there."

"Mr. McGrath? You want to quarrel with me? All right, quarrel! But if you think that I going to burst my clothes and mash up myself to suit, you, you mad. Listen to me, Mr. McGrath . . ."

"Boysie Thomas, don't make me have to throw you out'a my place. Don't make me have to . . ."

Look here, man, McGrath is not supposed to talk to me like that. I was wild, man, wild!

I said: "Touch me, Mr. McGrath. Just touch me. Get up out of your chair and try to put your hand on me."

McGrath was as frightened as hell. Too frightened even to talk to me.

To hell with McGrath. This is a free country; and if McGrath thinks that I am going to burst my clothes and rip off my white shirt to suit him, he is stark, staring mad. Worthless man: clowning around with all the dirty little girls in the world.

Man, I'm back in Manteca Bay, man. Christmas Eve Night. Fillies prancing all over the sidewalk and Boysie Thomas full of money and vim. To hell with McGrath.

I hailed a taxi fellow from over by the railway and told him to drop me off at Posy, fast. Posy was so glad to see me that he could hardly hold the bottle of Appleton steady.

"Boysie Thomas, you bushman, we're going to raise hell in this town tonight, boy—hell!"

"Posy Williams, you think you know everything. You think you know everything that's going on in this town?"

Posy puts the bottle down and lights a cigarette. There is Posy—standing and puffing and looking smart. Puffing cool, man: cool, man. You know the style, slow-like.

"Posy Williams," I says, "you think you are the smartest fellow in the world; but I've been talking to a watchman out at New Port who has nothing to do but keep an eye open and study all the vehicles rushing by."

"Boysie, what the hell are you trying to tell me?"

Cool. Still cool.

"I'm trying to tell you that what you *think* you know about Eustace Brown is a pack of foolishness. Sybil Thorpe is getting all she wants from McGrath."

"Lie," says Posy.

"How you mean lie?"

"Ignorance," says Posy, "listen to me, Boysie. You're a bushman—so listen to me. Sybil Thorpe is making a baby for Eustace Brown."

O.K. Barracks Road was buzzing with rumours. But Boysie Thomas will tell you no rumours; for Boysie Thomas does not like to spread rumours, true or false. So here's what I know.

I know that on the Second of January the ignorant and sinful shoemaker collared the apple of his eye and poured a pile of ugly blows on her supple back. I know this because that night I was sitting on a certain veranda on Barracks Road and heard the blows and the bawling and recognized the two voices concerned, and hopped over and looked.

I know that on the Fourth of January McGrath was talking on the telephone to the Manager of the Casa Verde for over half an hour.

I know that on the Twentieth of January Eustace Brown and Sybil Thorpe got married at the Baptist Church on Duke Street, and Boysie Thomas was sitting on his bicycle across the street and had to laugh.

I know that on the First of February Eustace Brown got a hell of a big raise of pay. Furthermore, I know the little baby girl. So I know that Eustace Brown is the biggest fool in Manteca Bay.

For this is a free country; and if any man comes tapping on your door with this style of guesswork, you have a right to hammer him all over his body and soul, and sling him out into the gutter.

R. O. Robinson

A Shirt Apiece

IF there's one thing Fred can kill you with, that thing is brains. Fred can kill you with brains; and a man who know how to use his brains is sure to have the edge all the while.

Take the morning when the slim Chinese fellow shuffle into the yard selling Peaka Peow tickets which, as you know, is against the law.

"Take a chance," says the fellow. "Take a chance and make a mark."

The fellow was a stranger, and he choose a wrong time to bother Fred. For just then Fred was ticking over fast, scheming for a drink to start off the day.

"Buy me a drink, no?" Fred suggest to the fellow; but he wouldn't pay him any mind.

All he did was to keep saying: "Is only sixpence a mark, man." That was all he kept saying: "Only sixpence a mark, man."

Fred don't like that sort of thing, you know.

"All right then, Big Boss," says Fred, pulling out a sixpence with his left hand. "You look lucky. You make the mark and I'll pay."

And as the fellow was busy reaching for his fountain pen Fred grab him by the waist and drape him clean off the ground.

"Buy me that drink," barks Fred, "or I'll haul you down to the station!"

And the fellow pluck out a shilling on the spot.

But that is nothing compared to the time when we make a shirt apiece. It was really Fred who did all the thinking, and all I had to do was to co-operate.

The station where he was going to haul the fellow was the Sutton Street station, you know. For Fred lives on East Queen Street, not two chains off the Sutton Street crossing. And another thing: he wasn't really trying to hurt the Peaka Peow fellow, you know, just trying to frighten him a little bit for what you might call a worthy cause. And as a matter of fact, after he drop the fellow he bought two tickets instead of one to sort of cheer him up. But that's not to say that Fred can't behave rough. It all depends—it all depends on how you rub him.

Fred enjoys a lot of sights on East Queen Street. The greatest one is the Children of the Earth—sort of Lodge people, burying each other cheap on monthly subscriptions. Every Sunday evening they have a march to the hall, which is right next door to Fred. Naturally, a march means a lot of dressing-up: black patent-leather shoes, a bright green sash as waistband, and a long black gown.

There is a tailor-man in front playing a sword; he is the official that makes the clothes for both the quick and the dead. What a man to fight up himself! There he is, twirling the sword like a harmless piece of wood, with the blade glistening pretty under the street-lamp. I tell you, this man is a working disaster!

Then right behind him struts a tall man. He is the only one that wears a hat: a hat with a point at both ends, and a green pom-pom cosy on top.

Now there's a garment that I love: a pom-pom. You can keep the sash and the creepy gown, but leave me the pom-pom.

Anyhow, this man is a known undertaker—a sort of President or Grand Master of the outfit. And it's no surprise to me, him being an undertaker, that he organized the Children.

Just behind him is a middle-age woman carrying a big-size paper bag in one hand and a little box in the other. Imagine making a woman lug that weight all the way down from Windward Road, which is a heap of miles away.

Mind you, if you ask them what's happening inside the hall, they won't tell you. There's always a lot of clanging and banging going on, but if you want to find out more you have to join.

It must be the sights that keep Fred sticking around East Queen Street, because the yard is too small to graze his animals. For like everybody else, there's two sides to Fred: he is a great lover of animals. Yes, old man, Fred is a great lover of dumb animals.

Funny enough, that's exactly why the police was after his blood. But blood or no blood, a man who know how to utilize his brains is sure to have the edge all the while.

Had a goat once, Fred. And the animal eat off all the grass in the yard, leaving it dusty in the process. Things reach a stage where Fred decide to graze him in the public park. Every morning early, and every evening religious, he used to walk that creature a good quarter-mile to the park, and just stand around watching him feed. Nice and fine, nice and fine till the night when the Constable made the mistake of tackling him.

"You, over there," says the constable, closing in on Fred Smith. "Don't you know that you can't graze goat on the Government?"

Then he come up and chuck Fred. Right away he chuck Fred again, pitching him towards the gate.

"You're a thief," says the constable.

And Fred said: "Like your mother."

And he pitch him rough again.

The best part was that Fred didn't like the particular officer, so he decide to serve him a hard sauce.

"All right, Champion," says Fred, getting sweet and cuddly. "You are doing your rightful duty and I should be doing mine. I'll come easy."

So everything was peaceful after that and they got round to talking real friendly by the time they reach the banyan tree in Victoria Park. Right there in the dark Fred punch him over, and pick up the rubber truncheon. And as the constable was rising, a wicked blow greet him across the ears temple.

All the while Fred had his left hand gripping the goat cord tight. That's a habit with him, you know: if he's got anything not so important to do, he'll do it with his left hand, leaving the right free for brain-work.

So Fred has a weakness for dumb animals, and all on account of that the police was after his blood. As I said: it all depends on how you rub him; and there's no doubt that the constable was rubbing him wrong, and with a net result that he'll never forget.

Fred didn't chance the park again. Next day he sold the goat. And the following Sunday found him looking across the fence at the Children of the Earth, Group One—that's what they call themselves, Group One—musing about this and that. The swordhandler came twisting through the gate, then the Grand Master, then the lady, and everybody else form a circle round them to the front of the hall. The Grand Master was looking as solemn as a judge, hold up his hand in the air and said:

"P-e-e-a-a-ce, Brethren!"

Then he turn to the lady. She pop the box open and take out a black book. If you ask them what's in that little black book they won't tell you, either. Anyhow, the Grand Master mumble-mumble something out of the book and hand it back to the lady. He give her a little time to put it one side, then he hold up his hand in the air and start to chant out:

"Oh, F-o-o-u-u-r W-i-i-nds!"

Listen to him. He talking dead slow, you know. Dead slow:

"Oh, Four Winds. Oh, Holy Seven Seas!"

At which stage everybody else bow low and says:

"Amen, we bring the grain, the sweat of our brows. Amen."

"We bring thee peace and love, praise and glory."

"Amen."

"We humbly beg of thee long life and happiness."

"A-a-a-men!"

Then the Grand Master reach across to the middle-age lady and take the paper bag.

Here's what the slimy undertaker does next. He opens the bag and pours a quart of grain over the ground. A whole quart of corn!

After this the procession march off into the hall, the swordhandler holding the door open for everybody else, and then bolting it cagey behind him.

Right away Fred took a decision. By the following Sunday he had a fowl, and switch the goat cord to the spur of this bird. Then, as soon as the banging and the clanging got going, he was easing the fowl over the fence, keeping his left hand glued to one end of the cord.

The fowl was as ready as anything: didn't even cluck at the start; just kept pecking steady at the grain with less noise than the softest of the Four Winds—not greedy, not rushing it, just cruising through. But a quart of corn is a tall order even for a hungry bird. So that after a while the cruise wasn't too comfortable, at which stage the fowl settle himself on the bottom step of the Children's Hall and give a little cluck of satisfaction. Fred jerk sudden on the rope, sort of trying to threaten and encourage him at one and the same time. But the poor fowl couldn't go up to it. Which means that Fred had to pull him in and get a mug from the house. Fred had to slide over himself and gather in the harvest for later feedings.

Not long after that he was bragging about the move in the barber shop. That was when I first heard about it. He was sprawling in the rocking-chair, bragging to any and everybody. So I took him outside to caution him.

"Look, Fred," I said, "you're being too careless about your private affairs."

But all he had to say was: "O.K.! O.K.! Don't worry 'bout that."

"It don't pay to be careless," I said.

"Is all right," said Fred. "Listen. I want to see you 'bout something smart. You listen to me. Something real smart. We sure to make a shirt apiece."

I listened all right, but I kept warning him about being careless. You know what? You listen. You listen, and judge for yourself whether I was being wise or not.

The very next day—listen—the very next day a burly fellow wearing a crusty bowler hat strolls into the undertaker shop. This pasero had a special constable badge on one sleeve and was looking dead serious—like he was out for blood.

"Morning, Missa Harris," he says, with a dead-pan face.

And Mr. Harris came over rubbing his hands. "What can I do for you?"—not so solemn this time, for it was during regular working hours and he was figuring that the speck of red in the constable's eye meant that he'd been crying over a dead.

Well, the constable rested a hand on a coffin and said: "I've got some information of the first importance."

But he said it so suspicious-like, no gurgling in his throat at all, that Mr. Harris could spot that he wasn't suffering from the usual complaint: death in the house.

"What information?" Mr. Harris wants to know, his face dropping a bit. "And if you don't mind," he says, "would you please not lean on the casket."

The constable stamp twice on the floor to dust off his brown-and-whites, and then start patting his rubber truncheon in a threatening sort of fashion.

"I've got vital information which you could use," he says, rugged as ever and still leaning. "About the grain," he says. "Somebody is stealing it and eating it."

"What grain?" barks Harris, getting impatient.

"The Holy Grain. The Consecrated Grain from the Children's Hall."

All of a sudden Harris look as if he was going mad. "The Grain!" he started bawling. "The Holy and Consecrated Corn! The food of the Four Winds!"

"Never mind the Winds," says the pasero, taking a seat on the casket. "We're after him, and by the look of things you're after him yourself."

By which time the undertaker was busy chewing on this vital piece of information, and he come to the conclusion that he was talking to a vital roughneck who he could use.

"Well, then, Constable," recovering from the fits, "suppose we apprehend in the act?"

"Just what I was figuring myself," says the roughneck, smiling for a change. "Right in the act. Evidence—we must have evidence. But . . . there's a little snag."

"Where's the snag?"

"Well," the pasero carries on, "being as I'll be operating on private premises . . ."

Mr. Harris could figure out what he was hinting at, so he promise him a whole pound for the catch.

At which time they got it all worked out how to apprehend Fred Smith.

Well, at last the crucial Sunday night came round—listen careful and judge for yourself—and they smuggle the special constable behind the hall without anybody noticing. Then as the procession was moving into the building, the Grand Master made a quick dodge round the side away from Fred's yard.

The constable was waiting for him, looking as fierce as a bull.

"You got the money?"

"Yes, but catch him first."

In no time the banging started and Fred ease over the bird as per usual. You'd think that the fowl was wise to the game by this time; but as soon as he saw the food he set up one big piece of clucking. Anyhow, you can't really blame the dumb creature; it's not every fowl that gets presented with a regular quart of corn.

Right away two people came out from hiding to take a peep. The undertaker got all excited: "Is only a fowl!" he's glad to whisper: "Is only a fowl! You can catch him if you like!" By which he means that his duty is done so far as the pay is concerned.

The big pasero grab him by the sash. "There's a master-mind behind the bird," whispers the pasero. "Just you wait."

And sure enough it reach a stage where the fowl was overloaded with corn, and Fred had to slide over with the enamel mug.

If feelings could kill, Fred Smith would be a dead man. When the Grand Master saw him treading on the Holy Earth and snatching the Consecrated Food, right away he put a curse on him for life. Imagine him standing there in the dark—in that creepy gown—mumbling a wicked curse against Fred. After that he grab off the hat and bend down. Using the front point of the hat he trace out an 'X' on the ground, then deposit a spit right in the centre of this 'X'.

Meanwhile the constable was busy smelling blood. He was advancing stealthily, stroking the rubber truncheon. Then he stop and turn round.

"Pay me the money now."

"Catch him first," says the undertaker, tracing a circle round the 'X'.

The constable pull him up off the ground. "This man is rough," he says. "Even if I don't hold him, he might damage me none the less. So pay me now."

Harris was rigid with venom and his eyeballs were rolling slow and wide, like he was going into a trance. So the constable started to get desperate for his pay, especially as Fred was shovelling up the grain fast. Watch what he do now. Watch him now. First he take the hat from the Undertaker hand and set it back on his head—making sure to steal the pom-pom in the process. Then he raise up the gown and fish out a pound note from the Undertaker side-pocket. Then he rush Fred with the truncheon at the ready, grip him from behind and said: "I arrest you in the name of the Law."

Fred didn't bother to struggle. The constable pitch him through the gate, pointing his nose in the direction of Sutton Street.

But wait! I haven't told you how we made a shirt apiece. That pasero: that pasero I've been calling a special constable all the while. That wasn't no police-man. That was me, man!

Donald Hinds (*Jamaica*)

Small Islan' Complex

Mrs. Imogene Mackfarlery's partner is the biggest in Brixton. The rules of this club are simple. Each week from Friday to Sunday Mrs. Mackfarlery collects three hundred and seventy-five pounds subscribed by some sixty-odd people from as far apart as Stoke Newington, Clapton and Ladbroke Grove. A 'hand of partner' or more commonly 'pardner' is worth five pounds. So a mathematical analysis shows that Mrs. Mack's pardner has seventy hands! Each week one of the sixty-odd members of the pardner collects a 'draw' of the aforesaid three hundred and seventy-five pounds. Very often Mrs. Mack would be rewarded with a pound or a bottle of whisky or just a profusion of thanks that made the good lady want to break down and cry. Mrs. Mackfarlery who was a life-long friend of my mother's threatened to stampede me into her pardner. She said she would walk behind me to the bank when it was my turn to get a 'draw', and after we had hoarded my money she would confiscate my bank book, just as my mother Mabel Hisla would have done if she was alive 'today day'. Mrs. Mack had done it to Noel and after three years he was able to buy a house in Saulton Road. She told me she would give me ample warning of when the seventy-fifth week is near at hand.

Gwenda, only child of Mrs. Macfarlery, and Pansie, friend of Gwenda's, acted as accountants. Sunday afternoons were spent smoothing out notes and arranging them for easy counting. The girls together contributed one 'hand' of the pardner.

There is a severe rule of Mrs. Mack's pardner, though: "No small islan' people." It is not because Jamaica is twenty-seven times the size of Barbados, and two times that of Trinidad. After all British Guiana is no islet.

"But Mama," Gwenda once said, "B.G. isn't an island and what is more, it is something as vast as some twenty-one times the size of Jamaica —your island continent!"

"I know what Ah know," Mrs. Mack said, shaking her head at the obstinate youth.

"But Mrs. Mack, what about your boy-friend Worrell?" Pansie asked. "He was born in Barbados."

To this Miss Mack pointed out that Frankie was a Lot who had the good sense to get out while the going was good. When Pansie pressed the point that the might of the West Indies Cricket team rests largely on small islanders, the old woman said rather innocently that what Pansie was doing to her was just not cricket.

There would not have been a major problem had not Mrs. Mack become well known for the delicious cakes she baked. Wonderful coconut cakes which the girls call 'drops' and buns with the sting of white rum in them.

Rupe had once tasted these cakes and now that he had come down for his forty-day leave he insisted that he should go to Miss Mack and get his share, which he believed would be bigger than I could afford to give him.

"I can't do it," I said. "Rupert, I will not smuggle a Small Islander into Mrs. Mackfarlery's house. That's spying. That's treason."

Rupe was preening himself before my mirror secure in the knowledge that I would give way sooner or later.

"You don't understand, Rupe," I pleaded. "A few years ago a Dominican who was throwing a hand in her partner—he had only thrown in seven weeks partner when she let him have a draw. He got well over two hundred pounds, and that was the last she heard or saw of him. She just takes it out of every small islander. Don't ask me to do this, Rupe."

"You know teacher Johnson who used to teach at Points Pen?" Rupe asked, giving a final pat to his hair, just like a girl.

"Cut it out, that Jamaican accent won't get you far. Who told you that Points Pen is anywhere near the place that Mrs. Mack is from?"

Rupe pushed me out of the room and locked the door, and we were off to Mrs. Mackfarlery's.

"Mama fry everybody in Egbert's fat. He carried her down, so if you are black and you aren't from Jamaica or America she calls you a small islander or an African," Gwenda explained.

"Well," drawled Rupe, "once bitten twice shy. Mrs. Mack jus' have to play cautious."

"Where you from then, sah?" asked Mr. Mack.

"Mandeville," said Rupe.

"Some fine people come from Mandeville," said Miss Mack.

"Mama, you just like those people who advertise rooms for rent in the newsagent's window and then say 'sorry, no coloured or Irish'."

"I keep me distant, that's all," said Mrs. Mack, handing Rupe a hefty slice of towto cake.

"True, true, you are just a nice kind ole liberal. Don't you see that this is the way the white people behave, too."

"We are all Jamaicans here," said Mrs. Mackfarlery, handing Rupe a glass of wine which was made from sorrel sent over from Jamaica. "I talk plain. I not fighting Bajans. Out there in the street, on the bus, we are one. I ready to stand by them in anything. But—and that is a big but—when it come amongst us I touch them with a long stick."

"Wash people pickooy, but no wash them back," Rupe said.

I sunk deeper in the chair. Somewhere Rupe will slip, and Lord help us when Mrs. Mackfarlery knows that I brought an alien into her house. I Shelton Hisla, son of one of her dearest friends, double-crossing a dear old lady. While I sunk deeper and deeper into the chair, growing worrier and worrier, I seemed to have left the room. I was reliving the time half a dozen of us shared the second and third floors in Notting Hill. After we had lived there for six months Rupert came in hot with anger.

"Jeezchrist, man you don' know what's goin' on here!" his accent native Barbadian as Kensington Oval. "This white man does charge us fifty shillings a week for a room, and the white couple on the first floor does pay twenty-five shillings per week. That ain' fair, man!"

"Don' you know that you got to pay for the colour o' your skin?" Peter asked.

"Ain' we goin' to do something about it?" Rupe asked.

We knew we could leave. We told Rupe that but he was not the type to pack and leave just like that. The fact was that Rupe was the only one of us who had no need to pack. Everything he possessed was in his suitcase, and Peter, who had had a look inside the case, told us that there was room in the case for more things. We knew the weekend when they were coming to throw out Rupe. Peter worked a rest day that Saturday so that he would not be around to see them throw out one of his countrymen. I stayed because of a sort of feeling which was more a morbid curiosity than wanting to stand by a friend in time of need.

The two men who knocked at the door were tough looking men with wide shoulders and wearing dark glasses. One was chewing gum, and generally flexing his muscles, and the other, the restraining spirit, announced their intentions.

"We want to see Rupert Ethane."

"Rupert?" asked Rupe, "what for?"

"He ain't been paying his rent," said the bruiser.

"Some of you darkies are okay, but some of you ain't nice at all, rocking the boat. We are sent to settle this peacefully with him. If he pays it, okay. If he doesn't we will ask him to leave."

"No rough stuff?" asked Rupe.

"Rough! Now whatever gave you that idea?"

"Where is Mr. Williams, who always collects the rent?" Rupe asked.

"He ain't with the firm no more," said the bruiser. "Now cut the lip and tell us if this guy Rupert is here."

"Yes, he is here," Rupe said. "He is in his room, I guess. Don't mix with guys like that."

"Very good," said the restraining spirit, patting Rupe on the cheek. "Bad influence, bad influence."

"His room is at the back," Rupe called out as the two men stumped up the stairs.

They were breaking down the door while Rupert snatched his case out of my room and took his leave. I did not know whether to make a run for it or to barracade my door and hope for the best. I was weak and buckling at the knees by the time the men came knocking at my door. I was trying to explain to the men that they had spent all five minutes in conversation with Rupert before he left, when we heard a loud knock at the door. The bruiser yanked it open, and two stout policemen were standing there.

"Someone telephoned that there was a fight here," one said.

"False alarm, officer," said the restraining spirit. "We were just leaving."

I left that very evening, myself.

I woke out of my reverie to hear Rupe laughing with Mrs. Mack-farlery.

"You ever heard the one about the Bajan and the hurricane?" he asked. "Well, there was a storm, you see? And this Bajan had a banana tree that had a bunch. Well this Bajan ran out in the storm and brace' himself against the banana tree and said, 'Dear Lord, Ah not going 'gainst you, but I just holding on 'til the storm pass by'."

"Lord, boy," said Mrs. Mackfarlery, wiping her eyes and checking her laughter into a happy smile, "boy, you will do, you will do. 'I just holding on 'til the storm pass by'."

When is he going to crack, I wondered.

"You ain't any bit lively today," said Mr. Mack. "What's matter, Shelton?"

"Nothing, sir," I said.

We were at dinner and Mrs. Mackfarlery had just served Rupe a drumstick. The other went to Mr. Mack. I wanted to confess.

Rupe was telling the others what life is like in the Air Force. He had just come back from Malaya.

"Just my luck, two winters running I was out in the tropics," he was telling them; then he went on to tell a funny story about a sergeant.

Rupe dislikes English winters. His parents always sent him rum in coconuts, rum in tins with hidden compartments, or sometimes just coloured and labelled 'fruit juice'. During the evenings of a week I spent with him in his basement room in Peckham I noticed that every night dead on eleven-thirty, Rupe would get up and put out the milk bottles. The third night it dawned on me that he only took one bottle of milk and should not have two bottles to put out each night.

"Look, Rupe, maybe is none of my business, but I notice that you have been putting out your milk bottles every night at eleven-thirty. Moreover you look cagey about the whole business. What's up?"

"A long story, boy," he said, pouring a little rum in a cup and the top of a thermos flask. He had no other drinking vessel. "One night I was coming home, tight, man, and two Teddy Boys started to rough me up, then a nice copper came along and took me home. Maybe he saw the flask in my pocket. Maybe he was just doing his duty. Well, he brought me home and sat in that very chair you are now sitting in and drank rum from that thermos cover. Boy, you know how cold it can be out on the street doing that graveyard shift? Well, we finish the rum and I promise him that I would get some more off my sister and leave it there beside the milk bottles the next night. I been doing it for two months now. He always warn me by a little note that he won't be around or so."

"Shelton boy, you lost you' appetite," Mrs. Mack said. "That sorrel wine was to open up you' maw not close it."

Dear Mrs. Mackfarlery, should you know that a small island man is now at your table eating your chicken and rice and peas and making eyes at your only child, what would you do?

At last the time came when I would be able to get the alien from out of Mrs. Mackfarlery's house. We were going to take Pansie and Gwenda to the pictures. We were out of the house, on the pavement, neutral territory, when I saw the great bulk of Mrs. Mackfarlery in the doorway.

"Sheltaaan!" she cooed, beckoning to me with the first finger of her right hand. I wanted to bolt down the road, but instead I walked back submissively. She hauled me into the house and slammed the door behind me and marched me into a room.

"I jus' want to tell you that I ain't blaming you. You see, I can't blame for Gwenda being mix-up with a small islan' man. I know about this boy-friend for a week or more. What I going to do? Fight my one child over the man of she choice? Don't look like you just done swallow a cow. You mean to say you never know that that small islan' man is foolin' round Gwenda?"

"Cross my heart."

"Ah say it morning noon and night that I have nothing to do with small islan' people. Ah hope you know what Ah mean now."

I ought to know, but the truth is that with Rupert Ethane you never know.

Donald Hinds

Busman's Blues

HE was a big fellow with a pale face and a network of veins in his cheeks. The blue veins stood out brightly on the back of his hands, and I mused quietly that at last I had found a true blue-blooded Englishman. His uniform was crumpled and dusty as if he had slept in it. The pockets of his coat bulged with his sandwiches.

"Sunshine," he said to me. "You with me today. First day you going out on the road on your own?"

"Yes," I said, and there was a plea in my voice.

"Never mind, the first forty years are the worst."

"Sambo," a squat little man with a head like pumpkin, wearing a pink skull cap, "you with ol' Tom Simmonds today?"

"Yes," I said.

"Look out, he kills conductors. He is responsible for creating a permanent shortage of conductors at London Transport. Just two months ago when ol' 'Arry Stout came in here and drop dead, the verdict was from over work. He was Tom's mate."

"True, Darkie," said another who looked like a broom. "How many conductors you killed, Tom?"

"Three. And two others retired," Tom said as deadly as if he was a wild west gunslinger checking the notches on his guns. "How is your heart, Sunshine?" Tom spoke without removing the stub of cigarette from his mouth. He kept on lighting this after flicking his lighter six or seven times. Tom was engaged flicking his lighter when another driver tip-toed up behind him, pursed his lips, placed his right hand to his mouth and:

"Prrrrpps!!"

Tom turned around, screwed up a corner of his jacket, and pointed it at the driver, holding it low to his groin.

"You passed that now, Tom," one said.

"They would have to lift you on and off."

"Blimey! he needs a step ladder. Prrrrpps!"

"Up the Arsenal."

"Prrrrpps!"

"Cheer up, Sunshine. Tom keep telling you that the first forty years are the worst. Look after the passengers, treat 'em nice, and they will die for you. Hi, Charlie, show Sambo the tie that that ol' girl gave you for Christmas."

"You mean a clip 'round the earhole? They give you that, Sunshine."

I pretended that I had not heard a word. The time had come for me to begin work as a public servant. I had to be calm, courteous, firm, and I was to be helpful, too! though I had arrived in England less than a month.

I got on the vehicle; it crept out of the garage into the swell of morning traffic and fought its way to the kerb. Passengers trooped on. Girls in bright cotton dresses, men in black suits carrying rolled umbrellas and wearing bowlers, working men with neck scarves and reading racing papers. What a romance, I thought, as I stood glued to the platform, neglecting to give the starting signal. Everyone settled down, then there were a few rustlings of papers and a few discreet coughs. I still stood my ground. A man came dashing around the corner and made a dive for the still stationary vehicle. What was I expecting? I didn't know either. Then Tom let the bus creep for a few yards and pulled up sharply; I did a swift dance to regain my balance, at the same time I pushed the bell button, ding-ding, a delayed action.

Here the busman's world comes near that of the young teacher taking over his first class. How does he know the problem child? How does the conductor know the problem passenger? I went nervously down the passage. Any moment I would be asked for places I never heard of. Given coins from which to take fares I did not know!

"Any more fares, please?" I asked, a pointless question, since I had not collected any yet. How strange was my voice! The man reading the morning paper said: "Westminster, please," his hand shot out mechanically giving me the money.

'Westminster', that was a vague name in my mind. How much was the fare: eightpence, tenpence, a shilling? Ah, I must consult my miniature fare chart. Out it came. But where was I? Oh yes, the garage was where he got on. Valuable minutes ticked away, passengers were hurrying on and off, taking advantage of my inexperience. At last the man who had had his hand stretched out all that time for his change and ticket, said:

"It's tenpence, conductor."

"Conductor," called out an honest woman, "you haven't taken my fare." She thrust the money on me, "I want to get off at the next stop."

"Threepence, please," said another.

"One to the Cut. I got on at Water Lane," declared another.

"Half to Charing Cross," chirrupped a schoolgirl with freckles.

"Hi, Conductor, I'm leaving my fare under the steps," called out a man coming from the upper deck. On and on it went. Now where were we, Brixton? . . . no . . . yes . . . no, but we have passed Brixton! That was the Oval we have just passed. Lord, when will it all end? I cried in desperation. At last an inspector got on. He looked at me, with inward amusement, I thought, when he found out that it was my first trip.

"Okay, relax. Go and collect those on the upper saloon. I'll watch out for those getting off down here," he said.

"My God," I said, as I started up the seven steps to the upper saloon, "I had completely forgotten that there are passengers up here, too."

The bus swayed as if it were the limb of a mango tree with a dozen small boys on it. "Stand with your knees slack," my instructing conductor had advised me. I loosened my stiff joints. Suddenly the vehicle slammed to a stop. I was propelled down the passage. I gripped a hand bar, swung around and ended up sitting on a lady's lap. She was flustered, the passengers were amused, and I very embarrassed.

"You'll soon learn the tricks of the trade, mate," said an old-timer with merry eyes. How true? Six months later I was telling a new recruit that the first five months are the worst! The conductor has got to be a cross between an adding machine and a psychiatrist to be able to please his employers and the public at one turn of the ticket issuing machine. But the conductor being more advanced in elementary mathematics than psychiatry, the public invariably gets the worst of him.

It has somehow got abroad that the favourite passengers are the merry charwomen of the earlier buses reaching the City of London. Why is that? It has been too long established for anyone to dispute. However, I found it true. They are chatty, bubbling over with laughter, and they always have the correct fare, a marked difference from the office clerks and the schoolchildren who travel on the later trips.

Like everything else, views on the subject are also conflicting. Some conductors are of the opinion that there are no good passengers, and many passengers declare that all conductors make up a big bad lot:

"They all ring the starting bell when you are almost at the bus stop," is their favourite complaint.

But I shall always remember the petite teenager whose eyes were laughing with mine for five minutes. At last she said: "Don't you remember me?" I did not, so I smiled broadly.

"Of course, you must," she went on, leaning closer to me, "three weeks ago I got on your bus, a number 49, I'd forgotten my purse, and had no money, I was in such a hurry, and you paid my fare for me. You didn't turn me off as that nasty old conductor did the old lady, yesterday. Here," she said, pressing her hand into mine, "here is half a crown, take it. Go on, please take it."

How could I tell her that I had never worked on route 49? I quietly returned the coin. "It was a long time ago," I said, pressing her hand, "it was sweet of you to have remembered."

"Treat 'em nice and they will give you presents . . ." one had said.

II

Her complexion was like the colour of earthenware and she was wearing an expensively tailored suit. I grabbed the case from her as soon as she approached the platform and stowed it under the stairs. That was a special service to old ladies, but equally prompt to pretty girls.

"I'm going to Hayter Road, Brixton. They tell me that this bus would take me there. Could you help me?"

"Yes, you will be all right."

"Thanks," she said.

My privilege, I said voicelessly.

I don't know, I thought she said, or maybe it was telepathic.

I am dying to say that I've seen you before. But that is a bit hackneyed.

Yes, it would be. Try something else.

I can't think of anything. You are a disturbing influence.

How often are you disturbed each day?

Not so profoundly in months.

It must be my legs.

That's not all. Where in Jamaica are you from?

Who told you I am from Jamaica?

All pretty coloured girls come from Jamaica. At least, I think so. You see, I'm from Jamaica myself.

I see. What else you know about me?

You are a nurse.

How did you know?

That is always the first guess.

Too true. I think I would guess that you are a bus conductor if I were to see you out of uniform.

It would be nice if we could meet when I'm out of uniform.

Perhaps. I don't think we ought to though.

Don't say that bit about strange men. Your own countryman is not a stranger in a strange land, not to you anyway.

"Conductor," the young lady said aloud, "this is Brixton, isn't it?"

"Yes."

"Don't let me pass my stop, you know."

"Your stop comes after the roundabout."

"Okay."

Shall we meet again, my soul said to hers as she stepped down on the platform.

No. Her soul told mine.

Why? Can't I even get your address in Hayter Road?

Perhaps I'm going there to get married.

That would be terrible.

Thank you very, very much.

I did not mean it that way. I'm jealous, that's all.

Crikey!

Anglicized? Can't I have your name. Go on, tell me that your name is Merle. It does not matter that it is a lie.

I really don't mean that much to you. I'm just a pair of pretty legs and a round behind, to you. In an hour you won't remember what my face looks like. Look! here is a pair of fine legs coming on.

What those! There is a run at the right knee!

See what I mean? Happy leg watching!

"Conductor, do you know Streatham Place?"

"Yes."

"Could you tell me when I come to it, please?"

"Yes. Sixpence."

She took off her left-hand glove. There was a wedding ring. She was not telepathic. I wonder if I will remember Streatham Place?

III

The old girl was about forty yards away. She was waddling towards the bus like a slow motion newsreel showing a ship riding the waves. I looked away as I reached for the button to press the bell, but the blue eyes of the blonde put me off. The old girl was waddling closer and closer towards the bus.

"Take my bag," she said.

"Thank you," I said.

"They don't wait for you, these conductors," she said.

"No, they do as they like, don't they?" a lady charged.

"I waited," I said.

"I know you did," said the old dear, "but you did it against your will." Is it done otherwise? I wanted to ask but did not.

"Know if the shops are opened in Brixton?" the old dear asked.

"Yes. But it will cost you more than threepence to get there."

"It was threepence the last time I went to Brixton."

"That was a long time ago."

"In the old days we could travel all day for sixpence."

I think she wanted to annoy me. I went back to the platform sulking.

"She reminds me of an aunt I have," said the blonde, getting off.

"The times have changed," mused the old girl. She was not going to Brixton after all. "Hand me out my bag," she said. "I say, you are not bad looking. You going with anyone for reg'lar?"

"I what!?"

"Look! he is blushing! I did not know that you people could blush. It is his eyes! Well, you going with anyone for reg'lar?"

My face was hot. The old rogue was laughing still when the bus was half-way down the road.

Donald Hinds

Any Lawful Impediment

THE first marriage service I ever attended was my parents'. I was ten years old, almost eleven. When I was older I learnt that most people never attended their parents' weddings and that their parents were always married some nine months or more before they were born. I attended my parents' wedding all right and was suitably attired and stood beside my father with the ring in a little bag which was slung over my shoulders. Later I was told that in most cases it was the best man who carried the ring. I often wondered what were my Uncle Kyah's duties, he was the best man. My parents did not have to get married on the day they did, and it was because of the day on which they got married which started my disliking for weddings. It was on a Wednesday, I remember, and Trinity Hill School was going on an outing to Kingston. I was one of the few from Carato Gully who was to have been on the trip. Of course, when it was later announced that my parents were to get married on the said Wednesday, I was obliged to drop out. The other children, when they returned, talked about such fairy-land things as visits to sweet factories, biscuit factories, the Institute, the museum, and a special matinee at a cinema. They were emphatic that in the cinema the pictures spoke and that it was not at all like the lantern slides they used to show us in the school. Why, oh why did my parents have to go and get married, and on that day, too? They were good parents, really. I was even a sort of favourite. They had vague ideas about my future. They wanted me to leave Carato Gully as soon as I was able to cope with the outside world, so they allowed me to attend school regularly enough.

Cisy, my sister, had suddenly become a member of the Bible Church of God. As a saint she had the alternative of leaving her young man and their two children or get married. So she decided that she would get married on a certain Sunday. When the word got around, some people close to religion said it was not the right thing if Cisy got married before our parents, so after weeks of deliberating they decided on the

Wednesday before Cisy's wedding as the day my parents were to be joined in holy matrimony.

Well, here I am playing best man at this wedding, and I'm hating it as much as I hated the first wedding I ever attended. I am wondering, too, why Bajo asked me to be his best man. We are not of the same age group or even friends. The fact that I am a relative of the bride does not signify, since the church is fairly populated with other relatives. I am thinking that it might be because of all the people who have escaped Carato Gully, mostly to Britain, I am the only one entirely independent of Bajo. His real name is Joseph, but at Carato we used to call him Brother Joseph, that is we wanted to, but we never did better than Bra' Jo, but more frequently we said Bajo.

I escaped from Carato Gully, thank God to my Aunt Dina. She was one of those fairy godmothers who are the envy of many Jamaican children. Aunty Dina had managed to get away to the United States of America three decades before I was born and she returned with great affluence when I was nearly thirteen. After she had held her court in Kingston and all the family had gone to pay homage, returning much pleased, and clad in gaudy hand-outs, Aunty Dina had by then seen all the family youngsters and for some reason (which pleased and confused me) decided that I was the one she wanted to live with her. The whole tribe of Potlits did not take it sitting down, in fact, they took it out of my mother and father, but applauded Aunty Dina's wisdom when the story was brought before her. If the Potlits had thought that I was on the way to becoming young dashing Prince Justice Potlit, they were wrong, but to me it was better to serve in Kingston than to reign in Carato Gully. I had no idea if Aunty Dina had anything in particular in her mind in respect to my future, but before I could summon courage to ask her, she took ill. My Harlem cousins, they were called McTurtles, became worried. The McTurtles came to Kingston with a swoop and carried off Aunty Dina back to the States. They did not really explain to me that they wanted their mother to have expensive medical care; I fancied that they wanted to be better placed in the old lady's will. I was left high and dry, much to the scorn of the McTurtles and what was termed cool justice by the residue of the Potlits. Even my parents claimed I was a bit high-toned of late. Anyway, some time passed and I was kicking around Kingston, or more to the point, I was being kicked around; at that time I was ordered to a lawyer's office and was placed in sole possession of Aunty Dina McTurtle's city house. It was too expensive a place for a poor young man of twenty-one, so I sold it and caught the first available plane for London.

Of course, while this scene of the drama of my life was being played out, Bajo had escaped the mountainous clutches of Carato. He is now well established in Brixton. When he bought his first house along a quiet, very English street, the neighbour to his left declared that the value of his place was plunging downwards, so he put it up for sale and Bajo bought it at an outrageous price. Then the neighbour to the right decided to sell and get out before he was unable to find a buyer, so he sold it to Bajo at a monumental price. Back in Carato Gully, Laboo, the lawyer acting for Bajo, had been planting 'no trespassing' signs all over the Gully.

Carato Gully never ask for much. It has its two churches. One for the Baptists and another for the Saints of the Bible Church of God. It has its school which is owned by the Baptists. Indeed, the Government never showed much interest in Carato Gully. A mile out of Trinity Hill there was a sign which warned motorists that to proceed on to Carato Gully was a very grave risk, and the responsibility was that of the driver. Truly, a politician had ventured in the Gully and had promised that if he was elected to the House of Representatives by the help of the good voters of Carato he would make it the Government's duty to care, but Carato never voted. Though it would be unfair to blame the adults of Carato for that ambitious teacher losing his election, they were left once again to their seclusion. But they were not really cut off from the rest of the world. Maxie, a daredevil with an ancient International truck, would always venture in to take the market women three times a week to Kingston. It was on one of those trips Bajo left. It is generally spoken of as a Monday. He left wearing his starched and ironed white-drill suit and folks had thought that he was going to Kingston to see the doctor who had lately been treating him for his chest-pains, but by the end of the week it was known that Bajo had gone to Britain. No one used to go to England. People had been known to go to Panama, to Cuba, even Costa Rica and, of course, 'gone away' generally meant to the States, but most certainly not to England, unless there was a war on, and the war had just been over, well give and take a few years. Bajo was not the type one would consider the emigrating kind. The parson never gave him tickets to take the tests for farm work in the United States. Bajo had left though, and a great controversy arose about how he raised the money for the passage. Most thought he sold marijuana. Years passed. His hut was tumbling down and Creek was feeding his cow and donkey all over the land. Suddenly Laboo the Indian lawyer sent in men who stuck notices everywhere on Bajo's acre and a half of hillside land, saying that trespassers would be prosecuted. Then Bajo took to writing to the Baptist parson and later to Creek. He sent pictures of himself and white people having wonderful time at the sea-side. He dropped dark hints and soon the Gully was humming with the rumour that Bajo was going to marry a white woman. That was a sure sign of status. The woman was expecting, they said. Well, why should people want to get married? Creek fell for it and told Bajo that he would like to give England a try. He suggested that he would mortgage his land to do so. Time passed and a summons to Laboo's office, and Creek was told he could have all he wanted to get him to London, if he handed over the deeds of his land to him. So Creek came to London and lived with Bajo. After him, Tom-tom handed in his land papers to Laboo and came to London, then Nana, then Ryland, then Sister Beah, then the thing really gathered momentum, and Laboo on behalf of Bajo stocked papers, until Bajo was in possession of lands second only to Squires, the white man whose family has owned Millington Abbey since Sir Henry Morgan governed Jamaica.

Very few found it worthwhile to honour the arrangements Laboo drew up. Many prefer to send for relatives, and Bajo was always ready to help. Of course, he was in legal possession of most of Carato Gully when it was discovered that the Gully was rich in Bauxite.

So here I am listening to the Vicar rambling on through the service. I look at Bajo and his face is a polished mahogany mask which does not hide his avarice and cruelty, from me. I am burning up inside for I am remembering that my parents died while I was lately come to England. Everyone had thought that I was doing well, so they never cut me out of the few acres of land which should have been mine. Indeed, I really wanted to be rid of them so I forgot them. The next I heard from my little sister Madge was that she was living in Brixton. That is why I am thinking that I might very well shout something when the Vicar warns those who have lawful impediments to stop this marriage now, or for aye hold their peace. I do not really know if it is lawful or not, but I have some strong objections to Bajo marrying my sister Madge!

H. Orlando Patterson (*Jamaica*)

The Very Funny Man: A Tale in Two Moods

THE FIRST MOOD: THE PRELUDE TO THE FUNNY MAN

FOR a moment his response had been blind, spontaneous, animal. He had been successful. It followed that he should be happy. Therefore he was happy. At the very least, he wanted desperately to be. And the consciousness of that alone should have satisfied him. Intent would be enough, would be everything. Why, he asked himself—somewhat self-embarrassed by a vague sense of artificiality—why should he pursue the unknown? For all he knew this strange unknown which he sought, and which he dreaded, may yet remain unknown by proving to be nothing. Here and now he had something tangible. The very thought, the very suggestion of happiness struck him as being slightly naïve, even bizarre. But there could be no doubting the reality of his intent. So why should he ask why?

But already, in the asking—and could he help himself; he was simply human?—he had trapped himself. Had been plunged headlong down into the bottomless pit of a little commonplace tragedy. A petty anti-climax, constantly seeing itself down. So the ridiculous question was posed. And what was he being left with? Anything else, he wondered, but a laughable, dismal monotony of self-consciousness?

Something in him revolted and he sought to shatter the confused trend of his thoughts with the hatchet of his consciousness. Blast it all! He had been very successful in his exams. He was happy. He was proud. Happy, proud, he repeated, blushed, and suppressed an urge to laugh. Yet he felt he longed for the holidays to be over so that he could be back at college to sit and watch the other students sitting and watching the lecturer. And he damned the crude reality of his mind that sought to remind him that as soon as the holidays were over and he was back only one desire would dominate his being—for the holidays to begin again so that he could long for college.

But sooner or later he knew that he would have to accept the crude reality of what he felt so deeply and which he now sought to deny by reducing to something no more than the flippant product of his thoughts. Then he would give himself up to weariness, to the deep, inner uneasiness that parched every semblance of achievement from him, that made him tired, so strangely tired that he would wish only to sink into everything and so be nowhere, that made him wish for everything—walls, carpets, chairs, ceiling, mirrors—to close in on him and in a moment (what sweet, self-killing joy, that moment!) crush him to complete depthlessness.

His emotions, as usual, drove him to pen, to paper, and to another of his funny attempts at expression. The story that clouded his consciousness then, struck him as the funniest he ever created. So he decided to call it The Very Funny Man. And so he wrote:

THE SECOND MOOD: THE MAKING OF THE FUNNY MAN

Once there was a very funny man. This man was neither short nor tall. This man was neither slim nor fat. This man was neither black nor white. He was just an average-looking Jamaican with average-looking features. Not even his dress betrayed any peculiarity. It possessed neither the tweedy waistcoated conservatism of those of light hue, nor the shabby exposure of those on whom the tar brush had been too lavish. No. He was just a normal-looking man on his normal way.

And yet, paradoxically, this man always caught your eye. It was very funny. So very strange. But if you happened to be on the same bus or train on which he travelled, inevitably your eye settled on him. Perhaps because he was so inconspicuous and unseeing. Or perhaps, in epitomizing the boredom and lack of interest in all the other faces his became the one most worthy of interest. But don't misunderstand, it was not as if in looking at him you really saw him. His was a sort of boredom ending itself in interest through sheer boredom. And that is why so many people afterwards while admitting to having spent an entire journey sitting opposite to him and actually staring at him could not, despite this, remember one solitary thing about the very funny man. That he existed almost everyone knew. But who and what he was, well, that was another matter.

The funniest thing about this very funny man was that he was always travelling. He never stopped. It was vital to his existence that he always found himself going. It didn't matter where. Not at all. The important thing, the essential fact, was that he should be going.

It is necessary for this tale to say that our man was fairly well off. And after all, this is not such an unreasonable assumption considering that it was widely rumoured that his father had been a successful politician. So the funny man, if he wished, could get most anything he wanted. He could eat all the nicest foods at all the nicest places where all the nicest people went. If he wanted he could have driven the biggest cars or he could have conquered the skies in his own private plane. But no. Space meant nothing to the funny man for the simple reason that he could be anywhere he wanted. And time meant nothing either, for he could get there in the moment he desired. Not that this funny man was a sorcerer or anything as extraordinary as that. In any case you needed faith for that sort of thing, and, this little is known of him: the funny man had absolutely no faith neither in anything apart from himself nor himself. It was just that to this funny man every moment, every thought, every action reduced itself into the present of his expectancy. This funny man could be everywhere for he never went anywhere except there—there —which was the expectancy of where he was ever going.

And so he passed his life. Always from one end of Jamaica to the other. Always on the narrow precipitous roads. But he never saw the rugged, passionate green hills that were about him, no matter how much they threw themselves at him with their tall peaks veiled in the distance with the mystic, remote, blue haze and topped with saintly flocks of clouds, he never saw them. Nor did he see the rich valleys with their entanglements of trunks and grass and thorns and huts and little plots of pitiable, dry farms beside the big-big sugar estates. Nor did he ever see the weary, downtrodden, black faces of the peasants, as stubborn as the basketed mules they drove. Not even the snug, brown faces of those in the city, though that might have been understandable, always hiding as they were behind the windshield of their enormous cars.

He just went on, passing from one place to the other, always coming to the point of reaching but never quite getting there, for there was never anywhere to get at, since to this funny man everywhere and everything began and existed in his expectation and everywhere and everything dwindled away with it.

Then one day a very tragic thing almost happened to the very funny man. That is to say, things conspired to make it so that on one occasion he almost did reach somewhere. Or thought he did. For as he assured himself afterwards it had all been a pretence anyway. A trick his mind had tried to play on him. None the less, it went like this.

One fine summer the funny man was suddenly struck with the idea of making a trip through Europe. He was hesitant at first. It seemed such a great idea. But he soon came to like it more and more and eventually was bubbling with joy just thinking about it. So then he went to all the travel agents. He collected all the travel pamphlets he could get and after reading them and making copious notes, added them to his large and ever expanding library of travel catalogues of which he was so proud. Then he drew up elaborate plans of the planes and ships and trains he would take and the places he would pass through, and, just to make sure, of the places he would not pass through.

Soon he was on his way. In the skies. Over the chiselled grey of the sleeping ocean. Relishing the sheer sweet joy of going, simply going. On the way he discovered to his delight that there was some error in his plans so when they landed in a place called England he rushed to the nearest hotel and for the next two days completely rearranged his schedules and times for travelling through Europe.

But then he found himself in France and it was there that it almost happened. After landing he had been escorted to the tourist office and there an elderly Frenchwoman, taking advantage of his ignorance of the language, had been wicked enough to arrange for him to take a guided tour of the city (perhaps it wasn't her fault, the funny man came to realize afterwards, yet, she should have warned him of the deceptive nature of the city). They had taken him to all the usual places—the Pantheon, the Notre Dame, Les Invalides, the Louvre, were those not their names?—and except for his annoyance with the Americans and their stupid obsession with getting to the places they were led to believe they were getting at, everything went, for a time, quite smoothly, especially since he had brought along a booklet explaining the delightfully intricate rail-routes of France.

However, the funny man eventually found himself in a place called the Palace of Versailles. At first he just walked along with the crowd through the large halls, not bothering to look at the massive, dreamy pictures on the walls and ceiling, or the carpets with their intricate, flowery designs, till they reached a point looking out toward the south end of the building.

But then, the funny man, for some strange reason, became more and more aware of the people around him. At first he could only stare at them in a kind of dazed disbelief. He saw that they were tall, that they had two legs and two arms, that they had smooth, pinkish, healthy faces, that the hair on the flat chested ones stood upon their heads like porcupines and those of the ones with bulging breasts and smoother, pinker skin tended to have it long. And then he became aware of the fact that he was actually in the middle of them. And they were squeezing him in; they who were all so much alike. He became terrified for a moment in the thought that there was a possibility that he might be like them too, and with the sweat creeping up on his brow, he looked down on his hands and found some slight relief in the relative darkness of its colour. But then, the clear, piercing voice of the Frenchman caught hold of him. He tried desperately not to, but he had to listen, had to hear him speak of the grand days of French diplomacy, had to hear him recall the many tribal wars of Europe, had to look at the rich, elaborate tapestry, had to stare outside at the vast, extravagant panorama of lawns and woods and steps and statues and lakes that confronted him.

Suddenly he knew, or felt he knew, that he was there, somewhere, in a land called France, near a city called Paris, in a palace called Versailles. And that they were all about him. He could not escape them. They terrified him. Utterly, completely. They shattered every crevice of his being. He tried desperately to think and to convince himself that he was different, something apart, himself. But this only drove him more and more to a self-destructive feeling of forlornness, of being somehow lost in the midst of them. So his soul was trapped in an abysmal paradox. For he could only escape them in the consciousness of his difference but in this very consciousness was an overwhelming sense of grief and abandonment. He was alone, the funny man, for the very first time that he could recall, he was alone in a vast world made up of their faces —pale, expressionless, indifferent—and he was terrified of being conscious even of himself, yet it was only of himself that he could dare to think, for if he moved, if he budged they would be about him, they would be closing in on him and they would all be screaming with horror what the Frenchman was now bellowing—that he was there, there in Versailles, seeing it, feeling it, smelling its antiquity, touching it, knowing in the moment nothing else but it and his relation to it.

The full terror of what had really happened suddenly crashed deep into him. He had been caught. Caught out of expectancy. No longer was there the sweet solace of going, of simply being in expectation. Gone in an instant were the passive joys of anticipation, the undemanding emptiness of the moment which knew nothing more than the expectation of what was only created by itself.

In his terror he began to scream, to shout that it was all a lie, a great farce. So everyone began looking round at him. And the encounter of their stares only drove him more to terror. He began to run.

"I must be going," he kept saying as he pushed them aside, "I must be going, I must be going."

Outside he dashed into a taxi and raced for his hotel. As soon as he was in his room he opened his suitcase and pulled out his catalogues and, sitting around the table with pencil and paper he continued until far into the night soothing his shattered nerves with a new, intricate plan of return to Jamaica.

Two weeks later he was back in Jamaica and had almost smothered the incident to the back of his mind though every now and then it forced itself up to the level of his consciousness. But soon it was completely forgotten. For the funny man had gotten back to his old routine and was happily travelling the length and breadth of the island again.

Moving along. Passing. Eternally going. Without joy, yet without sorrow, without fear. He knew no one. No one seemed to know him. And so his journey went, passed, continued. And he never reached, that funny man, and he never left . . .

H. Orlando Patterson

One for a Penny

SHE gripped the flesh around her belly tightly and gave a sharp, deep grunt of grief. Involuntarily, her head dropped to her knees and there it rested, limply, carelessly. Her brown eyes had now become a darkish red; sad beyond tears as they stared vacantly somewhere between the lines of the bare wooden floor.

In the streets close by, yet appearing to be far away, a fish-vendor was screaming, "Feeesh! Feeesh!" in the raw, wild, languishing manner of her kind. At intervals, a gush of wind would dash the withered leaves of the almond tree against the window pane giving a muffled, irregular sound which seemed somehow annoyed with itself. Then the wind stopped. The fish-vendor had gone away. Now there was only the dry, vibrant heat of the silent June day.

Frank, the boarder, had left the day before. And that seemed to have completed the barrenness and misery of the house for her. Not that she had liked him all that much though she had taken to calling him her son. At times he was even becoming tiring with his endless talk on the cosmos and the problems of evil and pain and suffering which he claimed only his Rosicrucian faith could resolve. But even he, despite his pretentiously stoic indifference to the trivialities of existence, had found the emptiness and misery of the house too oppressive. Yesterday he had come home from work. Apologetically, and with sincere qualms of guilt he had paid her for his keep and told her he was leaving. He had packed his bag and he had left. He hadn't said where he was moving to.

Now there was a misery that cancelled out all misery. The misery of total barrenness. Everything had finally soared to a climax of nothingness. As she walked around the house with a wet rag tied around her head, as she sat and stared at the vacant walls, her whole life seemed to lay itself bare before her. And it was all one worn nostalgic melody of despair. She listened to it, she laughed with it, she wept with it, but the more she listened and the more she laughed and the more she wept, the more she separated herself from it, till somehow her past had emptied itself out from her and she remained merely a thing, sensing, an aimless, drifting entity, a barren consciousness, totally unrelated to anything, present, future or past.

Perhaps it was better with the quarrelling and the fights. His cruelty and his torture did some little good in that she at least forgot herself in her attempt to survive his onslaughts. But suddenly he seemed to have had enough of her. Even of hating her. Two days before Frank had left he had stopped. The cursing, the abuse, the hate which had made them cling together like a vice had all dried up. Just so.

He went to the rum-bar and got himself drunk and came home and slept. She wet the rag in the ice-box and covered her forehead with it and drifted about the house till it needed wetting again.

Then, she put away the rag and sat on the side of the bed with her head on her knee. She vaguely recalled that she was waiting for someone, or something. She tried to think what it was. In vain. For everything was clouded in one unrelated mass. Perhaps it was the fish-vendor. Perhaps it was the parson who had promised to call. Perhaps it was the teacher who had asked her and the rest of the class to prepare her nine-times table. Perhaps it was the spread that needed mending. Or perhaps the common . . . yes . . . at last there was something positive . . . an open space in the mist . . .

They said it was a common and she had always thought it was. But mama had told her that a common was a place with lots of nice green grass and fairies running in between the blades. Of course you couldn't see the fairies because they were invisible but they would protect you from the rolling-calves and other evil spirits of the day when you walked by the cotton tree. But now, where were the green lawns? Aunt Matilda had said that if it didn't rain soon it would surely be a sign from God. People too wicked and bad these days. Them live in sin too much. So them must make to suffer. She had never liked the big black wart under Aunt Matilda's left eye. But the common with the green grass . . . no more. Now only dry, arid expanse. The fairies had all fled. There remained only the evil spirits. They would inveigle her to them with their wicked cunning. They would suck the life from her. So she had to run. Run from the common that was now only a dry, evil waste . . .

"Aunt Daphne!"

"Who that?"

"Me," expressed with some surprise at the lack of recognition.

"Who?"

"Tom."

She turned her head slightly to look up at the young man.

"Oh, is you. How you do?"

"Fine. Mama send me."

"What she say?"

"That she hear about a good room; if you want her to get it for you."

She looked away from him, then stared vacantly through the door in the direction of the dining-room. She glanced back at him, her expression a mixture of pain and shame. Then she smashed her face in her palms and burst into tears.

"So it come," she sobbed. "Me back where me begin. Back in one room. A careless, insignificant, single woman in some dirty single room. Oh Jesus Christ, look what me come to."

The youth stared at her awkwardly. He would like to have helped. But he was not the type to console. He made a gesture of encouragement, said something about only trying to help and that all was for the best, but in the end only fell back in embarrassment. He knew she was a woman that rarely cried and realized, if ever so slightly, the depth of her present suffering which only made him feel stupid at his incapacity to do anything for her. Furthermore he did not like to see other people suffer, not out of kindness, but out of selfishness, as his lack of any real sympathy—and his subsequent incapacity to console—made him feel guilty, and his guilt drove him to irritation which intensified yet more his lack of sympathy and further heightened his guilt. Confronted with her suffering his only thought was to flee the place. Unfortunately, a too highly developed conscience held him back.

"Aunt Daphne, Auntie," he said, his voice ringing with impatience and confusion, "please, try and control yourself. You must try; it make no sense crying."

"Oh God, Tom, I suffer too much. One person never make to suffer so much. I know that life is one long suffering, Tom. I don't mind sharing my burden. But I get too much. It not fair, it not fair."

She fell into another spasm. He walked towards the door to see if her husband was anywhere around, but half-way towards it realized the stupidity of his act. He turned and walked back towards her, held out his hand and touched her on her shoulder, almost at once recoiling in a shock of embarrassment and revulsion.

"Please, Aunt Daphne, try——"

"You is a good boy, Tom. You mother is a good woman too. She is me own sister. I never hate her, Tom. She good lookin', she have a good husban' an' she have you. Have nothing against her. You hear me . . . you hear me Tom . . . I have nothing against you or your mother or anybody else . . . but, but you must understand how I feel . . . someone must understand how I feel . . ."

Suddenly her countenance achieved an expression of urgency. She looked from one end of the room to the other but what she sought seemed to have evaded her; she looked towards him, but somehow he was not there. Something in her stomach seemed to have given way and a hard lump took its place. She swallowed hard, but her throat was dry and bitter . . .

You stand in front of one another and you press your palms together. Then you clap each other's palms and you move them away and you clap them behind you and above you and sideways. But you must concentrate. Or you miss your clap. So you must time the claps. That's partly what the rhyme is for:

> Orange in the market, one for a penny,
> Queen Victoria reign for many;
> Anybody, anybody, trouble me lover,
> I take out me knife and stab the bugger.

"Who tell you is 'Orange in the market'?" Peggy said, "it's 'Orange in England'."

"I don't care if is 'Orange in England'. I say is 'Orange in the market' an' I don't care what you or anybody else say. Is so me learn it."

"Daphne!"

She stared nervously round at her father who was oiling the whip he used for his mules. He was a tall, black man with a large, prominent nose which he proudly declared to be Scottish. He was a very angry, confused man who somehow hated her as much as he loved her elder, lighter sister who was pretty and who he said would one day marry the son of the Custosrotulorum of the parish.

"An' me, who I going to marry, Daddy?" she had inquired hesitantly as she always did whenever she dared to address him.

"You," he had laughed, "you is for the booga-man down at the pond."

And they had all laughed. Peggy and Sam and Aunt Matilda and even Mama though she knew Mama meant no harm. They had all laughed.

"Yes, yes, Daddy," she answered now.

"Is dat de way you speak to you elder sister? You mischievous little brat. You head tough like coco. Listen to what you sister have to say and learn. She have more sense than you. Listen, an' do t'ings de right an' proper way. Now Peggy darlin', tell her again."

Peggy had a cruel grin of triumph.

"Yes, Daddy." She cleared her throat and spoke in the ludicrously affected manner which Teacher Reynolds had said was 'the King's English': "Orange in England . . . Orange in England . . . Daddy, see she don't want to say after me."

"Daphne!" he bellowed, "repeat after you sister an' don't be damn rude. Don' mek me lose me temper, you hear me!"

"Orange in England," Peggy continued.

"Orange in . . ." No. She would not. She could not. She would die first. Let them all kill her.

"Daphne. I is orderin' you to say after you bigger sister, or so help me——"

"Orange in England," Peggy gave her cue once more.

"Orange in . . . in . . . in the market! In the market!" she screamed rebelliously.

The father fumed with rage. For a moment he forgot himself, lifted the whip and lashed it down beside her. The tip of the whip dug into her cheek. She screamed under the sting and threw herself to the ground. Out of the corner of her eye she could see that her father was frightened. She knew he had really meant only to frighten her and had hit her accidentally. For the first time in her life she felt she had her father where she wanted him. He was frightened, he was guilty, he was confused. She realized that the more she screamed the more she shattered him. And it was easy to scream for the sting of the whip still lingered. But now it became a pain of pleasure. Their eyes were all upon her and she had them at the mercy of her suffering. So she rolled and twisted and screamed in the dust till Mama came out running. Fair, silently suffering Mama who hated him and loved her.

"You . . . you hit her with that thing . . . your own daughter. How could you . . . how?"

Mama took her up. She clung to her and between her screaming she yelled: "Orange in the market! Orange in the market!"

"Aunt Daphne! Aunt Daphne! Get out of it. Control yourself. Please."

"Orange? . . . What? I was saying something?"

"You keep mumbling something about orange in the market."

Suddenly they both turned to look at the tall, dark figure of her husband which appeared at the door. For a brief moment her face twitched with hate as she looked at his bloodshot, drowsy eyes. A meaningless smile flashed across his face. Then she looked away, forgetting he was there. Silently, he left.

Tom's irritation had left him. For she was beginning to frighten him.

"Take the room, Aunt Daphne. Things will get better soon. But you must leave him if you to make a fresh start. Come on, take the room and leave."

"Him fling me out of him house the year after me mother dead, Tom. It was only she that was keeping him back. Go fend for yourself, him say. Is time you support yourself. You is big woman. You always been going on like you is big woman before your time. Alright, kirr-out now. That's what him say to me. Me poor gal pickney only sixteen. Know nothing 'bout life. What we must do? Only to take up man. Nothing else left for me to do, Tom. Only to take up man——"

"Auntie, please, you don't have to tell me all this, please."

"Him was old enough to be me father. I fall for him sweet-mouth and make him take advantage o' me. Him fall me, Tom——"

"Auntie!——"

"Him fall me and I had to marry him. Had to beg him too. Had to fall down on me knees and beg the dog. Him marry me and then me hell really begin. Oh Christ Almighty, why? Why me alone?"

She was staring towards heaven and she saw the ceiling with the cobweb. She spoke her thoughts with a loud voice and they seem to echo back at her, meaningless and strange . . .

Why had the drought been so long that year? Why had the common become so dry and empty? The year before, when it was green, they were playing with the little boy and the little girl from Kingston. The little boy wore socks, the little girl only wore shoes. Then her sister and her brother had told on her. They told how she still sucked her finger, and how she still wet her bed, and how the booga-man from the pond would marry her, and how the comb broke in her hair the other day when Mama was combing it. They screamed with laughter, ran after her and held her down, then they smelled her thumb and laughed again. After that she went and hid herself.

"Listen Aunt Daphne," Tom began to sound desperate, "I'll pay the first month rent for you. Leave the blooming place. It will send you crazy. Aunt Daphne."

"I lost my baby. Not even that I could have. I lost my baby and the doctor said I couldn't have any more——"

"What I want to know," Tom suddenly said, a bit angrily, "is why the devil you came back to him. You had a good job in England. Why you come back here to him?"

"I had to," she said, appearing to answer him, but speaking more to herself, "I didn't like England. I had to."

"Yes, but why back to him?"

"Him needed me. Him was sick and him needed me."

"But tha's crazy. After all the wrong he did to you."

"Him needed me. Him beg me to come. I had to come. I hate him so. I needed him to . . . to need me. Someone had to. Besides, it was cold over there. And somebody had to——"

She broke off and a long, unbearable pause followed. He stared vacantly round the room. Though he had been there several times before everything in it somehow seemed strange, alien. The walls, the dirty walls with the green paint stripping off them; the bed with the washed-out linen and the dirty pillow-cases. And there was the old mahogany table with the dog-eared Bible; the watermarked bureau with the oblong mirror through which he could see, reflected from the other room, the smeared door of the ice-box with the colour of sheep's wool. In the silence something in the reflection suddenly moved. It was an old, brown cockroach crawling dizzily down the smeared door of the ice-box. He shuddered a little and felt that he must go.

"Aunt Daphne, I'm gone. What I must say to Mama?"

"Tell her," she said, not looking at him, "tell her thanks, but not to bother with the room."

"But for God sake, Auntie, why? Why?"

She shook her head a little.

"There's no point," she said in a voice devoid of all emotion, "there's no point."

Then she fell silent. And he left.

Michael Anthony (*Trinidad*)

The Valley of Cocoa

THERE was not much in the valley of cocoa. Just the estate and our drying-houses, and our living-house. And the wriggling little river that passed through.

And of course, the labourers. But they didn't ever seem to speak to anyone. Always they worked silently from sunrise to evening. Only Wills was different. He was friendly, and he knew lots of things beside things about cocoa and drying-houses.

And he knew Port-of-Spain. He knew it inside out, he said. Every day after work he would sit down on the log with me and would tell of the wonderful place.

As he spoke his eyes would glow with longing. The longing to be in that world which he said was part of him. And sometimes I knew pain. For Wills made the city grow in me, and I knew longing too.

Never had I been out of the valley of cocoa. Father was only concerned about his plantation, and nothing else. He was dedicated to wealth and prosperity, and every year the cocoa yielded more and more. So he grew busier and busier, building, experimenting, planning for record returns. Everything needed out of the valley was handled by Wills—for people who knew Port-of-Spain could handle anything. Business progressed. The valley grew greener with cocoa, and the drying-houses were so full that the woodmen were always felling timber to build more.

Wills, who one day had just returned from ordering new machinery in Port-of-Spain, sat talking with me. The sun had not long gone down, but already it was dusk. Wills said it was never so in Port-of-Spain. Port of-Spain was always bright. He said as soon as the sun went down the whole city was lit by electric lamps, and you could hardly tell the difference between night and day!

And he explained all about those lamps which he said hung from poles, and from the houses that lined the million streets.

It was thick night when we got up. In the darkness Wills walked straight on to a tree, and he swore, and said, By Jove—if that would have happened to him in Port-of-Spain! He said one of these days I'd go there, when I got big, and I'd see for myself, and I'd never want to come back to the valley again.

The machinery arrived soon afterwards.

It came in a shining new van, and the name of the company was spelt in large letters on the sides of the van. The driver was a bright, gay-looking man and when the van stopped he jumped out and laughed and called, "Hey, there!'

Wills and father went down to meet him and I eased up behind them. I was thrilled. It was not every day that strangers came to the valley.

Father looked worried as he spoke to the man about payments and he complained that business wasn't doing well and the machinery was so expensive. But the man was laughing all the time, and said who cared about payments when father had all the time in the world to pay. Father was puzzled, and the man said yes, father could pay in instalments. Wills said it was true, that that was what they did in Port-of-Spain. The man made father sign up for instalments and while father signed, the man pulled at my chin and said, "Hi!"

Father was paying the first instalment. The man stretched his hands for the money and without counting it put it into his pocket. Every time my eyes caught his he winked.

"Hi!" he said again.

I twined round father's legs.

"Bashful," he said, and he tugged at the seat of my pants. I couldn't help laughing.

He opened the door of the van and the next moment he was outside with father and Wills. I noticed a bright-coloured packet in his hand and the next moment I felt something slide into my pocket. I looked up at him. "Like sweets?" he whispered. I turned away and grinned.

From about father's legs I watched him. He pulled out a red packet of cigarettes marked 'Camel' on top. He passed the cigarettes to father, then to Wills, and as he lit theirs and lit himself one, he seemed to be taken up with the estate below.

"All yours?" he asked after a while. "The whole thing?"

Father nodded.

He shook his head appraisingly: "Nice—nice, Old Man."

The evening was beginning to darken and the man looked at his watch and said it was getting late and he'd better start burning the gas. Father said true, because Port-of-Spain was so far, and the country roads were bad enough. The man claimed there were worse roads in some parts of Port-of-Spain. And he laughed and said what's a van anyway, only a lot of old iron. Father and Wills laughed heartily at this, and the man turned a silver key and started the van. And he said, well cheerio, cheerio, and if anything went wrong with the machine he'd hear from us.

The days that followed were filled with dream. I continually saw the gay city, and the bright, laughing man. Port-of-Spain, I kept thinking. Port-of-Spain! I imagined myself among the tall red houses, the maze of streets, the bright cars and vans darting to and fro; the trams, the trains, the buses; the thousands of people everywhere. And always I heard the voice. "Hi!" it kept sailing back to me. And every time I heard it I smiled.

Months passed, and more and more I grew fed-up with the valley. I felt a certain resentment growing inside me. Resentment for everything around. For father, for the silly labourers; even for Wills. For the cocoa trees. For the hills that imprisoned me night and day. I grew sullen and sick and miserable, tired of it all. I even wished for father's fears to come true. *Witchbroom*! I wished that witchbroom would come and destroy the cocoa and so chase father from this dreary place.

As expected, the machinery soon went wrong. It wouldn't work. Wills had to rush to Port-of-Spain to get the man.

I waited anxiously towards that evening, and when in the dusk I saw the van speeding between the trees I nearly jumped for sheer gladness.

From the hill father shouted saying he didn't know what was wrong but the machine wouldn't start. The man said, all right, and he boyishly ran up the hill to the house. He stopped, and made fun with me and I twined round father's legs, and he tickled me and we both laughed aloud. Then he gave me sweets in a blue and white packet, and he said he'd better go and see to the machine because the machine was lazy and didn't want to work. He made to tickle me again and I jumped away and we laughed, and father and Wills and he went to the shed. They had not been there five minutes when I heard the machine start again.

*   *   *

The labourers had changed a little. They had become somewhat fascinated by the new machine. It seemed they sometimes stole chances to operate it, for the machine went wrong quite a number of times afterwards. And so, happily, the man often came to us.

In time father and he became great friends. He gave father all the hints about cocoa prices in the city and about when to sell and whom to sell to. He knew all the good dealers and all the scamps, he said.

He knew all the latest measures taken to fight cacao diseases and he told father what they did in West Africa, and what they did here, and what they did there, to fight this, that, and the other disease.

With his help father did better than ever. And he was so pleased that he asked the man to spend a Sunday with us.

"Sure!" the man had agreed. And I had run out then, and I made two happy somersaults on the grass.

That Sunday came, and I was grazing the goats when from the hill I heard the voice.

"Kenneth!"

I turned and looked around. Then I dropped the ropes and ran excitedly up the hill. "Coming!" I kept saying. "Coming!" When I got there the big arms swept me up and threw me up in the air and caught me.

Directly father called us in to breakfast and afterwards the man put shorts on and we went out into the fresh air. The whole valley of cocoa nestled in the distance below us. The man watched like one under a spell.

"Beautiful!" he whispered, shaking his head. "Beautiful!"

"And the river," I said. Strange! I had hardly noticed how pretty the river was.

"Yes," the man answered. "Yellow, eh?"

I grinned.

"The water good?"

"Yes," I said.

"Sure, sure?"

"Sure, sure."

"Well, come on!" He took me by the hands and we hastened into the house.

The next moment we were running down the hill towards the river, the man in bathing trunks and me with my pants in my hand and sun all over me. We reached the banks and I showed where was shallow and where deep, and the man plunged into the deep part. He came to the surface again, laughing and saying how the water was nice and there was no such river in Port-of-Spain. He told me to get on his back, and he swam upstream and down with me and then he put me to stand in the shallow part. Then he soaped my body and bathed me, and when I was rinsed we went and sat a little on the bank.

He sat looking around at the trees and up at the hill. I looked too at the view. The cocoa seemed greener than I ever remembered seeing them, and the immortelle which stood between them, for shade, were like great giants, their blooms reddening the sky.

I looked up at him. We smiled.

Quietly then he talked of the city. He told me the city was lovely too, but in a different way. Not like it was here. He said I must see the city one of these days. Everything there was busy, he said. The cars and buses flashed by, and people hurried into the shops, and out of the shops, and everywhere. He said he liked the city. It had shops, stores, hotels, hospitals, Post Offices, schools—everything. Everything that made life easy. But sometimes he grew tired, he said, of the hustle and bustle and nowhere to turn for peace. He said he liked it here, quiet and nice. As life was meant to be. Then his eyes wandered off to the green cocoa again, and the immortelle, and here at the river, and up again to our house on the hill.

And he smiled sadly and said he wished he was father to be living here.

We went back into the water for some time, then we finished, then the man dried my skin, and his, and we went up to the house.

After we had eaten father took us into the cocoa field.

It was quiet there between the trees, and the dried brown leaves underfoot, together with the ripening cocoa put a healthy fragrance in the air.

It was strange being so near those trees. Before I had only known they were there and had watched them from the house. But now I was right in the middle of them, and touching them.

We passed under immortelle trees with the ground beneath red with dropped flowers and the man picked up the loveliest of the flowers and gave them to me. Father broke a cocoa pod, and we sucked the seeds and juicy pulp, and really, the young cocoa was as sweet as Wills had told me. The man sucked his seeds dry and looked as if he wanted more, so I laughed, and father who was watching from the corners of his eyes, knew, and he said, "Let's look for a nice ripe cocoa."

And it was already evening when we took the path out. Father and the young man were talking and I heard father ask him what he thought of the place.

"Mr. Browne, it's great," he had answered, "I mean, it's first-class, I'm telling you!"

★   ★   ★

Late, late that night I eased up from my bed. I unlatched the window and quietly shifted the curtain from one side.

The valley lay quietly below. The cocoa leaves seemed to be playing with the moonlight, and the immortelles stood there, looking tall and lonely and rapt in peace. From the shadows the moonlight spread right across the river and up the hill.

"Beautiful . . . !" the voice sailed back to my mind. And I wondered where he was now, if he was already in Port-of-Spain. He was sorry to leave. He had said this was one of the happiest days he had known. I had heard him telling father how he liked the valley so much, and he liked the little boy.

I had cried.

And now it swept back to my mind—what he had told father just as he was leaving. He had said, "Mr. Browne, don't be afraid about witch-broom. Not a thing will happen. Just you use that spray, and everything will be all right."

Quickly, then, I drew the curtains and latched the window. And I squeezed the pillow to me, for joy.

Michael Anthony

Pita of the Deep Sea

PITA panicked. There was nothing he could do. He was trapped. Trapped with hundreds of others. The Monster had come and was slowly, surely, dragging them from the deep. He swam through the excited crowd to try the bottom. Then he tried the top again. The great Monster had encircled them completely. There were millions of holes in its great hands, but none large enough. If only they were a little larger. Pita tried to push himself through one of the holes again. He squeezed and squeezed. Great tails lashed around him. Not only he but the whole crowd were in desperation. He tried to ease himself through. The thread-limbs pressed against his eyes. If only his head could get through. He pushed again, hard, and the pain quivered through his body. Down to his tail. He turned around. But it was no use trying it from that end. His tail was much wider than his head. There was nothing he could do. He heard the breakers roaring above now. That meant they were nearing the shore. Pita whipped his tail in fury. The Monster was gradually closing its hands. The crowd was being heaped against each other. He was knocked about by the giant tails. Good thing he was so small and could avoid being crushed. Around him were his friends and his dreaded enemies. The bonito was there, the killer shark was there. None of them thought of him now. They were all trying to escape. The killer shark, too. Shark, bonito, herring, cavali—they were all the same to him. A giant swordfish charged the threads desperately. The shark turned on its belly in vain to swallow the Monster. It swallowed a jellyfish. There were cries now above the surface. Below, the Monster grated on sand. The shore! They had reached the shore! Frantically Pita flung himself against one of the tiny holes. He gave a cry as the scales tore from his back—then a cry of joy. He was free! Free!

He lunged forward below the surface. He could feel the density of the breakers pushing down on him. He could hear the terrible roar which from the deep had sounded like a whisper of music. He looked back a little. There was only a tiny streak of blood behind him. He would be all right. He would be all right. Down, he went. Further away and down. Faster, faster he swam. His tail whipped the white foam, pushing him forward like a spear. Down he sped, rejoicing in his tinyness. If he was only a little bigger he would have been dying on the shore now. The fateful shore! There had been those who had actually come back from that world. This was one of the greatest mysteries. It was hard to believe that any fish had come back from the shore. But some said they had been there, and had talked of that awesome place. A place of no water and no fish. It was hard to believe this. But so had it been to believe about the Monster. But the Monster was real enough now. His mother had always warned him. He looked back a little. There was no more blood now. Down, he swam. Deeper, further. Deep, deep, until the sound of the breakers was only a bitter memory, and the sea was not sandy but blue and clear, and until, far, far away in the distance, green with the fern and the tender moss, he saw the rocks of home.

A thrill ran through him. He squirted through the water as if a new verve had possessed his body. His tail whipped the foam white and frothy. "Mother!" he thought, "Mother!" And he dived headlong towards the green rock.

"Mother, I am home," he gurgled.

The mother stared at him between the rocks. She noticed the bruised back. She was cross, yet the very fact that he had returned made her feel happy inside.

"Pita!" she exclaimed.

"I am home," he said.

"Wherever have you been to? Whatever happened?"

She was sure he had gone among the rocks playing and had lost his way. And that he had bruised his back swimming carelessly, or romping with the shingles. Pita was like that. He had always gone away far and played. He had always run away to meet the corals and the anemones and his other friends of the deep sea.

"Where have you been?" she said.

"Mother—" Pita hesitated, "Mother—the Monster."

The mother went cold with shock. Her eyes gleamed white and there was fear and horror in them.

"Pita, I warned you! I warned you! You wouldn't hear! Why did you go near the surface!"

"Mother——"

"Keep away from the surface, I always tell you! Keep away from the shore!"

"Mother, the Monster is everywhere."

"He can't come between the rocks. He never comes here."

"Mother, I can't stay all day between the rocks. I have friends everywhere. This morning I promised the corals——"

"This morning you promised nothing!" gulped the mother. "You nearly promised your life. Keep here between the rocks. Play with the moss and the fern. Here you are safe."

"The Monster isn't always here," said Pita. "Sometimes I swim out to my friends. We see the wonderful things. Sometimes we go up to the surface to see the sun. It is dark here below. Up there it is bright and very strange. When I grow up I will go often to see the sun, and to hear the music of the waves, and to watch the winds play on the roof of the sea."

"Hush up," the mother gulped. "It is more beautiful here between the rocks. It is more beautiful here because it is safe. Tell me, how did you escape? It is very odd. No one escapes the Monster."

"Oh," said Pita, and he told her. He told her how he was just playing and how very suddenly he found himself against the Great Hands of the Monster. He told her how terrified he was and how he swam down to the bottom to escape, but he could not. And even at the top he could not. For the hands were everywhere. The hands with the million tiny holes. He told her how there were hundreds of others caught like him, even the killer shark. She gulped, and shrunk back, and he said yes, the killer shark. And he told her how the Great Hands had gradually closed around them and pushed them all together and how they were all frightened and desperate, even the killer shark. He told her how the breakers had pounded over them and how they were dragged on the sands of the shore, and how he had actually heard the voices of the shore. Then he told her how he had flung himself desperately against one of the holes, while the thread-limbs cut at him and the pain shot through him, but how he had discovered himself free at last in the wide ocean. And he laughed as he said this part for he remembered himself speeding through the water, faster than barracuda, faster than anything.

But the mother did not laugh. In fact she was gloomier than before. For Pita was a wayward fish. She knew she couldn't change him. She knew that with all her advice she couldn't prevail upon him to keep away from the open deep, and from the surface, and from the sound of the breakers near the shore. She knew, too, as well as he, that it was his tinyness that saved him. But he was growing fast. In the next few months he would be no baby any more. She shuddered to think what would happen then if he made such a mistake again. Certainly that would be the end. Yet, as he grew he would become quicker. The fully-grown carite was perhaps the fastest fish in the sea. But as far as she had heard, the hands of the Monster were deep and wide and stretched far beyond the bounds of speed. Therefore she turned away sadly and swam to a dark corner of the rock to meditate.

*   *   *

The fully-grown carite was, indeed, the fastest fish in the sea. Pita no longer feared the barracuda, the shark, the swordfish. In the earlier months these had seemed to him so very fast. Now, with his long stream-lined body, he could outstrip them with the greatest ease.

The mother was so proud. Pita was as handsome as he was enormous. But he was not so enormous as to be ungainly. Sometimes at play, or just to be showing off, he would go past the rocks like a silver flash. And she would smile. Yes, he had grown up but he was still fond of play. And now he was so popular that his friends would not leave him alone. Every day he sported with the dolphins and corals and the anemones. And at night he came back to dream among the ferns.

Secretly his mother would be amused with his tales. Sometimes she stayed up just to hear.

"Quiet," she would say, "be quiet and go to sleep!" And he would gurgle teasingly among the rocks, and she would listen to his tales of the deep, about his pranks with the pretty corals and anemones. But about his new friend, the moonfish, Pita said nothing. He had met her at the distant rocks.

As the days passed he thought of the moonfish more and more. She was whom he dreamed of when he lay among the ferns. There he saw her eyes again, sparkling like the crystal depths. There again he saw her tinted scales, gleaming like mirrors of silver. She was Iona, the Pride of the Sea. Thinking of her, Pita became more and more wistful till even his mother noticed and was puzzled. But Pita kept silent. All his friends of the deep knew, though, and together they talked about it. They talked of how Pita stared blindly into water, and how once he nearly swam in the way of a killer shark. They talked of Iona the Beautiful, and they envied her.

For they knew what would be. And now the dolphins waited on the reefs in vain, and the corals, broken-hearted, murmured their low, sad song.

Eventually Pita spoke to his mother, for he would go away. She wept because she, too, knew what would be. She asked who was this Iona and Pita was surprised. All the sea knew, he said. In the heights and in the depths. From the waters near the shore, to the waters of the limitless bounds. Even the wonderful moon in the wind-water above the sea knew of her, for they had played together and he had given his magic to her.

He said he would go away to the distant rocks and before many tides he would return. Then would he bring back, he said, the greatest treasure of his days. He would bring back his bride and her daughter—the Pride of the Sea.

The mother listened with great pain. She realized that in this way Pita was lost to her. And she knew that she could not forbid this marriage even if she would have wanted to. Therefore she warned him again of the open sea, for it was still the terrible season of the Great Hands. And she told him of the ways to go. The ways which were difficult but safest. Then her heart lifted a little, for the marriage was good. As for the Monster of the Great Hands, the Providence which guided Pita so long would guide him again. She swam through the rocks looking about her busily. For now she had to prepare a home for her son, and for the beautiful Iona— the Pride of the Sea.

*　　*　　*

The bay was deep and wide and the winds played on the floor of the ocean. It was a beautiful month for the fishing, although it was the mating season. In the mating season you did not catch the fish plentifully, but if you were young and you went out with the sea calm and the breeze fresh, and with the sun lighting up the palm-fringed shore, sometimes you laughed aloud for the sheer joy of living and you hardly thought of the fish at all.

Thus had it been with these fishermen crossing the breakers. But now they cast their nets out with some enthusiasm because of the unexpected sight below. Half-way down, the water was foamy and rippling. The sign of fish.

Quickly they encircled the fish. They watched the leaden weights of the nets sink to the bottom. This would make their day. It came almost too easily. They watched each other, for it was very unusual to come upon a school of fish in the mating season.

Soon they were back on shore hauling the catch in. They hauled as the fish struggled in the nets and the breakers chattered along the bay. They pulled and pulled still amazed at their fortune, and when the nets dragged on sand and they could see the host of fins and tails flapping and lashing up the water, they were even more astonished.

They dragged the catch right out on dry beach. There were hundreds of fish and crabs and corals. Even anemones.

"Look," said one of the fishermen, pulling out a shiny flat fish from the living heap. Nearby a carite beat violently, gulping and leaping about the sand. The fishermen were looking at the shiny fish.

"It's ages," said the one with the fish, "years—since we brought in one of these." He held the fish high. Its eyes gleamed as sparkling as the crystal depths and its scales were like mirrors of silver.

"Moonfish," he said, more to himself. He was experienced and he knew it. "Look at her! Pretty eh?" he smiled. "She's like some—like some Pride of the Sea!"

The carite nearby beat furiously.

C. L. R. James (*Trinidad*)

Triumph

WHERE people in England and America say slums, Trinidadians said barrack-yards. Probably the word is a relic of the days when England relied as much on garrisons of soldiers as on her fleet to protect her valuable sugar-producing colonies. Every street in Port-of-Spain proper could show you numerous examples of the type: a narrow gateway leading into a fairly big yard, on either side of which run long, low buildings, consisting of anything from four to eighteen rooms, each about twelve feet square. In these lived the porters, the prostitutes, cartermen, washerwomen and domestic servants of the city.

In one corner of the yard is the hopelessly inadequate water-closet, unmistakable to the nose if not to the eye; sometimes there is a structure with the title of bathroom, a courtesy title, for he or she who would wash in it with decent privacy must cover the person as if bathing on the banks of the Thames; the kitchen happily presents no difficulty; never is there one and each barrack-yarder cooks before her door. In the centre of the yard is a heap of stones. On these the half-laundered clothes are bleached before being finally spread out to dry on the wire lines which in every yard cross and recross each other in all directions. Not only to Minerva have these stones been dedicated. Time was when they would have had an honoured shrine in a local temple to Mars, for they were the major source of ammunition for the homicidal strife which so often flared up in barrack-yards.

No longer do the barrack-yarders live the picturesque life of twenty-five years ago. Then, practising for the carnival, rival singers, Willie, Jean, and Freddie, porter, wharf-man or loafer in ordinary life, were for that season ennobled by some such striking sobriquet as The Duke of Normandy or the Lord Invincible, and carried with dignity homage such as young aspirants to literature had paid to Mr. Kipling or Mr. Shaw. They sang in competition from seven in the evening until far into the early morning, stimulated by the applause of their listeners and the excellence and copiousness of the rum; night after night the stickmen practised their dangerous and skilful game, the 'pierrots', after elaborate preface of complimentary speech, belaboured each other with riding whips; while around the performers the spectators pressed thick and good-humoured until mimic warfare was transformed into real, and stones from 'the bleach' flew thick. But today that life is dead. All carnival practice must cease at ten o'clock. The policeman is to the stick-fighter and 'pierrot' as the sanitary inspector to mosquito larvae. At nights the streets are bright with electric light, the arm of the law is longer, its grip stronger. Gone are the old lawlessness and picturesqueness. Barrack-yard life has lost its savour. Luckily, prohibition in Trinidad is still but a word. And life, dull and drab as it is in comparison, can still offer its great moments.

On a Sunday morning in one of the rooms of the barrack in Abercromby Street sat Mamitz. Accustomed as is squalid adversity to reign unchallenged in these quarters, yet in this room it was more than usually triumphant, sitting, as it were, high on a throne of regal state, so depressed was the woman and so depressing her surroundings.

The only representatives of the brighter side of life were three full-page pictures torn from illustrated periodicals, photographs of Lindbergh, Bernard Shaw and Sargent's 'Portrait of a Woman', and these owed their presence solely to the fact that no pawn-shop would have accepted them. They looked with unseeing eyes upon a room devoid of furniture save for a few bags spread upon the floor to form a bed. Mamitz sat on the door step talking to, or rather being talked to by her friend, Celestine, who stood astride the concrete canal which ran in front of the door.

"Somebody do you something," said Celestine with conviction. "Nobody goin' to change my mind from that. An' if you do what I tell you, you will t'row off this black spirit that on you. A nice woman like you, and you carn't get a man to keep you! You carn't get nothing to do!"

Mamitz said nothing. Had Celestine said the exact opposite, Mamitz's reply would have been the same.

She was a black woman, too black to be pure Negro, probably with some Madrasi East Indian blood in her, a suspicion which was made a certainty by the long thick plaits of her plentiful hair. She was shortish and fat, voluptuously developed, tremendously developed, and as a creole loves development in a woman more than any other extraneous allure, Mamitz (like the rest of her sex in all stations of life) saw to it when she moved that you missed none of her charms. But for the last nine weeks she had been 'in derricks', to use Celestine's phrase. First of all the tram conductor who used to keep her (seven dollars every Saturday night, out of which Mamitz usually got three) had accused her of infidelity and beaten her. Neither the accusation nor the beating had worried Mamitz. To her and her type those were minor incidents of existence, from their knowledge of life and men, the kept woman's inevitable fate. But after a temporary reconciliation he had beaten her once more, very badly indeed, and left her. Even this was not an irremediable catastrophe. But thenceforward, Mamitz, from being the most prosperous woman in the yard, had sunk gradually to being the most destitute. Despite her very obvious attractions, no man took notice of her. She went out asking for washing or for work as a cook. No success. Luckily, in the days of her prosperity she had been generous to Celestine who now kept her from actual starvation. One stroke of luck she had had. The agent for the barracks had suddenly taken a fancy to her, and Mamitz had not found it difficult to persuade him to give her a chance with the rent. But that respite was over: he was pressing for the money, and Mamitz had neither money to pay nor hope of refuge when she was turned out. Celestine would have taken her in, but Celestine's keeper was a policeman who visited her three or four nights a week, and to one in that position a fifteen-foot room does not offer much scope for housing the homeless. Yet Celestine was grieved that she could do nothing to help Mamitz in her trouble which she attributed to the evil and supernatural machinations of Irene, their common enemy.

"Take it from me, that woman do you something. Is she put Nathan against you. When was the quarrel again?"

"It was two or three days after Nathan gave me the first beating."

Nathan then had started on his evil courses before the quarrel with Irene took place, but Celestine brushed away objection.

"She musta had it in her mind for you from before. You didn't see how she fly out at you . . . As long as you livin' here an' I cookin' I wouldn't see you want a cup o' tea an' a spoonful o' rice. But I carn't help with the rent. . . . An' you ain't have nobody here."

Mamitz shook her head. She was from Demerara.

"If you could only cross the sea—that will cut any spirit that on you . . . Look the animal!"

Irene had come out of her room on the opposite side of the yard. She could not fail to see Celestine and Mamitz and she called loudly to a neighbour lower down the yard:

"Hey Jo-jo! What is the time? Ten o'clock a'ready? Le' me start to cook me chicken that me man buy for me—even if 'e have a so' foot . . . I don't know how long it will last before 'e get drunk and kick me out o' here. Then I will have to go dawg'n round other po' people to see if I could pick up what they t'row 'way."

She fixed a box in front of her door, put her coal-pot on it, and started to attend to her chicken.

Sunday morning in barrack-yards is pot-parade. Of the sixteen tenants in the yard twelve had their pots out, and they lifted the meat with long iron forks to turn it, or threw water into the pot so that it steamed to the heavens and every woman could tell what her neighbour was cooking— beef, or pork, or chicken. It didn't matter what you cooked in the week, if you didn't cook at all. But to cook salt fish, or hog-head, or pig-tail on a Sunday morning was a disgrace. You put your pot inside your house and cooked it there.

Mamitz, fat, easy-going, and cowed by many days of semi-starvation, took little notice of Irene. But Celestine, a thin little whip of a brown-skinned woman, bubbled over with repressed rage.

"By Christ, if it wasn't for one t'ing I'd rip every piece o' clothes she have on off 'er."

"Don' bother wid 'er. What is the use o' gettin' you'self in trouble with Jimmy?"

Jimmy was the policeman. He was a steady, reliable man but he believed in discipline and when he spoke, he spoke. He had made Celestine understand that she was not to fight: he wasn't going to find himself mixed up in court as the keeper of any brawling woman. Celestine's wrath, deprived of its natural outlet, burned none the less implacably.

"I tell you something, Mamitz, I goin' to talk to the agent in the morning. I goin' to tell 'im to give you to the end of the month. Is only five days . . . I goin' to give you a bath. Try and see if you could get some gully-root and so on this afternoon . . . Tonight I goin' give you . . . An' I will give you some prayers to read. God stronger than the devil. We gon' break this t'ing that on you. Cheer up. I goin' send you a plate with you' chicken an' rice as soon as it finish. Meanwhile burn you little candle, say you' little prayers, console you' little mind. I goin' give you that bath tonight. You ain' kill priest. You ain' cuss you' mudder. So you ain' have cause to 'fraid nothin'."

Celestine would never trust herself to indulge in abuse with Irene; the chances that it would end in a fight were too great. So she contented her self with casting a look of the most murderous hate and scorn and defiance at her enemy, and then went to her own pot which was calling for attention.

And yet three months before Mamitz, Celestine and Irene had been good friends. They shared their rum and their joys and troubles: and on Sunday afternoons they used to sit before Mamitz's room singing hymns: 'Abide With Me', 'Jesu, Lover of My Soul', 'Onward! Christian Soldiers'. Celestine and Irene sang soprano and Irene sang well. Mamitz was a naturally fine contralto and had a fine ear, while Nathan, who was a Barbadian and consequently knew vocal music, used to sing bass whenever he happened to be in. The singing would put him in a good mood and he would send off to buy more rum and everything would be peaceful and happy. But Irene was a jealous woman, not only jealous of Mamitz's steady three dollars a week and Celestine's policeman with his twenty-eight dollars at the end of the month. She lived with a cab-man, whose income though good enough was irregular. And he was a married man, with a wife and children to support. Irene had to do washing to help out, while Mamitz and Celestine did nothing, merely cooked and washed clothes for their men. So gradually a state of dissatisfaction arose. Then one damp evening, Mamitz, passing near the bamboo pole which supported a clothes line overburdened with Irene's clothes, brought it down with her broad, expansive person. The line burst, and nightgowns, sheets, pillow-cases, white suits and tablecloths fluttered to the mud. It had been a rainy week with little sun, and already it would have been difficult to get the clothes ready in time for Saturday morning: after this it was impossible. And hot and fiery was the altercation. Celestine who tried to make peace was drawn into the quarrel by Irene's comprehensive and incendiary invective.

"You comin' to put you' mouth in this. You think because you livin' with a policeman you is a magistrate. Mind you' business, woman, min' you' business. The two o' all you don't do nothing for you' livin'. You only sittin' down an' eatin' out the men all you livin' wid. An' I wo'k so hard an' put out me clo's on the line. And this one like some cab-horse knock it down, and when I tell 'er about it you comin' to meddle! Le' me tell you . . ."

So the wordy warfare raged, Celestine's policeman coming in for rough treatment at the tongue of Irene. Celestine, even though she was keeping herself in check, was a match for any barrack-yard woman Port-of-Spain could produce, but yet it was Mamitz who clinched the victory.

"Don't mind Celestine livin' with a policeman. You will be glad to get 'im for you'self. An' it better than livin' with any stinkin' so'-foot man."

For Irene's cab-man had a sore on his foot, which he had had for thirty years and would carry with him to the grave even if he lived for thirty years more. Syphilis, congenital and acquired, and his copious boozing would see to it that there was no recovery. Irene had stupidly hoped that nobody in the yard knew. But in Trinidad when His Excellency the Governor and his wife have a quarrel the street boys speak of it the day after, and Richard's bad foot had long been a secret topic of conversation in the yard. But it was Mamitz who had made it public property, and Irene hated Mamitz with a virulent hatred, and had promised to 'do' for her. Three days before, Nathan, the tram-conductor, had given Mamitz the first beating; but even at the time of the quarrel there was no hint of his swift defection and Mamitz's rapid descent to her present plight. So that Celestine, an errant but staunch religionist, was convinced that Mamitz's troubles were due to Irene's trafficking with the devil, if not personally, at least through one of his numerous agents who ply their profitable trade in every part of Port of Spain. Secure in her own immunity from anything that Irene might 'put on her', she daily regretted that she couldn't rip the woman to pieces. "Oh Jesus! If it wasn't for Jimmy I'd tear the wretch limb from limb!" But the energy that she could not put into the destruction of Irene she spent in upholding Mamitz. The fiery Celestine had a real affection for the placid Mamitz, whose quiet ways were so soothing. But, more than this, she was determined not to see Mamitz go down. In the bitter antagonism she nursed against Irene, it would have been a galling defeat if Mamitz went to the wall. Further, her reputation as a woman who knew things and could put crooked people straight was at stake. Once she had seen to Jimmy's food and clothes and creature comforts she set herself to devise ways and means of supporting the weak, easily crushed Mamitz.

Celestine's policeman being on duty that night, she herself was off duty and free to attend to her own affairs. At midnight, with the necessary rites and ceremonies, Ave Marias and Pater Nosters, she bathed Mamitz in a large bath pan full of water prepared with gully root, fever grass, lime leaves, *guerin tout*, *herbe a femmes*, and other roots, leaves and grasses noted for their efficacy (when properly applied) against malign plots and influences. That was at twelve o'clock the Sunday night. On Monday morning at eight o'clock behold Popo des Vignes walking into the yard, with a little bag in his hand.

Popo is a creole of creoles. His name is des Vignes, but do not be misled into thinking that there flows in his veins blood of those aristocrats who found their way to Trinidad after '89. He is a Negro, and his slave ancestor adopted the name from his master. Popo is nearing forty, medium-sized, though large about the stomach, with a longish moustache. He is dressed in a spotless suit of white with tight-fitting shoes of a particularly yellowish brown (no heavy English brogues or fantastic American shoes for him). On his head he wears his straw hat at a jaunty angle, and his manner of smoking his cigarette and his jacket always flying open (he wears no waistcoat) will give the impression that Popo is a man of pleasure rather than a man of work. And that impression would be right. He has never done a week's honest work in his life. He can get thirty dollars for you if you are in difficulties (at one hundred per cent); or three thousand dollars if you have a house or a cocoa estate. During the cocoa crop he lurks by the railway station with an unerring eye for peasant proprietors who have brought their cocoa into town and are not quite certain where they will get the best price. This is his most profitable business, for he gets commission both from the proprietors and from the big buyers. But he is not fastidious as to how he makes money, and will do anything that does not bind him down, and leaves him free of manual or clerical labour. For the rest, after he has had a good meal at about half past seven in the evening he can drink rum until six o'clock the next morning without turning a hair; and in his own circle he has a wide reputation for his connoisseurship in matters of love and his catholicity of taste in women.

"Eh, Mr. des Vignes! How you?" said Celestine. The inhabitants of every barrack-yard, especially the women, knew Popo.

"Keeping fine."

"Who you lookin' for roun' this way?"

"I come roun' to see you. How is Jimmy? When you getting married?"

"Married!" said Celestine with fine scorn. "Me married a police! I wouldn't trust a police further than I could smell him. Police ain't have no regard. A police will lock up 'is mudder to get a stripe. An' besides I ain' want to married the man in the house all the time, you go'n be a perfect slave. I all right as I be."

"Anyway, I want you to buy a ring."

"Rings you sellin' in the bag? I ain' have no money, but le' me see them."

Popo opened his bags and displayed the rings—beautiful gold of American workmanship, five dollars cash and six dollars on terms. They had cost an Assyrian merchant in Park Street ten dollars the dozen, and Popo was selling them on commission. He was doing good business, especially with those who paid two dollars down and gave promises of monthly or weekly instalments. If later the merchant saw trouble to collect his instalments or to get back his rings, that wouldn't worry Popo much for by that time he would have chucked up the job.

"So you wouldn't take one," said he, getting ready to put away his treasures again.

"Come roun' at the end o' the month. But don't shut them up yet. I have a friend I want to see them."

She went to the door.

"Mamitz!" she called. "Come see some rings Mr. des Vignes sellin'."

Mamitz came into Celestine's room, large, slow-moving, voluptuous, with her thick, smooth hair neatly plaited and her black skin shining. She took Popo's fancy at once.

"But you have a nice friend, Celestine," said Popo. "And she has a nice name too: Mamitz! Well, how many rings you are going to buy from me?"

Celestine answered quickly: "Mamitz can't buy no rings. The man was keepin' her, they fall out, an' she lookin' for a husband now."

"A nice woman like you can't stay long without a husband," said des Vignes. "Let me give you some luck . . . Choose a ring and I will make you a present."

Mamitz chose a ring and des Vignes put it on her finger himself.

"Excuse me, I comin' back now," said Celestine. "The Sanitary Inspector comin' just now, an' I want to clean up some rubbish before he come."

When she came back des Vignes was just going.

"As we say, Mamitz," he smiled. "So long, Celestine!"

He was hardly out of earshot when Celestine excitedly tackled Mamitz. "What 'e tell you?"

"'E say that 'e comin' round here about ten o'clock tonight or little later . . . An' 'e give me this." In her palm reposed a red two-dollar note.

"You see what I tell you?" said Celestine triumphantly. "That bath.

But don' stop. Read the prayers three times a day for nine days . . . Buy some stout, Mitz, to nourish up you'self . . . 'E ain't a man you could depend on. If you dress a broomstick in a petticoat 'e will run after it. But you goin' to get something out o' 'im for a few weeks or so . . . An' you see 'e is a nice man."

Mamitz smiled her lazy smile.

Celestine knew her man. For four weeks Popo was a more or less regular visitor to Mamitz's room. He paid the rent, he gave her money to get her bed and furniture out of the pawn-shop, and every Sunday morning Mamitz was stirring beef or pork or chicken in her pot. More than that, whenever Popo said he was coming to see her, he gave her money to prepare a meal so that sometimes late in the week, on a Thursday night, Mamitz's pot smelt as if it was Sunday morning. Celestine shared in the prosperity and they could afford to take small notice of Irene who prophesied early disaster.

"All you flourishin' now. But wait little bit. I know that Popo des Vignes well. 'E don't knock round a woman no more than a month. Just now all that high livin' goin' shut down an' I going see you Mamitz eatin' straw."

But Mamitz grew fatter than ever, and when she walked down the road in a fugi silk dress, tight fitting and short, which exposed her noble calves to the knee and accentuated the amplitudes of her person, she created a sensation among those men who took notice of her.

On Sunday morning she went into the market to buy beef. She was passing along the stalls going to the man she always bought from, when a butcher called out to her.

"Hey, Mamitz! Come this way."

Mamitz went. She didn't know the man, but she was of an acquiescent nature and she went to see what he wanted.

"But I don't know you," she said, after looking at him. "Where you know my name?"

"Ain't was you walkin' down Abercromby Street last Sunday in a white silk dress?"

"Yes," smiled Mamitz.

"Well, I know a nice woman when I see one. An' I find out where you livin' too. Ain't you livin' in the barrack just below Park Street? . . . Girl, you did look too sweet. You mustn't buy beef from nobody but me. How much you want? A pound? Look a nice piece. Don't worry to pay me for that. You could pay me later. Whenever you want beef, come round this way."

Mamitz accepted and went. She didn't like the butcher too much, but he liked her. And a pound of beef was a pound of beef. Nicholas came to see her a day or two after and brought two pints of stout as a present. At first Mamitz didn't bother with him. But des Vignes was a formidable rival. Nicholas made Mamitz extravagant presents and promises. What helped him was that Popo now began to slack off. A week would pass and Mamitz would not see him. And no more money was forthcoming. So, after a while she accepted Nicholas, and had no cause to regret her bargain. Nicholas made a lot of money as a butcher. He not only paid the rent, but gave her five dollars every Saturday night, and she could always get a dollar or two out of him during the week. Before long he loved her to distraction, and was given to violent fits of jealousy which, however, were always followed by repentance and lavish presents. Still Mamitz hankered after Popo. One day she wrote him a little note telling him that she was sorry she had to accept Nicholas but that she would be glad to see him any time he came round. She sent it to the Miranda Hotel where Popo took his meals. But no answer came and after a while Mamitz ceased actively to wish to see Popo. She was prosperous and pretty happy. She and Celestine were thicker than ever, and were on good terms with the neighbours in the yard. Only Irene they knew would do them mischief, and on mornings when Mamitz got up, on Celestine's advice, she looked carefully before the door lest she should unwittingly set foot on any church-yard bones, deadly powders, or other satanic agencies guaranteed to make the victim go mad, steal or commit those breaches of good conduct which are punishable by law. But nothing untoward happened. As Celestine pointed out to Mamitz, the power of the bath held good, "and as for me," concluded she, "no powers Irene can handle can touch my little finger."

Easter Sunday came, and with it came Popo. He walked into the yard early, about seven the morning, and knocked up Mamitz who was still sleeping.

"I t'ought you had given me up for good," said Mamitz. "I write you and you didn't answer."

"I didn't want any butcher to stick me with his knife," laughed Popo. "Anyway, that is all right . . . I was playing baccarat last night and I made a good haul, so I come to spend Easter with you. Look! Here is five dollars. Buy salt fish and sweet oil and some greens and tomatoes. Buy some pints of rum. And some stout for yourself. I am coming back about nine o'clock. Today is Easter Saturday, Nicholas is going to be in the market the whole day. Don't be afraid for him."

Mamitz became excited. She gave the five dollars to Celestine and put her in charge of the catering, while she prepared for her lover. At about half past nine Popo returned. He, Mamitz and Celestine ate in Mamitz's room, and before they got up from the table, much more than two bottles of rum had disappeared. Then Celestine left them and went to the market to Nicholas. She told him that Mamitz wasn't feeling too well and had sent for beef and pork. The willing Nicholas handed over the stuff and sent a shilling for his lady love. He said he was rather short of money but at the end of the day he was going to make a big draw. Celestine cooked, and at about half past one, she, Popo and Mamitz had lunch. Celestine had to go out again and buy more rum. The other people in the yard didn't take much notice of what was an everyday occurrence, were rather pleased in fact, for after lunch Celestine had a bottle and a half of rum to herself and ostentatiously invited all the neighbours to have drinks, all, of course, except Irene.

At about three o'clock Irene felt that she could bear it no longer and that if she didn't take this chance it would be throwing away a gift from God. She put on her shoes, took her basket on her arm, and left the yard. It was the basket that aroused the observant Celestine's suspicions for she knew that Irene had already done all her shopping that morning. She sat thinking for a few seconds, then she knocked at Mamitz's door.

"Look here, Mamitz," she called. "It's time for Mr. des Vignes to go. Irene just gone out with a basket, I think she gone to the market to tell Nicholas."

"But he can't get away today," called Mamitz.

"You know how the man jealous and how 'e bad," persisted Celestine. "Since nine o'clock Mr. des Vignes, is time for you to go."

Celestine's wise counsel prevailed. Popo dressed himself with his usual scrupulous neatness and cleared off. The rum bottles were put out of the way and Mamitz's room was made tidy. She and Celestine had hardly finished when Irene appeared with the basket empty.

"You see," said Celestine. "Now look out!"

Sure enough, it wasn't five minutes after when a cab drew up outside, and Nicholas still in his bloody butcher's apron, came hot foot into the yard. He went straight up to Mamitz and seized her by the throat.

"Where the hell is that man you had in the room with you—the room I payin' rent for?"

"Don't talk dam' foolishness, man, lemme go," said Mamitz.

"I will stick my knife into you as I will stick it in a cow. You had Popo des Vignes in that room for the whole day. Speak the truth, you dog."

"You' mother, you' sister, you' aunt, you' wife was the dog," shrieked Mamitz, quoting one of Celestine's most brilliant pieces of repartee.

"It's the wo'se when you meddle with them common low-island people," said Celestine. Nicholas was from St. Vincent, and Negroes from St. Vincent, Grenada and the smaller West Indian islands are looked down upon by the Trinidad Negro as low-island people.

"You shut you' blasted mouth and don' meddle with what don' concern you. Is you encouragin' the woman. I want the truth, or by Christ I'll make beef o' one o' you here today."

"Look here, man, lemme tell you something." Mamitz, drunk with love and rum and inspired by Celestine, was showing spirit. "That woman over there come and tell you that Mr. des Vignes was in this room. The man come in the yard, 'e come to Celestine to sell 'er a ring she did promise to buy from 'im long time. Look in me room," she flung the half doors wide, "you see any signs of any man in there? Me bed look as if any man been lyin' down on it? But I had no right to meddle with a low brute like you. You been botherin' me long enough. Go live with Irene. Go share she wid she so' foot cab-man. Is woman like she men like you want. I sorry the day I ever see you. An' I hope I never see you' face again."

She stopped, panting, and Celestine, who had only been waiting for an opening, took up the tale.

"But look at the man! The man leave 'is work this bright Easter Saturday because this nasty woman go and tell 'im that Mr. des Vignes in the room with Mamitz! Next thing you go'n say that 'e livin' with me. But man, I never see such a ass as you. Bertha, Olive, Josephine," she appealed to some of the other inhabitants of the yard. "Ain't all you been here the whole day an' see Mr. des Vignes come here after breakfast? I pay 'im two dollars I had for 'im. 'E sen' and buy a pint o' rum an' I call Mamitz for the three o' we to fire a little liquor for the Easter. Next thing I see is this one goin' out—to carry news: and now this Vincelonian fool leave 'e work—But, man, you drunk."

Bertha, Olive and Josephine, who had shared in the rum, confirmed

Celestine's statement. Irene had been sitting at the door of her room cleaning fish and pretending to take no notice, but at this she jumped up.

"Bertha, you ought to be ashame' o' you'self. For a drink o' rum you lyin' like that? Don't believe them, Nicholas. Whole day—"

But here occurred an unlooked for interruption. The cabby, hearing the altercation and not wishing to lose time on a day like Easter Saturday, had put a little boy in charge of his horse and had been listening for a minute or two. He now approached and held Nicholas by the arm.

"Boss," he said, "don't listen to that woman. She livin' with Richard the cab-man an' 'e tell me that all women does lie but 'e never hear or know none that does lie like she—"

There was a burst of laughter.

"Come go, boss," said the cabby, pulling the hot, unwilling Nicholas by the arm.

"I have to go back to my work, but I am comin' back tonight and I am goin' to lick the stuffin' out o' you."

"An' my man is a policeman," said Celestine. "An' 'e goin' to be here tonight. An' if you touch this woman, you spend you' Easter in the lock-up sure as my name is Celestine an' you are a good-for-nothing Vincelonian fool of a butcher."

Nicholas drove away, leaving Celestine mistress of the field, but for the rest of the afternoon Mamitz was depressed. She was tired out with the day's excitement, and after all Nicholas had good money. On a night like this he would be drawing quite a lot of money and now it seemed that she was in danger of losing him. She knew how he hated Popo. She liked Popo more than Nicholas, much more, but after all people had to live.

Celestine, however, was undaunted. "Don't min' what 'e say. 'E comin' back. 'E comin' back to beg. When you see a man love a woman like he love you, she could treat 'im how she like, 'e still comin' back like a dog to eat 'is vomit. But you listen to me, Mamitz. When 'e come back cuss 'im a little bit. Cuss 'im plenty. Make 'im see that you ain't goin' to stand too much nonsense from 'im."

Mamitz smiled in her sleepy way, but she was not hopeful. And all the rest of the afternoon Irene worried her by singing ballads appropriate to the occasion.

"Though you belong to somebody else
Tonight you belong to me."

"Come, come, come to me, Thora,
Come once again and be . . ."

"How can I live without you!
How can I let you go!"

Her voice soared shrill over the babel of clattering tongues in the yard. And as the voice rose so Mamitz's heart sank.

"Don' forget," were Celestine's last words before they parted for the night. "If 'e come back tonight, don't open the door for 'im straight. Le' 'im knock a little bit."

"All right," said Mamitz dully. She was thinking that she had only about thirty-six cents left over from the money des Vignes had given her. Not another cent.

But Celestine was right. The enraged Nicholas went back to work and cut beef and sawed bones with a ferocity that astonished his fellow-butchers and purchasers. But at seven o'clock, with his pocket full of money and nothing to do, he felt miserable. He had made his plans for the Easter: Saturday night he had decided to spend with Mamitz, and all Easter Sunday after he knocked off at nine in the morning. Easter Monday he had for himself and he had been thinking of taking Mamitz, Celestine and Jimmy down to Carenage in a taxi to bathe. He mooned about the streets for a time. He took two or three drinks, but he didn't feel in the mood for running a spree and getting drunk. He was tired from the strain of the day and he felt for the restful company of a woman, especially the woman he loved—the good-looking, fat, agreeable Mamitz. At about half past ten he found his resolution never to look at her again wavering.

"Damn it," he said to himself. "That woman Irene is a liar. She see how I am treatin' Mamitz well and she want to break up the livin'."

He fought the question out with himself.

"But the woman couldn't lie like that. The man musta been there."

He was undecided. He went over the arguments for and against, the testimony of Bertha and Olive, the testimony of the cab-man. His reason inclined him to believe that Mamitz had been entertaining des Vignes for the whole day in the room he was paying for, while he, the fool, was working hard for money to carry to her. But stronger powers than reason were fighting for Mamitz, and eleven o'clock found him in the yard knocking at the door.

"Mamitz! Mamitz! Open. Is me—Nicholas." There was a slight pause. Then he heard Mamitz's voice, sounding a little strange.

"What the devil you want!"

"I sorry for what happen today. Is that meddlin' woman, Irene. She come to the market an' she lie on you. Open the door, Mamitz . . . I have something here for you."

Celestine next door was listening closely, pleased that Mamitz was proving herself so obedient to instruction.

"Man, I 'fraid you. You have a knife out there an' you come here to cut me up as Gorrie cut up Eva."

"I have no knife. I brought some money for you."

"I don't believe you. You want to treat me as if I a cow."

"I tell you I have no knife . . . open the door, woman, or I'll break it in. You carn't treat me like that."

Nicholas's temper was getting the better of him, he hadn't expected this.

The watchful Celestine here interfered.

"Open the door for the man, Mamitz. 'E say 'e beg pardon and, after all, is he payin' the rent."

So Mamitz very willingly opened the door and Nicholas went in. He left early the next morning to go to work but he promised Mamitz to be back by half past nine.

Irene, about her daily business in the yard, gathered that Nicholas had come 'dawgin'' back to Mamitz the night before and Mamitz was drivin' him dog and lance, but Celestine beg for him and Mamitz let 'im come in. Mamitz, she noticed, got up that morning much later than usual. In fact Celestine (who was always up at five o'clock) knocked her up and went into the room before she came out. It was not long before Irene knew that something was afoot. First of all, Mamitz never opened her door as usual, but slipped in and out closing it after her. Neither she nor Celestine went to the market. They sent out Bertha's little sister who returned with beef and pork and mutton, each piece of which Mamitz held up high in the air and commented upon. Then Bertha's sister went out again and returned with a new coal-pot. Irene could guess where it came from—some little store, in Charlotte Street probably, whose owner was not afraid to run the risk of selling on Sundays. In and out the yard went Bertha's little sister, and going and coming she clutched something tightly in her hand. Irene, her senses tuned by resentment and hate to their highest pitch, could not make out what was happening. Meanwhile Celestine was inside Mamitz's room, and Mamitz, outside, had started to cook in three coal-pots.

Every minute or so Mamitz would poke her head inside the room and talk to Celestine. Irene could see Mamitz shaking her fat self with laughter while she could hear Celestine's shrill cackle inside. Then Bertha's sister returned for the last time and after going into the room to deliver whatever her message was, came and stood a few yards away, opposite Mamitz's door, expectantly waiting. Think as she would, Irene could form no idea as to what was going on inside.

Then Mamitz went and stood near to Bertha's sister; and, a second after, the two halves of the door were flung open and Irene saw Celestine standing in the doorway with arms akimbo. But there was nothing to— and then she saw. Both halves of the door were plastered with notes, green five-dollar notes, red two-dollar notes, and blue dollar notes, with a pin at a corner of each to keep it firm. The pin-heads were shining in the sun. Irene was so flabbergasted that for a second or two she stood with her mouth open. Money Nicholas had given Mamitz. Nicholas had come back and begged pardon, and given her all this money. The fool! So that was what Celestine had been doing inside there all the time. Bertha's sisters had been running up and down to get some of the notes changed. There must be about forty, no, fifty dollars, spread out on the door. Mamitz and Bertha's sister were sinking with laughter and the joke was spreading, for other people in the yard were going up to see what the disturbance was about. What a blind fool that Nicholas was! Tears of rage and mortification rushed to Irene's eyes.

"Hey, Irene, come see a picture Nicholas bring for Mamitz last night! An' tomorrow we goin' to Carenage. We don't want you, but we will carry you' husband, the sea-water will do 'is so'-foot good." Celestine's voice rang across the yard.

Bertha, Josephine, the fat Mamitz and the rest were laughing so that they could hardly hold themselves up. Irene could find neither spirit nor voice to reply. She trembled so that her hands shook. The china bowl in which she was washing rice slipped from her fingers and broke into a dozen pieces while the rice streamed into the dirty water of the canal.

C. L. R. James

La Divina Pastora

O^F my own belief in this story I shall say nothing. What I have done is to put it down as far as possible just as it was told to me, in my own style, but with no addition to or subtraction from the essential facts.

Anita Perez lived with her mother at Bande 1 'Est Road, just at the corner where North Trace joins the Main Road. She had one earthly aim. She considered it her duty and business to be married as quickly as possible, first because in that retired spot it marked the sweet perfection of a woman's existence, and secondly, because feminine youth and beauty, if they exist, fade early in the hard work on the cocoa plantations. Every morning of the week, Sundays excepted, she banded down her hair, and donned a skirt which reached to her knees, not with any pretensions to fashion, but so that from seven till five she might pick cocoa, or cut cocoa, or dry cocoa, or in some other way assist in the working of Mr. Kayle-Smith's cocoa estate. She did this for thirty cents a day, and did it uncomplainingly, because her mother and father had done it before her, and had thriven on it. On Sundays she dressed herself in one of her few dresses, put on a little gold chain, her only ornament, and went to Mass. She had no thought of woman's rights, nor any Ibsenic theories of morality. All she knew was that it was her duty to get married, when, if she was lucky, this hard life in the cocoa would cease.

Every night for the past two years Sebastian Montagnio came down from his four-roomed mansion, half a mile up the trace, and spent about an hour, sometimes much more, with the Perez family. Always he sat on a bench by the door, rolling cheap cigarettes and half-hiding himself in smoke. He was not fair to outward view, but yet Anita loved him. Frequently half an hour would elapse without a word from either, she knitting or sewing steadily, Sebastian watching her contentedly and Mrs. Perez sitting on the ground just outside the door, smoking one of Sebastian's cigarettes and carrying on a ceaseless monologue in the local patois. Always when Sebastian left, the good woman rated Anita for not being kinder to him. Sebastian owned a few acres of cocoa and a large provision garden, and Mrs Perez had an idea that Anita's marriage would mean relief from the cocoa-work, not only for Anita, but also for her.

Anita herself said nothing. She was not the talking kind. At much expense and trouble, Sebastian sent her a greeting card each Christmas. On them were beautiful words which Anita spelt through so often that in time she got to know them by heart. Otherwise nothing passed between the two. That he loved no one else she was sure. It was a great consolation; but did he love her? Or was it only because his home was dull and lonely, and theirs was just at the corner, that he came down every night?

As the months slipped by, Anita anxiously watched her naturally pale face in the little broken mirror. It was haggard and drawn with watching and waiting for Sebastian to speak. She was not young and her manner was not attractive. The gossiping neighbours looked upon her as Sebastian's property. Even in the little cocoa-house dances (Sebastian never went because he did not dance) she was left to herself most of the time. And then, she loved him.

It came about that Anita's aunt, who lived at Siparia, paid her a surprise visit on Sunday. She had not visited North Trace for years, and might never come back again. Consequently there were many things to be talked about. Also the good lady wanted to know what Anita was doing for herself.

"And when will you be married, *ma chère*?" she asked, secure in the possession of three children and a husband. Anita, aching for a confidante, poured forth her simple troubles into the married lady's sympathetic ear. Mrs. Perez expatiated on Sebastian's wordly goods. Mrs. Reis, you remember, came from Siparia. "Pack your clothes at once, girl," she said, "you will have to miss this week in the cocoa. But don't mind, I know some one who can help you. And that is La Divina."

Of La Divina Pastora, the Siparia saint, many things can be written, but here only this much need be said. It is a small image of some two feet in height which stands in the Roman Catholic Church at Siparia. To it go pilgrims from all parts of the island, at all times of the year: this one with an incurable malady, that one with a long succession of business misfortunes, the other with a private grudge against some fellow-creature to be satisfied, some out of mere curiosity. Once a year there used to be a special festival, the Siparia fête, when, besides the worshippers, many hundreds of sightseers and gamblers gathered at the little village, and for a week there were wild Bacchanalian carouses going on side by side with the religious celebrations. This has been modified, but still the pilgrims go. To many the saint is nothing more than a symbol of the divine. To more—like the Perez family—it possesses limitless powers of its own to help the importunate. From both parties it receives presents of all descriptions, money frequently, but ofttimes a gift from the suppliant—a gold ring, perhaps, or a brooch, or some other article of jewellery. Anita had no money; her aunt had to pay her passage. But she carried the little gold chain with her, the maiden's mite, for it was all that she had. It was not fête time, and quietly and by herself, with the quiet hum of the little country village in her ears, Anita placed the chain around the neck of the saint and prayed—prayed for what perhaps every woman except Eve has prayed for, the love of the man she loved.

That Sunday night when Sebastian reached Madame Perez's house, the even tenor of his way sustained a rude shock. Anita was not there, she had gone to Siparia, and was not coming back till next Sunday, by the last train. Wouldn't he come in and sit down? Sebastian came in and sat down, on his old seat, near the door. Mrs Perez sat outside commenting on the high price of shop goods generally, especially tobacco. But Sebastian did not answer; he was experiencing new sensations. He missed Anita's quiet face, her steady, nimble fingers, her glance at him and then away, whenever he spoke. He felt ill at ease, somehow disturbed, troubled, and it is probable that he recognized the cause of his trouble. For when Anita landed at Princes' Town the next Sunday, Tony the cabman came up to her and said: "Sebastian told me to bring you up alone, Anita." And he had to say it again before she could understand. During the six-mile drive, Anita sat in a corner of the cab, awed and expectant. Faith she had had, but for this she was not prepared. It was too sudden, as if the Saint had had nothing to do with it.

They met Sebastian walking slowly down the road to meet them. For an hour he had been standing by her house, and as soon as the first cab passed started, in his impatience, to meet her on the way. The cab stopped, and he was courageous enough to help her down. The cabman jumped down to light one of his lamps and the two stood waiting hand in hand. As he drove off Sebastian turned to her. "Nita," he said, shortening her name for the first time, "I missed you, Nita. God, how I missed you!"

Anita was happy, very happy indeed. In her new-found happiness she came near to forgetting the saint, whose answer had come so quickly. Sebastian himself was very little changed. Still he came every night, still Mrs. Perez smoked his cigarettes, ruminating now on her blissful future. But things were different. So different in fact that Sebastian proposed taking her to the little cocoa-house dance which was to come off in a day or two. It was the first time that they were going out together since that Sunday. Everybody who did not know before would know now, when they saw Sebastian taking her to a dance, a thing he had never done before. So she dressed herself with great care in the blue muslin dress, and what with happiness and excitement looked more beautiful than she had ever seen herself. Then, as she cast another last look in the mirror, she missed something. "How I wish," she said with a genuine note of regret in her voice, "how I wish I had my little gold chain." Here her mother, determined not to jeopardize her future, called sharply to her, and she came out, radiant.

The dance continued till long after five o'clock, but Anita had to leave at three. Sebastian got tired of sitting down in a corner of the room while she whisked around. He felt just a trifle sulky, for he had wanted to leave an hour before, but she, drinking of an intoxicating mixture of admiration, success and excitement, had implored him to stay a little longer. They went home almost in silence, he sleepy, she tired, each thinking the other offended. It was the first little cloud between them.

"It is nothing," thought Anita, "we shall make it up tomorrow night." She thought of something and smiled, but as she peeped at Sebastian and saw him peeping at her, she assumed a more serious expression. Tomorrow, not tonight.

Once inside the bedroom she started to undress quickly, took out a few pins and went to the table to put them down in the cigarette tin in which she kept her knick-knacks. Her mother, who was lying on the bed and listening with half-closed eyes to Anita's account of the dance, was startled by a sudden silence, followed by the sound of a heavy fall. She sprang down quickly, bent over the prostrate form of Anita, and turned to the little table to get the smelling-salts. Then she herself stood motionless, as if stricken, her senseless daughter lying unheeded on the floor. There, in its old place in the cigarette tin, lay a little chain of gold.

George Lamming (*Barbados*)

Birds of a Feather

THE silence was heavy and ominous as we waited for the strumming to continue. It came intermittently, a fine, wheezing sound like the blacksmith's pump in the distance, making us aware of our own existence. The dog gave a loud, insistent bark outside, and was on the verge of repeating the noise when the wind came in a powerful gust, flooding his lungs and muffling all sound. Through the iron bars which reinforced the walls of the dungeon it streamed like a torrent, powerful and uninterrupted, driving out the foulness and falling on us cold and refreshing. It revived our efforts at self-recovery. When the strumming reached us again it seemed less hazy. It possessed rhythm and meaning this time. In fact, it was no longer a mere strumming. But our uncertainty was so general and unlimited that no one hazarded a guess as to the kind of instrument it might be. Perhaps no one could. The wind rose again, more powerfully, and the sound was hushed immediately.

Dalton began to cough, a thundering noise which issued its echo around the walls. There was no peace for him. It seemed that the wind had shattered his inside. He always slept with his mouth open; a very awkward thing to do we often told him, but that was unavoidable on this occasion. He couldn't avoid anything. Neither could we. Three were no better than one in that infernal dungeon where the wind came pelting like a cold, stinging shower and loitered for a moment before leaving us to the impenetrable blackness of the walls and the foul space which enveloped us. Poor Dalton! He was coughing continually and knocking his fists against the wall. We could hear the clamping sound over and again. He turned heavily on his chest and vomited profusely. I wanted to shout at him, but there was no strength left to make my voice audible. He vomited again before dropping his head on the pavement.

What was our misery and the hours it lasted no one could say for certain, but we were sensible enough to know that we had been huddled together and isolated, if not with care at least with the conviction of our gaolers that we could no longer disturb the peace of our surroundings. What we did to justify the anguish we suffered loomed beyond the farthest bounds of our imaginings. It had to be endured until we had fully regained our senses. Dalton was in the worst shape. Sometimes I felt a vague fear that he would vomit up his life and spit it out, detested and unwanted, into the corner. It must have been his maiden voyage on the treacherously placid seas of liquor. A young, robust American, born in the tumbling storm of life and gaiety, was not expected to accept that kind of defeat so effortlessly and shamelessly. His countryman, Hendrickson, was an example of American toughness. Nothing seemed to affect him except the lingering sickliness of that overdose. He was silent and quiet, and had I not felt him easing his body now and again to render Dalton and me less uncomfortable, I would have thought him dead. There were people whom I had always been taught to regard as different from the sweltering mass of my countrymen. Either by heritage or some other device of nature they were marked as symbols of a certain way of living; and they set the standards by which those in lower layers of society were judged. Such were the Flennings. It wasn't unnatural therefore that I should feel uneasy in accompanying Dalton and Hendrickson to their party. Moreover it must have been the cry on every lip which jabbered in those cliques pinned here and there around the dancing hall that I had found my way into company to which my calling and station of life could not grant me access. I knew it and I felt it very keenly. Dalton and Hendrickson didn't. And Americans were quite unmanageable when they were caught in a situation which, no matter how serious in its impact, made no impression on their minds. Their gaiety and exuberance of spirit seemed to contain an element of revolt to that delicate organism which is West Indian society. And you couldn't ask them to conform to the serenity and apparent feebleness which characterized our atmosphere. There were many who declared that they were bent on disrupting the foundations of a society which seemed to them too delicate and enfeebled for use. I thought otherwise. They made no conscious demands; they imposed no standards. The freedom and hilarity in which they were steeped proved intoxicating in the calm and sobriety of their new surroundings. That was how I always felt. But the Americans had quickly become a type which aroused fear or disdain or admiration according to the peculiar slant of the mind which judged them. And so I kept near to my companions this night, not because I needed their protection momently, but I found it amusing and consoling alternately to watch them.

There was, I remember, a fair exchange of oaths between Dalton and a young man who had taken objection to his dancing methods. The young man, a West Indian, was broad and muscular with long, curved hands which showed streaks of blue veins. His hair was cropped low in his neck, almost in line with his collar, and his eyes wrathful and pitiless measured Dalton at a glance. Dalton muttering a friendly oath offered him a drink and was repaid with what seemed nothing short of an insult. Hendrickson seemed very uneasy, and thought that he should settle his nerves with another whisky and soda. He drank two in quick succession and was ordering the third when Dalton tumbled his glass on the floor amid a series of muttered interjections. The West Indian asked him to tidy the room and, more politely, to find a type of company which would be less unprepared for his vulgarity.

"Your job," said Dalton with a sardonic smile, indicating the broken glass. He kicked the pieces from under his feet and ordered a brandy.

"And wha'll you have, ol' boy?" he said, turning to face the West Indian. Hendrickson smiled and moved nearer the two men. His face quickly became a blank, and his eyes, cold and unseeing, were set in the corners of his face like bits of glazed marble.

"What about you, ol' bean?" Dalton asked him. "A straight one, I guess, old male as you are, always going straight, straight as a road. Why don't you bend that back of yours sometimes?" Hendrickson looked at him through eyes which seemed to have lost all communication with the brain.

"Joe," Dalton grinned, shoving me in the direction of the West Indian, "what?"

"Falernum and soda," I shouted, pretending to be drunk.

"Tell it to the Bobby Soxers," he screamed uproariously, "the Bobby Soxers'll tell you what to do with that."

"You won't drink any more here," the West Indian protested. "And look about getting out."

"Playing tough, I'll say," Dalton challenged, cracking a glass on the table. There was a rapid exchange of glances, sharp and incisive. Hendrickson stood firm, his teeth a faint glimmer of white beneath the pale, furrowed lips. He looked from Dalton to the West Indian, from the

West Indian to Dalton, and if those eyes weren't so lifeless, so void of expression, I would have said that he was smiling. And when Dalton and the West Indian in the agony of passion gripped, he burst an empty bottle against the latter's head and walked quietly, unperturbed, into the dancing hall. That was the prelude to the final onslaught and our ultimate expulsion.

The incidents which led to and climaxed that demonstration were broken and disconnected, and no picture of the episode remains clear to my mind. Each of us buried in that cell suffered a vague feeling of dehumanization. There was no contact with life, and it might have been less disconcerting if the wind and that instrument with its lingering melody flowing from the richness of civilized life around us had not brought us a sense of estrangement and isolation. I felt that life was slipping away from me, and were it possible I would have acted traitor to Hendrickson and Dalton. They had nothing to fear, nothing to regret. Their security was something impervious to attacks from external forces. If they transgressed the law, they would be dealt with very carefully. Society had nothing to offer them but a scowl. They were Americans. That was their defence, their protection. That was all. I, on the other hand, was a native, and a native of little worth in the judgment of those who formed the élite of my countrymen. The services I rendered my community might be winked at, but my shortcomings could not escape the searching eyes of those who held me in their power. That was the unhappy plight of natives like me. Tradition! System! We lived under the awful shadow of those Gods. And then there was the war, and mingled with the gifts it brought to these parts was the treasure of the Americans. The Americans came and moved about our community like new brooms around a dust-laden room. And not a few were suffocated and choked and poisoned against them. None were ever fully convinced that it was the dust which had obscured the lives of the neglected natives which was blinding.

I wondered what the other two beside me were thinking, and I envied them. It was silly to recapitulate all the Americans had done. To linger on the brief past was useless. What I had to achieve was a way of escape. The Americans could be left to confront their difficulties alone. We had to meet again, but treachery was nothing new to them. It was the outcome of fear, and fear is an emotion innate in each of us. My eyes opened and closed. The surface of the pavement on which I lay seemed rougher and harder. Time had slipped away slowly, very slowly, I thought, and opening my eyes again I caught the faint glimmer of an early sun peeping at us through the iron bars. For a moment it seemed to reveal the indecency and stupidity of the night's adventure, and fear, like sudden claps of thunder, shook me through and through. Outside the tall, slender willows stood solemn and unhappy in their silence. Not a breath of air to graze the placid dignity of their demeanour. I tottered on my feet for a while, and fully gaining my balance stood erect on the solid pavement. The room contained all the fear and despair of the dungeon I had hitherto thought it. For a moment I felt more neglected and forlorn than the immobile willows. The melody of that instrument was straining to my ears again. Dalton sat up and shot a wondering glance at Hendrickson who lay smiling a deadly, unfeeling smile. Soon the sun was streaming down on us.

"I didn't expect it of either of you," I heard Mr. Waite remonstrating some days after. His voice was fine and clear, and leaked through every crevice of his office. I was sitting in an adjoining room sorting cards, and the continual ringing shriek was most disturbing. "Be gay, certainly, do what you like," he argued, "but keep your head on. Look out for the circle in which you are swinging. Move with the tide, you know what I mean. You've been living in this place long enough to know things for yourselves. Go ahead now."

I heard the jeep drive off, and when I reached the windows the vehicle was all but lost in the spiralling dust. Mr. Waite cleared his throat twice in quick succession, and soon I heard the door slam violently. From where I sat I could see his slim, angular body ambling along the gravelled path. Small puffs of smoke wafted over his shoulder, thinned out and melted quietly in the air. He was born in Texas, Mr. Waite, an accident which greatly facilitated his labours in these parts. The natives viewed him with awe, for the sons of Texas, it was alleged, were not to be trifled with. But he was not unjust or dictatorial. He had lived in New York for more than six years and in Europe for a similar period. It was during the First World War when he served in the Merchant Navy that he had gathered most of his experience. He professed a knowledge of men, their inconsistency and their indeterminateness, and his actions bore testimony to the veracity of his professions. Of course he had his prejudices and dislikes, but he always made an honest attempt to guard his judgment against their demands. His manner was firm and decisive however, and that was what the natives on the base discussed among themselves. They did not like a firm and decisive manner.

A week passed before I saw Dalton and Hendrickson again. They had gone south, nearly a hundred miles from the base, in connection with the transportation of petrol from the oil refinery. They were as radiant as ever. Dalton always in exuberant spirits hailed me with a shout that sent a shiver to my spine. They were sitting at a small, round table in the Balalaika. The air was warm and moist, and the soft red light fell lightly on their faces. An army man was pounding a Jerome Kern tune on the piano, while people tripped to and fro in the crowded room. I looked at the two Americans sitting before me, and wondered what eternal spark within them gave their faces that glow of warmth and happiness.

"Hello, you prison rat," Dalton shouted and threw an empty cigarette box into my face. He shouted to the waiter and gave an order.

"So old Flenning was out for us," he remarked, squinting his eyes. "Sent a long, nasty letter to the boss. Thought all hands would have been fired."

"I guess so," I said.

"Prisoners must be pretty tough in these parts," Hendrickson observed.

"The place stinks," Dalton snarled. "How in the name of Christ you put a man in this dug-out? Where are the law and the prophets this side?"

"Dead," Hendrickson said and drained his glass.

"Old Waite kicked hell," Dalton said. "Talked of the dignity and so and so of the American flag. The stars and stripes and stripes and stars. Waite's a good boy," he continued, sipping his drink, "he's got the real American spirit, a damned nasty spirit when it starts to pounce on you."

He passed an indolent hand through his dishevelled hair and dropped it heavily on the table. Hendrickson sneezed powerfully, and parted his lips in a derisive smile.

"A drink?"

Dalton looked at him out of furtive, questioning eyes. "The gaol's no blasted fun in these parts," he said and shouted to the waiter again.

"We are bound for New Jersey next week," Dalton said, patting me on the shoulder. "It's going to be fun."

"New Jersey," I exclaimed in genuine surprise.

"Yes, sir," Hendrickson said slowly.

"Probably old Flenning's letter had something to do with it," Dalton said irritably. He surveyed the room with longing eyes. Hendrickson sat in his chair, a silent, incalculable weight, weary of the world. Now and again he tapped his thick, hirsute fingers on the table. This world of men and women seemed so small and delicate for him. It was dangerous to join too freely in the trifles which diverted those around him. A drink was enough. He felt a secret, unexpressed pleasure in knocking his glass against another's and listening to the mellifluous jabbering of those uncontrollable tongues. But he could not descend from his pedestal for fear of crushing the little heads that bobbed around him.

"Say," he exclaimed, turning to Dalton, and for a moment seemed to struggle against the tide of emotion that surged within. "An old friend." Dalton looked round dreamily.

"Remember me?" he shouted, and his voice trailed above the confused sounds that mingled within the room. The young man turned friendly, understanding eyes on him, and smiled. It was the young West Indian we had met at the Flennings! He groped through the shifting, excited crowd, and drew a chair to our table. Dalton gave him an amicable slap on the shoulder and motioned to the waiter.

"So you let us have it wholesale," Dalton said, propping his hands on the table. The West Indian coloured, and gave Hendrickson a portentous glance. The silence that lingered between us had a greater impact than the noise around.

"Forget it," Dalton said and passed the drinks. "I'm Dalton, Joe Dalton," he muttered quickly, extending his right hand to the young man. Hendrickson eased himself from his chair and whispered his name.

"Dickson, Arty Dickson," the young man said, and sat down quickly.

"Had no trouble?" he asked.

"Forget it," said Dalton.

"The truth is," he began.

"Forget it, I said," Dalton repeated.

It was warmer than ever at the Balalaika. I could feel my shirt slipping against my back when I moved in the chair. The Americans opened their shirts and let the water trickle through the wiry sprigs of hair that covered their chests. People were moving around, a seething mass, heedless of time or the depressing heat of the tropical weather. And as we talked, Dalton always energetic, Hendrickson, a silent, concentrated listener, the music wound its way through the senses, sometimes softly, often jarringly and in discord.

"New Jersey for us within a week," Dalton said.

"New Jersey by all that's wonderful," Hendrickson muttered.

Dickson lit a cigarette and made circles with the smoke. "Pity I didn't get to know you fellows better," he said.

"Pity," Hendrickson assured him, and I wondered what he meant. Dalton laughed, a hollow, empty sound.

"Of course, you'll remember this old place," the West Indian said smilingly. Dalton for a moment pensive rolled his glass on the table. The waiter, a clean, fierce-looking Negro, looked at us out of eyes which held no meaning. The music came again, a slow, monotonous melody. The Balalaika grew vague and hazy within, and the couples traipsing like imbeciles to the languid rhythms became undistinguished shapes.

"The gaol, you mean," Hendrickson smiled, "of course we couldn't forget it."

It was two o'clock when we parted with life enough to take us twenty yards where the last jeep parked. Dickson, the young West Indian, sat on the pavement waiting for the driver to help him in the taxi, and the wind flowing along his face, warm and forceful, kept his eyes open. He smiled, a painful contortion of the lips, and waved both hands at us. We saw him totter and fall, a dead, inflexible weight, in the car which belched its steam at us and drove away.

Our jeep moved lightly along the narrow, undulating road. The driver, silent and morose, glanced from us to a frail, crumpled figure that lay beside him. The moon shed its light, a haze of white on the pitched road, and the wind rushed against us in desperation. For a second I could hear the muffled croaking of the invisible frogs. Dalton and Hendrickson crouched on either side of me, and I could feel their breath, heavy and regular, along my face. Perhaps they were asleep, dreaming of New Jersey and the unique joy of meeting old acquaintances. It was sooner than we expected, but we were sure the time would come. They had been moving out gradually, and I dreaded the day they would all be gone. The time had come for Dalton and Hendrickson to go, and I felt it keenly. The base would be in the future a different place for me, as it had become different for those whose services it needed no longer. It was human to feel the loss of companions like Dalton and Hendrickson, but their departure had more serious implications. As had been the case with their arrival, it was going to strike the very foundations of my society. It was probably in the nature of our destiny that we, born in these parts, should know and feel the violence of these changes.

"No chick feed this time, ol' boy," was the triumphant cry from lips which had once been bloodless and dry. "Dish it out, dish the dough out, or do it yerself."

That was a dangerous symptom. I didn't belong to the land, it was true, but it wasn't going to be pleasant pounding at typewriters after what I had known and enjoyed. I knew it, and all those who shared my comfort and delight during the past few years knew it too. It seemed that there was nothing to hope for. Life would be much like the monotonous humming of the jeep along this smooth road. I was content to live the present to the fullest. I was going to look upon the drama of life in an hour of intoxication. I would extract its last ounce of sweetness, and while that sweetness remained feel that it was all I knew and all I would ever grow to know. When all was gone, well, there would be memory, the memory of all I had known and felt. I hadn't lost the faculty of remembering, of reflecting, and feeling satisfied with all that rushed back to me in an odd moment. That was something to be thankful for. It would be the same in the future. I would have with me the memory of what I was before the Americans came, the memory of what they made me suffer no less than what they helped me to enjoy. And I would be all the wiser. I would have the memory of Hendrickson's inscrutable eyes and Dalton's ebullience. They were in themselves a well of life from which I could draw in the future. And there was Dickson, my own countryman, who would have meant nothing to me had we met under different circumstances. Under that cloak of hypocrisy in which he was vested by those to whom he had sworn social allegiance there was yet some fundamental goodness. He was the prototype of an army, a symbol of the age in which he lived. I was glad to have known him. And that lifeless figure that crouched against the driver, lost to the world, insensible to the surrounding air, he, too, would be remembered. I would have liked to see his face, but the incident was enough. And the old Balalaika would find its treasured spot in the memory. It served its purpose well. Let the Americans go if their work was done. All would be absorbed in the melting-pot to form another link in the chain of experience which would encircle my days.

The old Balalaika had set my imagination aflame and how much sense there was in all that had passed through my slumberous mind could not be assessed by one in my condition. The little wooden jeep increased its speed. I looked at my watch and was aware of nothing but its faltering tick. The driver kept his eyes fixed on the narrow road. The light of the moon revealed his long, slender fingers on the steering-wheel, shivering like a delicate lily against a mild breeze. His body, lean and erect, held the sacredness of some hallowed spot on which one is forbidden to trespass, and for a moment he seemed to bear the awful responsibility of preserving the world from destruction.

The village of Assam lay before us like a sleeping child. Withdrawn from the din and bustle of city life, it seemed another world. The humility of its aspect and the dignity of its silence were like memories of the past. Encircled by a grey, undulating wall of precarious strength, the church of St. George nestled beneath a cluster of huge mahogany, and beyond it I could see a plane soaring to the base. In the distance it looked like a fixed light set against the pale sky. I closed my eyes and waited for Assam to pass by.

And then it happened; that terrible shriek which rent the stillness of the air and struck us senseless and dumb by its suddenness. Words will not portray the horror. I was thrown forward, my head clinched tightly between Dalton's legs, while Hendrickson lay heavily on top of us. The man who lay in the front was jerked from his seat into the open canal that bordered the road. The driver held his seat, firm but speechless. Seconds passed, and each seemed to wait for the other to reveal the mystery of our plight. I heard a voice, a brawling, gulping sound, nearby, but the words were indistinct. The driver stepped from the jeep, and I raised myself from the weight that pressed on me and followed him. Dalton and Hendrickson soon came, and we stared in silence at the figure which lay in the road within a yard of the vehicle. It was incredible.

"Bastards," the voice muttered, "Americans . . . drunken bastards . . . respect . . . no . . . respect . . . law . . . citizen . . ." Our driver raised the body and dragged it to the side of the road. It spat and kicked violently. "Law . . . no . . . days wonderful . . . dogs."

"Shut up," the driver shouted, and that seemed to bring him to his senses.

"Shut up," he droned; "you say . . . shut . . . up. I didn't tell you shut up," he said articulately. "I asked Waite to do that. Waite . . . old bitch . . . drunken bitch."

"Old Flenning!" Dalton exclaimed, bringing the man's head under the light. "Old Flenning, Hendrickson," Dalton repeated.

"Flenning," the man bawled, "old . . . drunk . . . Flenning . . . Tell Waite . . . write letters . . . Waite . . . drunk . . . Waite."

Hendrickson lifted him carefully and rested him in the canefield nearby, and for the first time we remembered the man who had driven with us from the Balalaika. He gave a painful groan and wriggled his body despairingly.

"Take care o'him," the driver snapped, and threw himself in the jeep.

"Dead drunk," said Dalton, helping him to his feet, and for a moment we could hear the stifled, disconnected words: "Bastards . . . Americans . . . Waite."

It was a distressing scene which made the driver's blood boil with anger. He sat, struggling defiantly against the tide of passion that wrestled within his breast.

"Nearly got it," Dalton said, panting.

"Flenning's in a bad way," I said to Hendrickson, in the hope of hearing his comment.

"Serve him well right," Dalton said quickly. "I could have crushed his guts out. And that's what you get for saving him."

"Lucky guy," said Hendrickson, clearing his throat.

"Drunken fool," Dalton answered hotly, and threw his head back.

"I can't believe it," I said with a great deal of feeling. "Over sixty miles from the city, and a man like Old Flenning, a man like him."

"Shut up," Dalton said, elbowing me in the ribs. "Do something for that dead one there in front, or sleep."

The wings of the American clipper glinted in the moonlight as we moved across the expanse of land. The cluster of buildings glimmered faintly around us. We motored slowly into the open shed that sheltered the vehicles, and the driver, stepping lightly from his seat, left me unnoticed to the sleeping men.

Jan Carew (*British Guiana*)

Hunters and Hunted

OLD man Doorne and his two elder sons walked through the swamp with the ease of men who had known the feel of mud and water all their lives. But Tonic, the youngest, splashed and stumbled every now and then. The afternoon sun, fierce and yellowing, flung shadows behind them long as fallen coconut palms. The old man was carrying a *wareshi*.★ His back was arched and the harness bit into his forehead and shoulders.

Ahead of them was Black Bush, a belt of dense forest which rolled inland like a green ocean. Leading into Black Bush was a sandy plain where the sun had consumed and the wind swept away all but a few clumps of grass and black sage.

They approached a reed bed where bisi-bisi and wild-cane had jostled the lotus lilies out of the way.

"Is how much farther we got to go?" Tonic asked plaintively.

"Don't ask stupid question, boy, save you breath for the walk," Doorne said.

"Nobody didn't beg you to come, so why you crying out with strain now? You, self, say you want to hunt. If you want to play man-game, then you got to take man-punishment," Caya, the eldest, said. His brother's whining angered him. It reminded him of his own tiredness.

"Ah! Lef him alone! The boy young and this swamp got teeth enough to bite the marrow of you bone out of you," Tengar growled from deep inside his belly and he added gently, "If you get too fatigue', boy, I will carry you over the last stretch."

"No!" Old man Doorne shouted. "Let the boy walk it on he own. I don't want no rice-pap mother's boy growing up under me roof." And he turned round and glared up at his second son who towered over him like a giant mora tree over a gnarled lignum vitae.

The rise and fall of their voices and the plop-plop of their feet sounded

★ A South American Indian haversack.

unreal in the silence. Far to their right negrocups* were grazing near a cluster of lilies. The birds stretched long necks to gaze at the intruders. A flock of ducks and curry-curries rose noisily from the bisi-bisi reeds ahead of them. But the negrocups stood moving their heads from side to side nervously and preening their wings for flight. The horizon behind those ostrich-like birds was a circle of mirages where the hazy green swamps melted away, calcinated by the sun before they merged with the sky.

As the old man and his sons drew nearer Black Bush they saw the jungle where tall trees, massed growths of bamboo and closely woven tapestries of vines and creepers had erupted out of the earth. The sight put Doorne in a good mood. In the middle of the bamboo grove was a dark hole: it was almost blocked up by new shoots but the old man recognized it. He had cut it out himself on his last trip. Huge yellow and blue butterflies danced before it. Against the dark background their wings were incandescent.

"Come on, Tonic, only lil' way to go now, boy. Brace yourself against the mud, keep you foot wide apart to fight it," Doorne said.

"Is how much farther we got to go?" Tonic asked again and his voice was listless like a man with fever.

"Don't worry, small-boy, I will carry you over the las' stretch," Tengar said, stopping to hoist his brother on his broad back.

"Lef' the boy alone, Tengar!" the old man said fiercely. "He got to learn to be a hunter. Even if he bright like moonlight on still water, is time he understand he can't live by book alone. He too black and ugly to be a book man."

"The boy is you son, old man, but he is me brother," Tengar said.

Tonic, his legs round Tengar's waist and his hands locked around his neck, looked like a black spider clinging to a tree trunk.

"Put the boy down!" Doorne insisted, blocking Tengar's path.

"Move out the way, old man, and stop making gar-bar," Tengar said, still good-natured.

"Put the boy down!" Doorne shouted, whipping out his prospecting knife.

"Old man, don't look for trouble, because when you searching for it that is the time it does ambush you. Don't bank on me vexation jus'

* A swamp bird of the heron family.

staying in me belly and rupturing me, jus' because we is the same flesh and blood."

Caya stepped between them and said, "All you two making mirth or what? Look, stop this fool-acting. Old man, you better put you knife away. If the small-boy too weak to bear the strain is you fault. You encourage he to full-up he head with white man book and all of we does boast how he going to turn doctor or lawyer. When turtle papa give he shell, nobody can change it."

Growling and muttering, Doorne sheathed his knife and Tengar moved on.

"Thank you, brother Tengar," Tonic whispered and the black giant grinned showing white teeth between well-fleshed lips.

Doorne's face looked like a sky threatening rain. He thrust his head forward and strode on.

A hundred yards from dry land, Caya burst out singing:

> "Kaloo, kaloo,
> Lef' me echo in the bush las' time.
> Was sundown when wind steal that echo of mine.
> Kaloo, kaloo,
> Sundown wind steal me echo
> And I tell Wind leggo me echo! Leggo!
> But wind wouldn't set me echo free.
> Wind hide me echo in the bowel of a tree.
> Wind wouldn't set me echo free.
> Kaloo, kaloo.
> A who-you bird set me echo free
> A who-you bird steal it from the tree.
> Kaloo, kaloo."

Caya sang with a deep bass voice and because this was their way of celebrating another victory over the swamps, the others joined in the chorus:

> "A who-you bird set me echo free
> A who-you bird steal it from the tree.
> Kaloo, kaloo."

Tengar made Tonic walk the last fifty yards and Doorne, although he pretended not to notice, understood that this was done to placate him. The gesture, however, irritated the old man.

"Eh, eh, you get so weak you can't carry you fly-weight brother couple yards," he jeered.

Tengar did not answer his father. Other people's malice was something he could never understand; that it should linger and rankle always baffled him. Perhaps it was his father's vindictive Amerindian blood, he thought.

Tonic staggered across the last stretch of water and as he forced his way through bisi-bisi and wild cane reeds, they tossed as if a storm had hit them. Looking at his brother, Caya burst out laughing.

"Go on, Tonic, go on. Go on, mother's boy," he said.

"Ah, leave the small-boy alone," Tengar said.

"Papa Tengar and he boy-child," Doorne taunted.

Tonic crawled up on dry land and lay down, his feet still trailing in the swamp.

"But is why I come on this brute-walk?" he sobbed.

"We tell you wasn't fun; this swamp got teeth, boy," Caya said.

"You only full of 'I tell you this' and 'I tell you the other,' but how was I to know that this sun was so hot, that this swamp would be me kinnah?"*

"All right, boy, all right. You hold out well enough," Doorne said, lifting him up and putting him on higher ground.

Against the whiteness of Tonic's eyeballs the brown irises were luminous. His face had the dark sheen of seal skin but his lips were powdered with tiny crystals of perspiration.

"Drink this!" Doorne ordered, holding a flask of bush rum to his lips. Tonic swallowed a mouthful and sat up coughing and spitting.

"It hot like fire," he said, opening his mouth wide and gasping.

"Nothing like it to pick you up," Doorne said, taking a swig and passing the flask to Caya and Tengar.

"This is bush-rum, father," Caya said appreciatively after he swallowed his drink.

"Is Chinaman the old man does get it from," Tengar said looking sideways at his father. Tonic lay still and shut his eyes but the sun pricked his eyeballs and he turned over on his stomach. The others sat near him with their backs to the sun. Doorne took out a delicately wrought, white clay pipe and used a dry stem of para-grass to clean it.

"We really take long to reach Black Bush this time," Caya said.

* Poison.

"All right, don't make bad worse," Tengar said. Tonic had fallen asleep and was wheezing softly. Saliva was running from the corner of his open mouth. The old man struck a match and puffed away at his pipe. In the afternoon sun his head looked like a beach strewn with patches of dirty foam. His face was shaped like an upturned pear—high mongolian cheekbones and hollow cheeks tapering down to a pointed cleft chin. It was lean as a harpy eagle's and the eyes, deep set, were restless. Veins stood out like bush rope at the side of his temples and Tengar could see them throbbing. Ever since he could remember, his father had had those bulging veins at the side of his head. When he was a boy he used to think that the old man had lizards puffing under his skin.

"We better start fixing up camp before a tiger snatch-up one of we tonight," Doorne said.

"Rest you bones, old man, long time yet before sundown," Caya said. He sat cross-legged, scratching his naked belly and chewing a black sage stem. His almond-shaped eyes were smoky—oriental eyes set in a negro face. Doorne's sons were all by different mothers and Caya's had been a Chinese-Negro mixture.

"Come on, get up!" Doorne ordered and he turned on Caya. "What I forget 'bout this part of the world you en't begin to learn yet. Who is you, boy, to tell you father 'bout when is time to pitch camp . . .?"

"All right, old man, all right. Stop frying-up you lil fat," Caya said standing up and stretching.

Tonic was rested and refreshed and he went to the edge of the forest to gather firewood. The afternoon sun had lost its sting and flocks of birds were flying home after feeding in the swamps or on the seashore. Parrots screamed and chattered in the nearby trees as Tonic hacked at dry branches with his cutlass. A snake with silvery scales slithered past him and he chopped it in two, watching the halves wriggle until his father bellowed at him to hurry up. Tengar and Caya had already driven uprights into the ground and were tying on cross-beams with bush rope.

"Go and bring some troolie palm leaf, boy, and do it bird-speed!" Caya ordered. Tonic obeyed quickly. He didn't want darkness to catch him too far away from the others. He heard the night wind in the trees and shivered.

Night fell suddenly. The lazy mosquitoes which had been sleeping under the trees all day came out in clouds. The old man and his sons crouched around a fire bathing their limbs in smoke. As soon as a tongue of flame escaped they smothered it with green leaves. Doorne left his sons and sat away from the fire. He heard Tonic alternately coughing from the smoke and slapping mosquitoes.

"You can't control yourself, boy?" he shouted.

"These mosquitoes stinging like pepper, papa."

"Damn balls!"

"You blood get old and bitter, old man, mosquito don't like it no more," Caya said.

"Don't make you eye pass me, boy," the old man said chuckling.

"They going to let up in a lil while, I can feel the wind clearing up the thickness in the air," Tengar said encouragingly. He inhaled the aromatic smell of wild mango in the wood smoke and remembered how his mother used to burn green limbs inside their hut to kill the stink of dirty bedclothes and sweat.

Dew fell noiselessly and the night wind grew chill. A piper owl sang to the new moon.

"They say them owl is jumbie bird, and nobody never see one," Tonic said hugging his knees tightly.

"I see plenty. They got big eye and they does eat small snake," Tengar said.

"When I was young I try to tame one, jus' to hear he sing when the moon come out, but the one I had never sing a note and he kill so much of the neighbour chicken that me mother drown he in a bucket of water," Doorne said.

They ate tasso and cassava bread for dinner and when Tonic complained that the tasso was like a car tyre, Doorne boasted, "I chewing up this tasso like it is fresh meat," and he added, spitting out a splinter of bone, "all you young boy teeth make out of jelly."

The fire burned steadily and the green logs hissed. In the firelight Doorne's face could have been a burnished mark nailed against the wall of night.

Tengar, Caya and Tonic lay in their hammocks. Tonic had fallen asleep instantly but his brothers watched the stars through holes in the thatch. They heard the piper owl fluting its melodies to the moon, a tinamou singing across the tree tops to its mate, howler baboons roaring and the wind in the bamboo trees. The sounds faded and died in sleep.

A family of red howlers feeding on bamboo shoots woke them up at daybreak. Doorne brought the dying fire to a blaze while his three sons went down to the edge of the swamp to wash. They sat down to a breakfast of turtle eggs, salted fish, biscuits and unleavened bread with bits of pork in it and they washed the meal down with tea.

"I had a funny dream last night," Tonic said, putting a whole turtle egg into his mouth. He always spoke quickly. His mind seemed to push his words out before tongue and lips had time to form them. "I dream that a lot of wolves was calling me."

"Was that tasso sitting heavy on you stomach, boy," Doorne said, drawing his forearm across his mouth and he added, "We got to get going."

"But that wasn't all the dream," Tonic said.

"Well, tell it quick. We got to go," Doorne said.

"There was an old black man on the other side of the canal and he had teeth like a shark, and every time he talk or sing he teeth was so sharp that they cut his tongue and he mouth was always dripping blood," Tonic said.

"Blood is a good thing to dream 'bout, boy. It mean that one of we going to make some money," Caya said.

They set out immediately after the meal. There was no washing up as they had used water lily leaves for dishes. Doorne led the way into the twilight of Black Bush. Once out of reach of the sun's rays there was no undergrowth and they moved swiftly, silently across a carpet of rotting leaves. Crouching slightly forward, the old man almost merged with his surroundings. He and Tengar had the hunter's ability of becoming more shadow than substance in the forest. Doorne noticed every movement, even the wind stirring in the leaves high above him. A green parrot snake slid down a mora tree in front of them and when Tonic pointed at it excitedly, his father signalled at him to be quiet. The snake disappeared in the underbush. A bush rabbit stopped in the middle of the trail, standing on its hind legs and examining them with quick darting glances. It sensed no danger. The parrot snake struck so swiftly that the watchers heard a cry and only then noticed that the snake had coiled the rabbit. Doorne whispered to his sons and they walked on quickly until he picked up a bush hog trail. He knelt down and examined the cloven hoof-prints carefully.

"They been passing by here couple days well," Doorne whispered. He followed the trail for a little distance, stopped and picked up a section of a snake's backbone.

"Them hog kill a big snake here. That parrot snake better watch out. Once he swallow the rabbit he can't move too far," the old man said in an undertone. He knelt down on the trail again. "This is tiger footmark here, fresh footmark. Is a big puss. He must be following the hog for a meal." His eyes scanned the trees. "Let we climb this one and wait."

Doorne led the way to a big tree with branches spreading over the trail. He wedged his *wareshi* between two branches. The others followed him and they built a rough platform and settled down to wait. Tonic was fidgety but his father and brothers sat alert and still. They were about twenty feet up and above them the tree grew for over a hundred feet boring through the forest ceiling to reach the sunlight. Tonic wormed his way from one end of the platform to the other and Doorne clapped a hand on his bony shoulder.

"Stay quiet!" he hissed. "If you go too near the edge and fall out even Jesus' weeping wouldn't help you."

"I hearing something," Tengar said and a moment later he pointed down the trail. A jaguar, moving with the ease of a river flowing across a plain, its power hidden under a smooth surface, emerged from the twilight. A marudi bird shouted a raucous warning and there were green fires in the jaguar's eyes as he sniffed suspiciously. He seemed to have picked up their scent. Tonic imagined that the jaguar's eyes and his own were making four all the time. Doorne loaded his fifteen-bore shotgun and waited. Tengar and Caya did not move. They trusted the old man's marksmanship.

The thunder of bush hogs coming down the trail broke the silence. The jaguar turned round and sprang on a branch hanging over the trail not far from the watchers.

"We going to have some sport. We got a hunting pardner," Doorne said and some of the tension inside him relaxed as he spoke. His sons laughed mirthlessly, never taking their eyes off the jaguar. The leader of the bush hogs appeared, then the flock, moving in a tightly packed phalanx with the sows and their young ones bringing up the rear. The earth shook with hoofbeats and the forest vibrated with atavistic grunts. Tonic clung to Tengar, the feel of his brother's warm, muscular body was reassuring. The jaguar waited until the main body of hogs had passed by and there were only about a dozen stragglers. He pounced on a fat sow and buried curved fangs into its neck. There was a piercing squeal cut short by a gurgle. The rest of the flock turned round and stampeded towards the attacker. Sensing danger, the jaguar sprang back on the tree, the hog still gripped in his jaws. The branch broke under the extra weight and the jaguar fell in the midst of the flock. Certain of his strength, he released the dead hog and snarled. The milling, grunting pack closed in on him and he began to force his way through with fangs and claws and fury, maddened by the scent of blood and the pain of his wounds. The hogs that could not reach their enemy turned on the wounded and dying of their own kind and devoured them. Four times it seemed as if the jaguar had cleared enough space around him to spring free, but each time they surged in again. The spot on which he fought became a whirlpool in the middle of a stream of hogs.

"He done kill 'bout twenty of them," Doorne said but the others did not hear him.

The jaguar went down twice more, but he came up and fought back in an impotent frenzy of ebbing strength. He snarled a hoarse admission of defeat and went down for the last time. The hogs played tug-o'-war with his intestines and when nothing was left but blood-stained skin and bones, they remained milling around uncertainly.

Whenever Tonic looked away from the scene of the fight, his eyes fell on the shotgun across Tengar's knees. He had been allowed to use it a few times but Tengar always complained that cartridges were expensive, and that a shotgun was not a small-boy's toy.

"Let me take a shot, Tengar," he pleaded but his brother either did not hear him or ignored him. Tonic felt that this was a good chance to bag one or even two of the hogs. He would be a hero at school if he did. He looked at Tengar and then at the gun. He reached for the gun and no one seemed to notice. Grabbing it, he raised the stock to his shoulder and fired quickly. He did not bother to aim or hold the gun close enough. The recoil flung him backwards and before Tengar could reach out to save him, he fell off the platform. The twenty-foot drop dazed him and he sat in the midst of the hogs, nursing a bruised shoulder and showing the lily bulbs of his eyes. The gun lay beside him with one barrel still loaded but he made no attempt to pick it up. The hogs closed in on him and he screamed. Fear gave him strength and cunning. He got up unsteadily and ran towards the base of the tree. If he reached it he could climb up a bush rope. The flock came after him. Tengar sprang down from the platform, a prospecting knife in one hand and a cutlass in the other. Most of the hogs followed Tonic but Tengar stamped his feet and shouted trying to call them away. Tonic, running like a tiger, sprang on to a thick liana, but it had too much slack and he dropped back. He saw the hogs baring their teeth below him and tugged frantically at the vine. Tengar fought the hogs off by crouching low and hacking at their legs. Doorne and Caya sat on the platform, looking on helplessly, the old man fingering the trigger of his gun, and Caya shouting encouragement.

"Hold on, Tonic! Climb up, boy! Don't frighten, small-boy!"

A big hog caught Tonic by the heel and hauled him down. Tengar had cleared a way to within ten feet of his brother.

"I coming, Tonic, I coming, boy!" he called out, sweat glistening on his limbs. Tengar's strength was invincible because he was unconscious of it. It was something vibrating in his body like anger or laughter. Many of the hogs had turned away from Tonic and were attacking him now. Every time they rushed at him he swung his cutlass, chopping off forelegs like twigs. Tonic was screaming and foam whitened his lips. Before Tengar reached him, the boy's legs suddenly seemed to melt, he grew shorter and shorter. His screams subsided into a rhythmic moaning. When Tengar cleared a path to his brother, all that was left of the boy's legs were frayed stumps gushing blood and protruding bones with jagged ends. Doorne and Caya joined them. The old man went down on one knee and fired into the flock until the barrel of his gun was too hot to touch. The hogs, their leaders dead, turned and ran. Tonic was lying face down with one eye pressed against a big, star-shaped leaf stained with drops of blood. Ants were scurrying up and down the leaf and before lapsing into unconsciousness, he saw them as huge monsters. Doorne tied a tourniquet around the stumps, cooing to his son all the time like a mother baboon nursing a wounded baby. The sweet and sticky smell of blood and death was everywhere. Caya helped his father to wash Tonic's wounds, but Tengar stood with his back against the tree holding the dripping cutlass in his hand. A sense of community was awakened between Doorne and his sons. He was again the father, the one in authority.

"You got some water in you balata pouch. Give the boy some and wash this froth off his mouth," he ordered and Tengar obeyed mechanically. Caya went around clubbing wounded hogs to death. The ground was slippery with blood. Tengar wet his handkerchief and mopped his brother's face. Tonic opened his eyes and said:

"Tengar, me don't want Mantop to call me yet but I feeling funny. Me head feel like a kite flying over me . . ."

"Don't talk so much, boy. Lie down quiet," Doorne said.

"Is why me foot feelin' so heavy, papa?"

"You get injure, boy, bad injure."

"Tengar!"

"Aye, aye, small-boy."

"Is how you does know when Mantop come for you?"

"You does jus' know, small-boy. You don't never need no prophet to tell you."

"Is how you does know . . . how you does know . . . how . . ." Tonic's voice trailed off. Tengar and Doorne stood over him crying softly. The skin around the stumps of Tonic's legs was turning yellow.

"You think he got a chance?" Caya asked.

"He loss too much blood," Doorne said. Tonic's breath was coming as if it was retched from his body. Suddenly it stopped and blood poured from his mouth.

"Small-boy! Small-boy!" Tengar called urgently. Tonic's eyes looked like eggs in a dark nest. Caya was calculating how much money the pork would fetch in the village. He did not notice when his brother died. Tengar covered the dead boy's legs with a dirty blanket and stood over the corpse.

"Is why folks like we does die so stupid!" he shouted, waving his arms about, challenging enemies in the forest whom he was sure lurked and listened everywhere. "Is why we folks does die so stupid? In other place, they say, people does die for something. But is why Tonic die, tell me that?"

Claude Thompson (*Jamaica*)

The Stragglers

Aʟʟ the parties they can find to gatecrash are over but no one feels like going home. To go home now after the emotion-packed hours would be flat. If it is to be a night out it might as well be a night out.

No one can think of anywhere else to go. The taxi driver replaces the cap on the gas tank, pays the gas station attendant, gets into the car and sits immobile. The gas man says—

"Don't block the driveway."

Someone shouts—

"Let us roll."

The taxi driver reaches for the switch key and presses the starter, saying—

"Where to?"

No one knows where to. The engine bursts into life and the car crawls off slowly. The driver is grumbling—

"Come on—make up your minds."

Still no one knows where to. The night is still theirs. They hold it in their hands. They are reluctant to part with it but they do not know where to spend the last precious hours of its black magic. They have danced and they have talked of everything under the sun they could have talked of in one night and in between have held many women in their arms and made love to them—love in their own way—'You take your chance baby. What the hell!'—but now it is all over unless they can find somewhere else to go—unless they can listen to the musical tinkle of ice in a glass and commence to talk again.

Even with the street lights burning, the black ooze of the night fills every nook and cranny and the crawling of the car into the pathway of its own headlights creates the impression of a giant beetle burrowing into it.

Someone has a brilliant idea. They will run the Guard—the Police Guard! They will crawl along and check up on the policemen!

"Ha—— Ha——!"

"Just keep moving and we will run the Guard."

"O.K. Inspector," says the driver, joining in the game, "O.K."

One policeman, two policemen, three policemen. Blacker than the night itself. Imponderable gloom lightened by little buttons that scintillate like fireflies when the smallest speck of light touches them. It gives them away, these buttons. They should be black. Black as the night, black as their tunic, black as themselves.

Someone shouts—

"All correct, officer——?"

The black man in black approaches the crawling car and grins.

"You boys havin' a hell of a time. Mind yourself."

"O.K. Officer," someone shouts, "keep both eyes open."

"Ha-ha——! Ha-ha——!"

And now the car is at an intersection of the street they are crawling along, with another street. Silence is everywhere—a somnolent silence. Suddenly it is broken. What is that? News! Everyone is sitting up. It must be morning. No. It is still night. They are getting the papers straight off the press. There is a frantic search for coppers and then there it is—. Why it is yesterday's paper—! Oh hell! Today or the coming day is Christmas Day. Yesterday's news is today's news.

Then it is that someone remembers—

"Let's go to Miss Emma's."

It is the bar that is never closed save by day. Any hour of the night you may have a drink. They will have their complete night after all before the children take over Xmas Day. They can still sit and talk in harmony with the sound of the tinkle of ice in a glass and so complete the affairs of the world.

*   *   *

The entrance is almost subterranean. It is a foul, much in need of white-wash, covered passageway with some sort of a light shining on the brick steps that lead up in the appropriate way of 'Old Kingston' to a 'Yard'.

They are suddenly in a terraced patio. A single tree flings its arms to the night sky and fights for the right to live through its roots embedded far beneath the man-made terrain.

On either side are houses. Who can possibly live in this rabbit warren of a place? The spoor of the night doubles almost back on its trail as they climb a final series of steps to a grime-smeared grey coloured porch directly above the passage by which they entered. A single unshaded electric light bulb performs the offices.

What a place! And yet someone makes here a home! They are in the roofs. To either side are the slanting slopes of their corrugated iron shapes and on one—beside the step—is a garden! God! Think of it! Here in this bare place someone has tried to make a garden! They all stare blankly. The flowers are growing as bravely as ever they would anywhere else in their makeshift flower pots made of discarded slop pails and pisspots! A garden! No-one can talk. Dawn is at hand. They have lost the night—they with their talk. The skylight of the neighbouring Chinese shop is like a belfry in the opalescent gloom.

*   *   *

They straggle down the street. They are but a ragged remnant of the gallant force that had marched but eight short hours ago. They have been killed by time. They are dead. They are ghosts marching fitfully. No more are there any rallying cries. No more any valiant answers. They peer wistfully at the faces of the passers-by. Were they too of the same army—a different battalion—that had tried to hold the night—the ONE NIGHT of the year—and got this? Look at the litter!

They come to the Park and the dawn is here. Not the voices of the children coming forth to greet the DAY or the burst of explosions of fireworks coming from all over the city like a mopping up operation clearing up spots of resistance and sounding like rifle fire, can recapture the vanished hours. Here in the Park the pale dawn is barely sight giving. It comes in feebly like any other day.

What is that over there? It cannot be lights so close to the ground. No. That is a street light over there. This is something much more golden. They must be drunk still—tight as hell! What a night! They are seeing shining lights close to the ground! No. It is—it is a bed of cannas glorious in all their golden bloom. A huge bed, yards long and yards wide of pure gold. They all exclaim! Gone is their weariness. The dew-drenched sward feels good beneath their feet. They walk close to the blooms eager to touch them but not touching them. On one side is a golden bed and on the other a crimson bed. On a single bench between the beds is a 'down and outer' sitting like a prince, in his rags, staring at the golden bounty. Dear God! Simple beauty! This is a thing beyond purchase—beyond wealth—that even a poor black beggar can enjoy. No quest—no talk can create it. It is or it isn't. They have lost the night—they with their talk! What a night! O God—what a night!

Claude Thompson

The House of Many Doors

IT all appeared to Marylyn like the closing of a door. She stepped into the bright noonday of the street and it appeared more than ever so. Here were the glare, the smells and the clangour and clamour of tropic life, and yet it was as if she had stepped into another world and not into the familiar trivia that she knew. She had been fired—fired! The word clanged hollowly as a door in some grim fortress from which those who entered never came out—never came out.

It was unbelievable—that this thing that was life should treat one thus. Here in a city you had a job and worked and, while you had it, life was bearable but when you lost it—when the very right to live that was yours by reason of the paltry pittance that you earned was taken from you, this thing called life became as a prison, a fortress, from which only the fortunate ever escaped—some fully, some never; some never beyond the grace of parole. You lived with terror all your days—terror—! A man born to walk upright, you scurried all your days down the dirty alleyways of existence—afraid; afraid lest that hideous phantom should strike again. Guilty or not guilty it asked no questions but like some dread secret police it came when you knew not. Perhaps you stood for the decent things of life and it was an affront in this changing world where a new order is afoot for anyone to think that there is justice or right against wrong, and some little dictator, God—think of it—exercises his right to decide whether you should live or not and you are sentenced! As sure as if your back were put to a wall you die, perhaps not physically, but nevertheless you died, for how can a man live when his spirit is dead?

Marylyn knew that this was the end. She had seen others—those sleep-walkers of the daily life, groping blindly along. From her stand on the ground she had seen them walking high on the skyline of the building that was the house of life, and then she had seen them fall without being able to help. She herself—God! She was asleep—in some coma. She saw the light of the sun but neither the glare nor heat of it touched her. She saw vaguely the other two-footed animals that like her lived in the jungle of civilization, but it meant naught to her for she was already dead. She was a stricken animal and those of her kind—the wolf kind—were only waiting for her to falter and then they would make the kill. They sheered aside from her but soon they would be snarling—

"Go away. How often must I tell you I have no work to offer you!"

—the death cry of the pack.

She panted along. She did not know what Jimmy her husband—himself now unemployed—and herself would do. He had been promised half a week's work sometime in the near future, but if he even got it what could it do, and until he got it what would they do? She had been expecting this sort of thing for a long time now. Someday she knew that fate would get the better of her and now fate had struck. Her amorous employer had moved up from veiled suggestion which she had long pretended to misunderstand, to something more, and she had slapped his face. Even now she could draw some satisfaction from the blank look that had appeared on his putty-coloured face at the explosion of her blow. The dirty dog! What a shock it must have been to him to discover that there are women and women! Now it was her turn to be stunned for anywhere you turned you lost. Remain and you became a filthy thing. Stand only on the paths of decency and you starved!

She had wanted so hard to help even though Jimmy had not wanted her to work. It had helped, and now she had lost the chance to help. What should she have done? Her spirit rose valiantly within her. If she had done this thing she would have killed Jimmy. Imagine! Just in order to live you——! She could see Jimmy's eyes. They were those of a stricken animal if ever she had done a thing like that in order to get bread. A man kept by a woman who——. Better a thousand times to die than to lose not only her self-respect but, greater than all, the self-respect a man must have in himself for himself. The things some women had to do to live! There were doors through which so many of them passed and were never the same again. The burnish—the sheen of them—was forever lost. There were doors that shut behind them and they went out into the outer darkness of no food, no clothes and accumulating rent because they refused to sell their birthright for a mess of pottage, and there—outside these doors—the good died young because they starved.

Marylyn laughed bitterly from the dim regions of that dark place where she now was. The good died young! Already she was a ghost, for who would care in a city like Kingston where it was every man for himself. Who cared what happened to Jimmy or herself? Look at them busy rushing in and out of doors! So busy closing and opening them in an effort to get at or escape what!

With a start she realized that she had reached the place she called home. The gate had banged to behind her and almost but not quite awakened her from the deadly languor that had crept over her. Now she was going up the concreted walk to the house. What a house! In the light of what had just occurred to her it was a house of many doors—a house of dreadful life—in which too many people were opening and closing these doors—doors of which they were not even aware themselves.

The front room was occupied by a sambo girl who 'played' with a Chinaman. She was a rather colourless personality who smiled always in a vague impersonal way and, either wandered at large like a lost soul on the veranda or, standing at the door of her apartment, gave an idea of arrested motion so that one never knew whether she was coming or going. As a matter of fact she appeared, owing to the manner of her living, rather like some caged animal allowed brief periods of fresh air and, as such, one might almost say she lived only to be an animal—a man's kept woman. She never appeared to speak to anyone and the only time Marylyn had heard her speaking was when, on the very few occasions herself and Jimmy went out, she had glimpsed her holding court in her apartment with the rather remarkable servant called Mattie whom she employed. Rather the court was held by Mattie because she sat on equal terms with her mistress in a rocking chair and dominated the talk as she rocked backward and forward. If one did not know their proper relationship one could not tell that they were not very intimate friends and the conversation beggared description. It was always about a certain relationship between men and women and was of such a candid type as to more than verge on the obscene. Jimmy voiced the opinion that Mattie was a retired whore fallen on evil times and chafing at the chains of domesticity. Marylyn had been laughingly shocked at the phrase. She had squeezed Jimmy's arm. He could put something in the frank manner of their age without appearing too vulgar and the words had just seemed to fit the occasion—

"—a retired whore fallen on evil days."

It had always been a wonder how varying were the people commencing from the front room who lived in the house in the various rooms thereof. Today her wonder was more than ever because her brain was thinking, in a great and dispassionate manner, about humanity in general. As she came along the semi-dark passage every smell seemed to have an individuality of its own. She knew them all as if they were all familiar friends. She knew them all and accepted them and, mixed along with them, the sounds of living. There was the murmur of voices behind closed doors, there was the smell of food and here—the inexplicable silence that sometimes falls on such a *mèlange* of life. There is the sudden explosion of a slamming door. The sound crackles through the ether like an electric spark and all the machinery of living in the house whirrs. It is as if it had awaited it. Here there was silence, in this room someone sighs, in the next a board in the flooring creaks, overhead there is the sound of running water, and all over there is the sound of a sudden scurry as even the rats are startled; for they too are life and this is a house warm with life—warm with living—and having many doors.

In the next room lived the unutterably sad brown woman full of years and with the resignation of those who have come a long way and know the path to be endless. With her lived her three grown children. Always her hands were crossed in her lap and she stared afar into a nothingness that was as blank as the vacuity that is nothing can be. Where the next meal was to come from was always a gamble with her, Marylyn knew, for if the sailor man to whom her eldest daughter was married never sent them the meagre pittance on which they kept body and soul together they had no recourse but to die, and this, thought Marylyn, was soon to be her, Marylyn's, fate; a gamble in which the stakes were food and shelter.

There was no work, or apparently they could find none. The son did none, while the daughters were definitely shiftless. They were too snobbish to do even their own work. The snobbishness of better times clung to them and prevented them from doing their own washing and cooking and cleaning, and they clung to this pretence of a possibly well-to-do past by even keeping a servant whom they could not afford to pay and never did pay, and even if they starved, it was something to know that they had a luckless lackey to wait on them—three women who sat with folded hands in their laps all day and did nothing but look at a door through which they could never return yet would not turn from.

Without the baby of the eldest daughter to relieve the monotony of their days they must, at least, have gone mad, but in this tragedy of life that was theirs, two generations of life took hope. They passed the child from hand to hand like a rosary, and it seemed that, to the old woman, regardless of all—regardless of her spoilt children—she had done well. She knew that death must soon come, but after her there was another and yet another generation. She herself was like the calm—the stillness—over the house, and the child was a slamming door waking them from their slumbers in the teeming house of life.

In the room across from this lived the short, pudgy, shoe clerk who, along with his motherless son, lived with a woman. Marylyn positively hated the man. He was a bully of the worst type—a little dictator who kept forever strutting across the stage of the little room that was his—in which he lived and moved and had his being. He bawled down the woman who was twice his size, and the boy who was one-fourth his size he thrashed morning, noon and night. Under the pretence of imparting to the little boy the rudiments of reading he thrashed him every second word that was read, and the sniffles became whimpers as the saddest little boy in the world prepared himself to be a man. He was not allowed to play with the other children. One stumbled over him in the gloom of the passage, lurking behind a door, or you passed him sitting on the steps with a book held rigidly before his eyes out of which he could not read because under his nose other little boys were wrestling in the dirt, running and hurling a ball and doing the hundred and one things that a boy should do but which he was not allowed to do. Marylyn had never passed him without patting his head. His eyes were like those of a cowed animal—large and luminous with fear—and lit up at even such a tiny gesture.

At night they sometimes—the shoe clerk and his woman—went out and left him alone, and woe unto him if they came back and found him asleep with the lights burning. It meant several unnecessary cuffs, and then a whimpering child falling asleep on a tear-stained pillow. That was what hurt most—to hear him whimpering, trying to hold back his sobs and just whimpering in a mute agony—just a little lonely boy. She could never erase the sight of him from her mind. She tried to picture his unhappiness, to think what would equate it in hers, and then the only picture she could visualize was the thought of her world without Jimmy. It was as if you had taken the sunshine and laughter away from the world and there were no green things, no blue sky, no fleecy clouds! She held the horror of the thought away from her and her anger redoubled, if it could be said so to do, against this father who could so treat his motherless son, and at the large vacuous woman who gave a cackling applause to all this sadism. Jimmy had more than once started to go over and remonstrate but each time he had sat down with a groan at the ineffectiveness of whatsoever he might do. He could not change the heart of the man, so even if he stopped him for a while it would go on again. Perhaps the man was a fool and some day he would learn to his cost, when it was too late, the folly of what he was doing today. Someday that boy would grow up and then that man would know. Perhaps that boy would not abandon him, but he would have lost something more priceless—the love and friendship and companionship of his son. Here was a man building a house of life, but where were the keys to it? When the door slammed he would awake to find himself locked outside—locked out of the heart of his own son!

Here on the left, side by side, were the rooms of the two bachelor tenants. One rarely saw them except at week-ends and sometimes not even then. They always appeared on the move. They came in late and left early, and sometimes they came in very drunk. You could tell from their exaggerated attempts at silence and from the sound of their staggering progress up the passage. Sometimes they laughed and sang a snatch of song, and one could be heard shushing the other, and then there was laughter—subdued laughter. They were like a pair of will-o-the-wisps. Even the servant who worked for both of them only saw them once a day before they left for work each morning, and sometimes one or the other she might not see for days at a time. They were past all understanding. They flashed in and out with different lady friends and sometimes they delayed going out until midnight and then there was the sound of an opening door and then silence! She wondered where they could be going at such an hour and once she had asked Jimmy but he had only grumbled about the inquisitiveness of women and turned his back to her—placed it as a barrier between himself and her inquiries. There seemed so many closing doors and she wondered at what lay behind them.

The only other persons on the ground floor were Jimmy and herself, and now this was their room before her. She paused with her hand on the door knob, then she entered, and, simultaneously with the act, there came a dull thud from overhead—from overhead where——

Upstairs lived the family of horror. The landlady also lived upstairs but for as far as that went she was non-existent now that the family of horror had installed themselves. They had started out as three persons and now there were eight persons in all living up there and later there had been added a dog to the lot. When it scratched itself at dead of night—it **never** left the house at any time—the sound of its tail thumping the floor was like the sound of someone knocking on the door. Twice Jimmy had got up to answer such a summons only to find no one before he realized where the sound came from. He had returned, swearing, to bed. That was, however, when one could sleep. The horrible family upstairs were always silent until sometime near midnight when they always commenced, according to Jimmy, their mobilization. What it was they did nobody knew. They tramped backwards and forwards overhead, like a battalion of Foot, for hours on end, and ever and anon they punctuated the man-oeuvres by dropping something that gave a loud thud. Then they were back at it again, including the dog, at their eternal movement. Jimmy swore to high heaven that they were practising witchcraft although he was once told that they were practising their livelihood of basket-making. What got him was the hour at which the whole show always commenced —midnight! He grumbled and he fumed and all the while Marylyn knew that he was fretting at the position into which he had brought her. What was this life if a man could not find the wherewithal to live in comfort or even just to keep alive? And then, always, he had turned his back on her and she had not dared to touch him.

*   *   *

Marylyn did not know how long she had slept. When she awoke she saw Jimmy coming in. She had already got the evening meal ready and had only sat down in a chair to rest for a while. One moment she was conscious and then a door closed and she was asleep. Now a door opened and she was awake again. She regarded Jimmy drowsily and then, as returning reason flooded back she became aware of that awful sick feeling that always came over her whenever she fell asleep in the afternoon and slept until after sunset and awoke to find the night around her. What caused it she did not know. She was always depressed mentally, physically and spiritually in every way. Along with this depression a great fear always yawned at her from nowhere in particular. She could feel the black abyss of it now—the vacuum of it—pulling at her, hauling at her. Some-day she knew she would be pulled through that opening to the stark terror that lurked there!

But there was Jimmy—Jimmy. She rushed to the haven of his arms. He would protect her, and nothing could harm her. For the moment there was only himself and herself against the world and she felt strong; as strong as only two people can feel from the refuge of each other's arms. The moment was theirs regardless of the worries of the day and tomorrow was another day. She gave him their password.

"Tonight," she said, "tonight is ours."

"Tonight," he echoed, "is ours."

Overhead a door slammed—the horrible family again—and the whirring machinery of life all over the house commenced to move. Marylyn snuggled closer to him. Somewhere she had read that—'the closing of one door is the opening of another'. Here a door slammed and life stirred anew; life, that warm pulsing thing that naught could really ever kill—never really obliterate, especially when you were young and it coursed through you like a madness with all its wild desire.

Suddenly of all the things in the world there was only Jimmy. She herself did not exist so selfless did she feel. She closed the door softly behind them and led him into the warm circle of light that sprung up at the touch of the light switch. Outside was sordidness, fear and despair, but it could not touch them at least for tonight. Perhaps it could not touch them at any time if they walked with their heads held high. One cannot choose what one wants to meet in a world where everything has to be made 'whole'. One could only avoid it for a time when one got into one's narrow corner and shut oneself in, for life was like the house in which one lived—a mansion of many doors.

Edgar Mittelholzer (*British Guiana*)

Miss Clarke is Dying

A sk anyone at Oistins in Barbados and they'll tell you. Miss Clarke? Yes, poor lady, she's dying. And if you inquire from what they'll tell you it's from an excess of white corpuscles.

Miss Clarke lives in a well-kept, not-too-shabby-looking grey shingled cottage that stands isolated in an extensive plot of land overgrown with brownish, drought-afflicted grass. Three straggly casuarina trees grow near the front door, relics of the days when a whole line of casuarina trees stood elegant guard along the driveway that leads to the cottage from the road.

Miss Clarke is fifty-two, and up to five months ago had thought herself in perfect health. So had her nephew, Basil, who works in a drug-store in Bridgetown. So had her sister, Mabel, who keeps a small guest-house at Maxwell (and does embroidery work as a side-line). In fact, it is likely that nobody would have known that Miss Clarke is dying from an excess of white corpuscles had not Basil tactfully suggested to his aunt one Sunday, when on a visit, that it would not be a bad idea if she were to have her life insured.

Miss Clarke was well accustomed to acting upon the tactful suggestions of her nephew, Basil, for Basil is a qualified chemist and druggist, and, to Miss Clarke, anybody who could be so clever as to learn enough about chemicals and drugs so that even the Government took notice and gave him permission to compound mixtures was a person to be looked upon with respect and confidence. Suggestions coming from such a person, Miss Clarke felt, could not be spurned or treated lightly. Indeed, one person only can claim predominance over Basil in Miss Clarke's scale of esteem, and that person is Doctor Corbin. For, naturally, a doctor is a man not only clever with chemicals and drugs but versed also in the secret workings of the human machine. It goes without saying, therefore, that Miss Clarke, when it came to the point of choosing a wise mentor, unhesitatingly accepted Doctor Corbin in preference to Basil.

When Basil suggested to Miss Clarke that she should have her life insured Miss Clarke had replied: "Insure my life? But, Basil! Whatever for, boy? I'm in the best of health. Why should you suggest such a thing to me all of a sudden like this, boy?"

Basil wriggled a little. He cleared his throat and said: "Well, you see, aunty, it's like this. It's because you're in such perfect health that I'm making the suggestion."

"You see, aunty," he went on, wriggling again and fidgeting in his chair and trying to show how concerned he was about her welfare, "I'm going to tell you something. I'm the kind of man who is known in educated circles as a psycho-pathologist." He paused in order to let the sound of this word reverberate impressively throughout her senses. Then when he thought that the desired effect had been achieved he said: "Yes, aunty, I'm a psycho-pathologist, and I can tell you this. I *know* from my extensive knowledge that when a person gets his life insured it always has a good effect both on his body and on his mind. A person who gets his or *her* life insured never dies in a hurry. And you see me here? I don't want you to die in a hurry, aunty. You're my *only* friend in this whole Barbados, aunty, and if you was to die life wouldn't hold anything for me no more. Nothing more no more."

Miss Clarke, in her guilelessness, was touched. She said: "You really that fond of your old aunty, Basil?"

Basil went off into more phrases expressive of deep devotion, and the upshot of the matter was that Miss Clarke decided that she would take immediate steps to have her life insured for two thousand dollars (Basil suggested the amount). And that Basil should be named sole beneficiary in the event of her death was also another decision she came to (again, with the help of another tactful suggestion by Basil).

She planned to go to town on Wednesday to see the insurance people, but as things fell out, on Monday evening Doctor Corbin her good friend dropped in to see her, and in the course of conversation she mentioned the matter to him, telling him of Basil's visit the day before.

Doctor Corbin expressed dismay and astonishment—almost alarm and annoyance. "Insure your life, Susan! But whatever for, child!" He leaned forward earnestly. "Look here, don't you go listening to that boy. Huh! To tell you the truth, Susan, I don't like that nephew of yours at-all, at-all. I well believe he has an ulterior motive in this thing."

"Ulterior motive?" Miss Clarke was shocked. Imagine her good friend Dennis saying such calumnious things of poor Basil! "But, Dennis, I'm surprised at you. How can you say such a thing! Basil is very fond of me.

213

I'm sure he has my welfare deep, deep at heart. He said it would help me in mind *and* body if I got insured—and that boy is no fool, Dennis. He has his good learning you see him there. He knows Latin, and he's a patho-something-or-the-other, besides. Everybody can't be a patho-whatever-it-is."

But Doctor Corbin wagged his finger at her. "I tell you, Susan, you listen to me. That boy may be clever in some things, but remember that I'm an older man and what's more I'm an L.R.C.P. and an L.R.C.S. You know what those letters mean? Huh! All right. You see Basil? He's only a druggist, you know. And I can tell you this, Susan, from my knowledge of the workings of the human body and the human mind, especially of psycho-therapeutics"—he paused for effect—"yes, especially of psycho-therapeutics, I can tell you this. That boy has an ulterior motive behind this thing. You listen to me, Susan. Listen to me as an old and wise friend, a Licentiate of the Royal College of Physicians and a Licentiate of the Royal College of Surgeons. You heed *my* words, Susan. I know what I'm talking about."

"But, Dennis, I've already promised him to do as he suggested. I can't back down now. It would hurt his feelings."

Doctor Corbin grunted pensively (remembering that as Miss Clarke's old and respected friend he was down for quite a substantial sum in her will). "All I know, Susan," he said in a tone of grave solicitude, "is that this thing doesn't smell good. That boy wants you to throw away your money on keeping up this policy so that he can benefit when you're gone along. But," he added quickly, noting her rising agitation and annoyance, "I tell you what, Susan. I'm going to make a little suggestion on my own now, and as a dear friend I can only hope you will grant it."

"Certainly, Dennis. I'm always willing to listen to anything you suggest."

"Very well. Well, Susan, before you go to Bridgetown let me give you a run-over first to see that your system is in good order. These insurance people are going to make you undergo an examination by their doctor, and since you look as if you're set on taking out this policy, well, it's no harm if I just give you a look over first to see that you're in sound health."

"But I am in sound health, Dennis. You know that very well. You examined me only last month and you said so yourself."

Doctor Corbin wagged his finger at her. "Look here, Susan child, you see me here? I'm an L.R.C.P. you know. *And* an L.R.C.S. Bear in mind my qualifications, Susan, when I tell you this. You see this thing the human body? It's a funny, funny thing, child. Today you can be in the best health—everything sound—and tomorrow? Huh; tomorrow everything turns topsy-turvy, and when you catch yourself you're treading straight on the high-road to your Lord and Saviour!"

Miss Clarke nodded, deeply impressed. "Yes, Dennis, you're right. You're quite right. I should have borne that in mind. Yes, you're a wise man, Dennis. Life can be very uncertain."

"I know I'm right, Susan. I *know* I'm right. And that's why I insist as your good friend who has your welfare at heart that I should put you through an examination before you go to town. Those Bridgetown doctors? Hoi! Susan, you don't know how wicked those men can be. They turn up their noses at us old retired country doctors, but they! More wicked men you couldn't wish for, child! It would be just like one of them to tell you that something was wrong with you and that the insurance company can't give you a policy. I know them!"

So Miss Clarke agreed to have Doctor Corbin give her an examination before her trip to town.

The doctor came on the following day, Tuesday, and he was in a jovial mood. "Of course, Susan," he said casually, "I know perfectly well that not a thing is the matter with you. You're a strong girl. You can't die just now. You have at least forty more years before you."

"Me, Dennis! Forty more years! Look, don't make fun of me! Have I ever told you I want to live to ninety-two?"

"We can't decide these things for ourselves, Susan. If we've got to live to ninety or a hundred we've got to live to that. And if we've got to live to forty-three all the wild horses in the whole world couldn't make any difference."

"That's true, Dennis. You're a wise man. A wise man."

As the examination progressed Doctor Corbin nodded and muttered in satisfaction, carrying on, so to speak, a running commentary on his findings.

"Heart sound—perfect." And later: "Yes ... Lungs—perfect. No dullness. No bronchi." And again: "Nerve reflexes excellent." ... "Spleen—splendid! No signs of enlargement."

But towards the end of the examination he suddenly stiffened and frowned and said: "Mm." He put his hand to his chin reflectively and after a silence said slowly: "Now, what's this? What's this at all?"

"What's what, Dennis?" asked Miss Clarke.

Doctor Corbin did not reply. He pursed his lips, looking grave. He uttered another ominous "Mm".

"Dennis, don't you hear me addressing a question to you? What's wrong? Why are you looking so serious?"

Doctor Corbin nodded with gravity and stroked his chin slowly. He said: "Mm" and shook his head. He sighed and muttered: "What is life? What is life?" At length, he told Miss Clarke: "Susan, I have something extremely grave to impart to you. I have made a grave discovery."

"A grave discovery?" Miss Clarke went pale. "What's that, Dennis? Something wrong with me?"

Doctor Corbin nodded slowly, wagged his head and sighed. "Susan, I wish it were not incumbent upon me to have to break this piece of news to your respected and dear self. But I have to inform you that you are in a most critical condition, Susan."

"A critical condition, Dennis?"

"Yes, Susan." Doctor Corbin averted his face and brushed hastily at his eyes. "It grieves me to have to tell you, Susan, but it is now useless for you to go to Bridgetown to try and take out that policy on your life. The doctors wouldn't pass you."

Miss Clarke paled again—this time in great alarm. The policy didn't matter now. What mattered was her health. "But, Dennis, what do you mean? What has gone wrong with me so suddenly?"

"To all appearances, Susan, you are in good health. In fact, I'm sure that even as you lie there you feel quite fit. But to a medical man, Susan— to an L.R.C.P., things are not always that which they seem to ordinary people. I have made a serious diagnosis, and I can tell you now with certainty that you are in a low state. You are suffering from a rare disease. You have an excess of white corpuscles."

"An excess of white what, Dennis?"

"White corpuscles. Phagocytes. But you won't know what I mean. You won't understand all these medical terms."

Miss Clarke, trembling now, asked: "But, Dennis, is it very serious? How serious?"

Doctor Corbin was silent for a moment, then looked at her and said, quietly: "Susan, I'm in a difficult position. What I mean is this: as your dear friend, it gives me great grief to have to tell you that it is now only a matter of time for you before the Lord calls you." Doctor Corbin's eyes were moist. He dabbed at them hastily, averting his face and heaving a sigh.

After a silence of profound dismay Miss Clarke looked at him and asked: "And how much longer have I got to live, Dennis?"

Doctor Corbin, seemingly too moved to reply at once, shook his head, fumbling for his handkerchief, his face drawn. At length, his face still averted, he said quietly: "It might be a year, Susan. Or it might be eight months. Or only six. You're a dying woman, Susan." His voice broke and he walked over to the window. "There's no cure, Susan," he said in a voice barely audible in the room.

"No cure?"

"No cure. Leucocythemia is beyond medical aid, Susan."

And that is why Miss Clarke never went to Bridgetown to see the insurance people about the policy. Her nephew, Basil, came to Oistins on the day after the examination to inquire what was the matter, and when he heard the facts he scowled and said: "Look, aunty! You don't worry with that man Corbin! He's only throwing dust in your eyes because he knows that you've got him down for a big sum of money in your will——"

"But, Basil! How dare you say such a thing of my old and treasured friend, Doctor Corbin! I won't have it!"

Basil, trying with difficulty to restrain his fury, said: "I know, aunty! I tell you, I know! That man Corbin! He's no good! And you listen to me and come to town and let another doctor examine you, and see if you don't hear a different, different story about what's wrong with you!"

"Then what you mean is that Dennis doesn't know his job! That's what you mean to tell me, Basil? Look here, boy, I've always respected you because I know you have studied your books and passed your examinations, but I'm not going to stand here, Basil, and hear you say all those things about a dear trusted friend of mine. I won't have it, Basil!"

Basil returned to Oistins on at least three other occasions to try to persuade his aunt to get another doctor to examine her, but on each occasion she proved firm and decided in her intention not to heed him. Furthermore, Doctor Corbin came every day to attend upon her, and he never failed to express what he felt about Basil.

"Hoi! That boy, Susan! He certainly hasn't taken after you. He's an evil-minded boy. You don't listen to him, Susan. Heed your old and wise friend. With me, Susan, you have nothing to fear. I shall attend upon you to the last. Never a day shall I desert you, my dear friend. Here, I have brought you a bottle of medicine which will relieve your condition, my dear. Take it three times a day after meals. It will make your end more easy when the hour strikes. I shall bring a bottle every week for you, Susan, free of charge. It is the least I can do for my old and dear friend."

And so Basil's visits ceased entirely, and the situation is exactly the same today, five months after the examination. Miss Clarke is dying— from an excess of white corpuscles. If you ask her she will tell you that every day she gets paler and paler and thinner. When a neighbour inquires after her health she says: "My dear. Just the same. The little white devils have got me looking paler than ever this morning."

And she sniggers and sighs philosophically!

Denis Williams (British Guiana)

A Long Long Pause

THE police were a long time coming. While I waited I asked the boy who it was had put him up to it. He whimpered, his hand limp in my grasp. His eyes, large and pink with crying, kept darting to the source of each sound entering the closed, shuttered house. We stood before the passage leading to the kitchen. Smell of scrubbed wood, gloom. Two or three threads of weak sunlight falling—you'd think tired—across the darkness, unobtrusive reminder of the dying fury of the sun outside. Even his agitation could not disturb the tranquillity of the house. Clean rooms, calm Caribbean evening. Through the open window could be seen the sea—could be heard voices calling children to bed, counting hens, admonishing goats and donkeys. Loose in-between moment. A long long pause.

The three threads of light became shorter each moment, drew spectrum-fringed ovals across the floor. The boy jerked slyly at my grasp to test it, and whimpered. I said again, "You little thief, who put you up to it, answer me," and belted him one.

Like before he only shrieked and repeated, "Nobody . . . mistake . . . let me go!"

He started struggling. I gave him another clout, good hard one this time, and watched him hang over in pain. Must've been seeing stars regular by now the way he kept blinking. I shook him. "How old y'are?' Couldn't be more than nine, ten, for sure, the little swine, but he said thirteen!

When the hell would the police come?

The fellow'd begun to tremble and I didn't like that; he kept an arm crooked over his brow the whole time in case I bashed him suddenly, watching me like I was a snake. I looked at his ugly little face. Not so dark as usual, but black just the same, blacker than mine. Old strains of Carib, Dutchman, Spaniard, no doubt, but not quite what you'd call a red nigger. Habitual fear had pinched the little face into a mask of suspicion and defensiveness. "Where's y'father?"

He shrank back. A new jab of terror sharpened his look. He didn't answer, so I smacked him another and shouted him down, "Who's y'father, tell me say?"

He shrieked again, "Let me go . . . mistake I tell you . . . let me go!"
And began blubbering.

So I gave him another good shaking and showed him how easy it'd been—the open outside backstairs climbing the house like a wooden step-ladder, the back door, the narrow skirting-board running round the walls to my bedroom window, the window itself forced, gaping open. The little swine!

"Who th'hell you think I am, millionaire or something?"

Raised my fist to fetch him another, but before it could land the old maiden lady from the room across the way opened her door and walked quietly down the passage. She disappeared into the gloom at the far end of the house.

The boy started violently and swung round. He looked down the passage, cowering. The big black lodger had appeared too at his room door. Weeks, months, since I'd seen the man. Surprised me now how he looked: kind of spreading round his illness, thickening. Most frightening the way people suffering from certain illnesses spread and put on weight while death's eating its way out from the inside. The fellow was just busting through the navy-blue vest and towering out of his khaki shorts, arms thick as my thighs, shoulders like an ox. He'd been a heavy-weight since way back at Engineering School and this rest-up on account of his illness wasn't doing him a lot of good anybody could see.

I looked into his eyes. Kind of glittering and set, like they had a separate fever of their own. His lips too, parched, whitish at the corners. Maybe reading too much, thinking too much, fooling himself. Wasn't much crazy, you couldn't rightly say though, about his eyes. But with him standing there holding the cup as high as his chin, glaring me straight like I'd done him something, I felt kind of a watering in the guts that made me sick.

What you should feel at a time like this about a man like that, you should feel something like pity; want to make way, move over, help him down the flight of stairs leading from his room even though they be only short and to be managed by anybody without too much fuss and loss of breath. But me, I felt nothing of the kind. I looked at him and could see that he knew. He was measuring the effort contact would involve, calculating the cost before spending.

He was for contacting me all right. From the way of his eyes, from the way he'd taken in the position with me and the boy and stood now just outside his door holding this cup and watching. He stood there and there was surely menace between us, and when he took the first step down it was terrible, like somebody coming. The boy leaped and bolted free. Down the passage to the kitchen door, and though I could easily have caught him as he fumbled with the lock, something about the big fellow just stood me there paralysed. I thought, for one thing, it'd please him me letting the little fellow free. But he only took another step. I heard the boy's footsteps down the backstairs. No matter: he'd stolen nothing.

The lodger came steady, planting one foot before the other like he had to think about each step. I didn't like the way he looked, glittering all the time into my eyes, so I felt I'd better answer, as though he'd asked a question. So I said, "No!" and when he kept coming without the faintest murmur I thought I'd better bawl it out real loud, so I shouted, "No, not me."

I think I was really trying to dissociate myself, to say I didn't know him, had no connection with him, something like that; clear the air.

But he only whispered, "Of course!" And that was terrifying. Because what the hell did it mean? He said "of course" and didn't stop coming. Slowly, but coming. I didn't feel I'd better let him. Not cowardice or anything, just the logic of the situation.

So I took a couple steps back and one sideways, trying to show nothing; nothing in my face: fear, alarm, nothing. Just watching him back steady, backing, inch by inch.

I wanted to repeat, "Not me," but I couldn't somehow—the silence between us was becoming practically solid. I didn't feel this helped one bit so I really bellowed, "Mistake . . ." and wanted to say more. But the man had cut me off. An enormous stride, just one, and he'd cut me off from the kitchen door. Now he stood blocking the passage. His neck, part of the stubby chin, the slope of his shoulders silhouetted against the window, blocked the view of the sea. A ship in port was unloading a motor-car. It glittered like a jewel in the sun. There must be all sorts of people watching that ship unloading that motor-car, it occurred to me, with not a thing on their minds.

I watched him. There'd surely been some kind of mistake. In his eyes, though, I could see only conviction. He was seeking me, stalking me. Sure. But why?

I eradicated any thought of escape from my countenance, watching to know what he was on to. He had forced contact all right; all I had done and said proved it, acknowledged it, but what was the man on to? The cup. Why hold on to it so carefully? Even in that giant stride across to the passage he'd been so mindful about the thing hadn't spilled a drop. Curious, I asked, "Your cup?"

"It is full," he whispered. And grinned.

That cup meant me no good. I said (or asked), "Harm," knowing it to be unnecessary. Fact is, practically every word possible between us seemed already spoken. So when, after a moment, he added, "Nitric . . ." I merely agreed, "Mmmmmh!" in the sense of "Sure!" There was agreement between us.

A sound down the far end of the corridor, and the old maiden lady began emerging from the gloom. I was relieved. I glanced quickly back at the man and noticed he hadn't taken his eyes off me. I could hear the woman's footsteps slacken as she tried to take in the situation. Much as, for my own reasons, I disliked her, I hoped desperately she'd say something, anything, that meant she'd taken a side. This seemed to me suddenly very necessary.

But she said nothing, took no side. I couldn't wait any longer. I leaped across to the open window. It was low, no more than a couple foot from the floor. Without thinking I was clean through it, on to the corrugated roof of the shed below. I gained nothing for my pains because the roof was surrounded on three sides by walls and on the fourth dropped straight into a piled-up junk-pit twenty, thirty feet below. Behind, the voice of the lodger urged, "Jump!"

He was already through the window approaching me like a cat, soft, the cup poised at near arm's length. I faced around towards him. Protests rose in my throat, elaborate explanations that I felt might right the situation, but the words my voice would form were limited. I heard myself moan, "Mistake . . ." pitiably. Nothing had registered on his face, nothing at all. He was only feet away, breathing with a whistling sound, waiting for his exhaustion to subside before the inevitable encounter.

Behind him the old maiden lady appeared at the window. I searched the tired blue eyes, rigid mouth, firm-set chin, for some attitude, some judgment. This seemed to me crucial; all now left was judgment. But she did nothing, could not understand. She was no help at all. This man and me, we were on our own.

I moved. I watched the cup. Held my breath. The man saw me blinded, writhing on the roof, a contemptible quibbler, so that my words, when again I shouted, were meaningless. "We're . . . *on our own*, you realize?"

He didn't move. Mutely he began raising an arm. "Mistake!" I shrieked, inching back, "Can't you understand?" And crooked an arm defensively over the brow. "Let me go . . ."

His arm began to descend, the movement bringing him to a slow crouch. His dark brown eyes seemed now almost indifferent, his thick lips easy. He could see the thing already done. I found I was trembling profoundly. I tried once more to make him understand "We're on our own . . ." but I could shout no longer; my voice issued in a croak. "Don't you understand."

"Jump!"

There was a confusion on the left and behind; the window filled up with sudden dark shapes. Three policemen tumbled on to the roof, and made for us, fanning out. The maiden lady's face reappeared at the window. Even now I hoped she would take a side, pronounce a judgment; I should destroy him otherwise. But her face seemed far away, like a diminishing cloud. She faded from my mind. I had no more words, no more time.

"Jump!"

His voice was so close it seemed to come from under my own skin. The police approached in a converging triangle, crouching fearful of scaring us off the edge of the roof; the lodger too was crouching in order to throw upwards. My skin began moving all on its own, like a snake. He was watching me like I was a snake about to leap. I could not leap; we had seconds to destroy this fear, I saw, poised between the policeman and the pit. I estimated again the distance into the pit, noted the jagged fragments of rusty metal piled there. I could edge no nearer the roofline; what with the slope and the police approaching, it was the ultimate moment.

I bent suddenly low, near the crouching man, the cup inches from my face. I spoke softly: "It was *you*, wasn't it?" And his eyes wavered, his lips twitched indecisively. "You sent him, didn't you?" His mouth fell right open. "Whose boy was it—you thought of *that*?" He hadn't. I was causing him to think now, perhaps, for the first time. He was shaking so violently the cup fell from his hands; between us the acid began foaming on the zinc. It brought me no relief, though, to notice the last of it trickle along the runnels of the roof and into the pit. "Now go on, tell *them*!" Straightening up I gestured towards the police. We were both trembling brutally.

Even before the first constable pronounced the words of arrest, I had surrendered myself.

O. R. Dathorne (*British Guiana*)

The Wintering of Mr. Kolawole

Mr. Kolawole was a Nigerian student I knew who lived, ate, studied and suffered in London. His studies were as mysterious as his source of income, indeed his entire existence. For some months we shared a kitchen. I had gone to live in a house, owned by a money-grabbing Greek who said to me as he led me up dingy stairs, flanked on both sides by darkness: "A good place here—very good place you have here." He tore away viciously at some cobwebs that obstructed his path and opened a door. "Much discrimination people make in London, but for me I make none—two pounds ten a week, one month payable in advance."

He dribbled liberally as he spoke and mopped at the excess with a cloth that might once have been a handkerchief. I paid him out of some money I had just claimed from a liberal firm of photographers, who had me going round the countryside asking farmers if they wanted to have their photographs taken. He counted it carefully, dribbling carefully over the notes, leaving his signature so to speak on each one.

"One thing," he said. "You share kitchen for the price—good price yes?—you share kitchen with Mr. Kolawole."

Then he disappeared. As for me I didn't care with whom I had to share the kitchen—I was so broke that I would have shared the same fire with the devil's wife. I had to get some examinations ready pretty soon and thought of settling down to some solid hard work. But such was not to be the case. Mr. Kolawole had different ideas about what I ought to do. At first he was just a near neighbour; I encountered him on the stairs, raced him to the lavatory and borrowed his salt and pepper when he was not there. But old Kolawole's neighbourliness did not end there where he was concerned. Just when I was getting down to a night's hard work the music would start. Kolawole had brought over some talking drums and they spoke every night, to me, to the people next door, to the neighbours, to the next few streets. I used to wonder if Kolawole was a music student doing research on the talking drums, for the amount of practice he used to get in nightly should have made him an expert in a few months. Once Mr. Kolawole started his nightly manoeuvres on the drums work was impossible and one by one you would see the lights go on in the neighbourhood as people tried not to sleep.

For Mr. Kolawole did not sleep. He played the drums early morning and late night and he played with such fierceness and energy that one might have thought that Mr. Kolawole had been expressly sent up from Nigeria on some sort of mission to keep the English continually awake. He played all August, he played through September, into October; and then in November, one night I didn't hear the drums. I had got so used to them that the silence distracted me. Let me say that I was even slightly annoyed that Mr. Kolawole had chosen to leave off playing the drums, for they had become such a regular part of my night, that to be without them was like being without something to quarrel about.

I went over to investigate, tore viciously at the cobwebs and knocked at my neighbour's door. As I was waiting to be called in, I observed our landlord making his wet way up the stairs.

"No drums," he complained bitterly to the banister, dribbling liberally over it. "Why he not play the drums tonight? I wait—I tell Isobella—I say maybe drums come later. We wait, we wait—" He shrugged fat, eloquent shoulders and spat emphatically across at me. I dodged in time as Mr. Kolawole cried out a feeble "Come in" to my second knock.

It was the first time I had entered Kolawole's room. Books were liberally scattered in all directions for he had been a student of every type—Law, Medicine, Arts, the lot—Kolawole had sampled a little bit here and a little bit there of knowledge. He is of the type that remain indefinitely in London and become permanent fixtures, like Buckingham Palace and the 'cuppa tea'. In years to come when visitors are shown round London they will witness the changing of the guards, the British Museum and Mr. Kolawole, for he is there for life. Anyhow when we entered his room, Kolawole lay shivering under a huge carpet.

"Not my carpet," the landlord interjected. "Please if you are cold I sorry—very sorry—but please not to use my carpet." He looked at Kolawole sadly and Kolawole returned a look of blank dislike.

"No drums?" he asked, shooting saliva at us. "Ah, very cold here, no fire. I go tell Isobella—no fire tonight, no drums, Mr. Kolawole very cold."

He tugged at the carpet and smoothed it back into place. Kolawole rose from his sitting posture. "The winter," he said profoundly to me, "is too too cold." I pointed out the discovery of fire, the advantage of having a matchbox, a matchstick, some coal. Kolawole shook his head. "No," he said. "I want to winter."

"Winter?" I asked sceptically.

"Yes," he said. "Like Churchill. Go somewhere warmer."

I laughed. "You have money?"

Kolawole looked at me: "What has money to do with it? Where shall I winter?" he asked himself pensively. I saw the drum in the corner among his books. He went across and picked it up. I was happy for a moment. Perhaps he would play. But he sat with it in his hands, saying nothing. I got up to go. Then suddenly the sound came, as usual.

"I know. I know," Kolawole said, between drum-beats. "I won't spend winter here. I'll winter elsewhere."

I spent some time pleading with him but to no avail. Kolawole was adamant. He was determined 'to winter' and to do it elsewhere.

"Central heating in the hotel, servants to attend on me, food for the asking . . ." Kolawole continued dreamily.

"You have money?" I asked again.

I was ignored. Kolawole made his drums talk and dreamt late into the night. I left him soon after for I thought to myself that perhaps too long a spell in England had caused him to have delusions of grandeur.

Events, however, were to prove Kolawole right. He did winter. Next morning he gave us the usual serenade on the drums and then I saw him go out. He was immaculate with three-piece suit and large suitcase and I saw him stride elegantly down to the corner of the street. He looked carefully round for some time and then he noticed that a bus had just come up and discharged its load of passengers. As they were coming towards him Mr. Kolawole decided to clutch his stomach and roll disconsolately into the ditch. There was a concerted rush for his person. I raced out of the house to observe Mr. Kolawole being fanned by solicitous observers, groaning on his back and clutching in frenzy at the pavement. "Do you know him?" one of the locals asked me, seeing a dark face in the crowd.

I was stooping near Kolawole at the time and before I could reply he pinched me violently in the posterior. I thought that perhaps this was another symptom of Mr. Kolawole's disease and looked round quickly. Mr. Kolawole gave me the barest of winks between groans.

"I don't know the man," I stammered out quoting in frenzy.

I was now sure that Kolawole was mad. The ambulance came and fetched him away to the Royal Free Hospital. I went to see him on Sunday. Kolawole was reading in bed, attended by two of the prettiest nurses. Near him central heating pipes swished discreetly. One of the pretty nurses fed him delicately. He sipped free government orange juice.

"He needs at least three months' rest," the nurse said.

Kolawole sighed contentedly and turned over a leaf. He was wintering.

Edward Braithwaite (Barbados)

The Black Angel

Now that I think back, the first time I thought the Black Angel unusual, to say the least of it, was when I went to call on Bee. Bee hadn't been to work for several days, and the foreman asked me if I would drop in on him on my way home and see what was the matter. I knocked at Bee's shack and when there was no answer, I pushed open his dark-painted galvanized door and went in. Bee lived alone, and as a bachelor, he had only a bed-sitting room and a kitchen: the Factory Committee never allowed a single man more.

The room was untidy: pots, pans and greasy plates left dirty on the table: in fact, there was a considerable unfinished meal there. Bee was lying on his bunk, unconscious, his head twisted a little to one side, and his eyes open showing the whites of them. Somebody had wrapped him, apparently, in the Black Angel; it had been carefully placed around his shoulders and tucked in under his arms, like a blanket. There was a faint smell, as of ammonia, in the air.

The Black Angel belonged to Kappa. Kappa had joined our camp some three months back. He was a dark and stocky fellow, with a rich, shiny moustache, dark hair and dark eyes; rather sullen in appearance though friendly enough when one got to know him. I had known him now for about a month. There was nothing, really, to distinguish him from the rest of the men at the camp, except the Black Angel, which was his leather jacket.

This jacket was a large affair, of faded black leather, very worn, but warm, which was the important thing in the cold, unfriendly climate around the factory, the cold, grey, bleak chill in the wood of beech and evergreens where we had our camp. The jacket was lined with a fluffy substance like wool, or its substitute, but was so dirty from long use that it was practically the same colour as the leather. I couldn't have said what the original colour had been. It was a jacket very much like what, later, I saw airmen use.

We gave it a name because, in the first place, it was the only one of its kind in the camp and we had never seen its like before; and because, when Kappa wore it, he kept the high collar sticking up like little ears or wings around his ears. We used to have some quite heated discussions on whether the collar more closely resembled wings or ears, until some-one hit on the idea of the Black Angel, and from then on everybody saw the collars as wings. Or perhaps it may have been the other way round. I can't remember; anyway we all accepted the name, and in the queer, fantastic environment of our lives, naming and identifying a jacket was one of the less extraordinary happenings.

For instance, none of us had ever seen the outer world. At least we certainly didn't know how near a proper town was. We were the off-spring of lovers, convicts, the poor; and had been brought to this forest by the Factory Committee in our infancy. Many of us were mad, some were idiots, and a few suffered from blood diseases as the result of the vicious internal breeding of our progenitors. The women in the camp, immune themselves, transported these diseases to the others of us.

But despite all this, we possessed (I know this now) an extraordinary innocence of soul; and though we were neurotically sensitive and sub-ject to depressions and profound hallucinations, we possessed a moral integrity and equilibrium which was quite astonishing; though I wonder still if 'equilibrium' is the word I want, since in our unspoiled souls there seldom was the need for balance, since the antagonism of tempta-tions, the wings of evil, were unknown to us.

For instance, in my then innocence, I was so upset to find Bee in this sadly fatal condition, that it never occurred to me to ask how Kappa's Angel came to serve him as blanket in his final illness.

II

Our only recreation at the camp was boxing. After work, in the even-ings, most of us went over to Gamma's shed where we did some general skylarking and a little serious shadow-boxing. Once or twice a quarter we arranged a more public spectacle in the form of championships, six to nine rounds a bout. Gamma was a ball-headed giant of about forty who fancied himself the descendant of a great and famous prize-fighter. Certainly his enthusiasm for the game made it impossible for any able-bodied man in camp to escape his shed for long.

One late afternoon, just before dusk covered the small area of our lives with its sticky smoke, Kappa and myself were walking down the hill which led from the factory back to our camp. His competitive bout was scheduled for the following night, and he was rather edgily, I thought, discussing his chances and his opponent's prowess. None of us ever took these bouts at all seriously, and I remember vaguely wondering why Kappa took it differently from the rest of us. And having thus nebulously differentiated him 'from the rest of us', I must have gone on, but only at a subconscious level, to wonder what he was doing here among 'the rest of us'. We were native here: either brought in early childhood, or born here. Yet only three months ago, a grown man, with a strange outstanding jacket had appeared among us. And in our innocent lunacy, not one of us had formulated the query which I, talking to the man, and reassuring him as we walked down the hill, had only just then dimly initiated.

Kappa usually cycled to town; he always referred to our camp as 'town'. 'Going to town?' he had asked me, catching me up as I walked through the yard from the factory. It turned out that he had offered his bike that afternoon to Alfie. Alfie had lost a leg two months before in a factory accident, and even though he had returned to work, he was by no means a fit man; so the use of Kappa's bicycle was a helpful turn of fortune for him.

At the bottom of the hill were some railings. We had erected them only recently, to serve as a road-sign and fence, because the hill was rather steep, and people cycling down from a late-shift at the factory, were liable, in the darkness, to run into the ugly thorny ditch at the bottom of the hill. So we had all put in overtime at the factory, making, with the Committee's permission, these railings, modest affairs of cast-iron, and measuring about four feet of height when we had staked them into the ground. Our one ambition was, one day, to make fine decorative heads for them. At the moment, they remained ashamedly un-attractive and blunt. The trouble was that we couldn't decide on a design for the heads. Some of us wanted a spear-shaped design, others a fleur-de-lis, while one man favoured the design of twined serpents, like those at the factory hospital gates.

But we did paint them white, which was a far more practical improvement. Now they could be more clearly observed in the dark, and did, in fact, prevent many a careless rider from crashing into them, reserving him from a more painful landing than falling into the original ditch. Those blunt, undecorated heads were dangerous.

Some intuition seems to have warned Kappa of my then only half-formed queries of him, because before we got much farther down the hill, he had turned the anxieties we had been discussing a moment before into a joke against himself, became quite flippant and vigorous; in fact, and challenged me to race him down the hill. We both came laughing, panting down, and at the bottom stopped, held on to the railings, recovering breath.

After that we fell to skylarking. I don't remember how it started. One of us slapped the other on the back. I think he was coughing, that was it. His cough caught up in his chest with his heaving breath. I slapped him on the back, we laughing, coughing, gasping all the while. He slapped me back. And before we knew where we were, our hilarious mood led us, quite seriously, but still clearly in jest, to a bare-fisted show of Gamma's pugilistic art. This queer, unaccountable hilarity, often leading to blows, was another normal feature of our unworldly climate and circumstances.

As I said, there was nothing much in this little scuffle, really. There was no anger, no intent, no ill will; we were both of us about the same weight, of the same level of experience and proficiency; my reach was longer but Kappa seemed to operate on interior lines, using short jabs and hooks; and at close quarters, confined to the narrow space at the bottom of the hill where the road sharply bent away from the railings, I could not keep him at more advantageous range.

Soon we were at it quite seriously, grunting and shuffling: but not yet sufficiently roused to exchange brute slug for fine art. Kappa kept his head well and correctly down, his face sinking into the high collar of the Black Angel which he was wearing, so there wasn't much of him I could hit. The jacket, with its thick woollen lining, was soft and pillowy around his body, so I couldn't make much impression on him there, either; and I didn't like hammering at his head with my bare knuckles. Besides, the man was my friend, and I didn't want to hurt him unnecessarily.

I didn't suppose that Kappa wanted to hurt me either, but he was certainly powerful on the short jab, and he was always finding my chin, just regularly tapping it. Each time I felt my head jerk back.

The strange thing was that I felt no pain. Or rather what I felt when he struck didn't have the sensation of physical pain. But—and I couldn't understand it—I could hear myself groaning. In spite of myself I was groaning, but the groans didn't come from my physical self. It seemed that each time Kappa hit me, he didn't actually hit my chin or my face, but that he hit something inside me: hit my innocence, my spirit or soul, if you like, and that it was this existence inside me which involuntarily groaned.

I can't say how long it went on like this. I remember struggling back against him with all my will. It was my will, not my physical strength I discovered I had to exercise; I remember once struggling against him with this inner force, that I saw my blows hit, not Kappa, but the Black Angel. This jacket, it appeared to me, had assumed an entity all its own; it seemed to have enveloped Kappa completely, so that it was not a man at all I fought, but some other with small sharp black wings, opposing me there in the dusk, at the bottom of the hill, by the railings.

I felt, too, that this other, opposing me, was intent to conquer me, to break me; that if Kappa continued to hit me as he did, this Black Angel, of which he seemed the agent or the incarnation, would wrench me out from the vital consciousness of my body, would, by this attack upon my consciousness and my will, gain an ascendancy over me, against the wishes of myself and reason.

But then I might have imagined all this: it might have been merely an hallucination, one of those complete acts of imagination to which all of us, as a recompense perhaps, for our strange solitude and situation, were so easily subject. I remember, as in a dream, helplessly, that I began to swoon, was losing will and conscious direction, still without being aware of any physical pain, when suddenly I realized that Kappa had stopped hitting me.

I found myself leaning against the railings, shaking my head slowly from side to side, wondering what had happened, and saw Kappa, standing some distance away from me, staring back up the now quickly falling dusk on the hill. He seemed tense, impatient, as if he were expecting something or someone to come down the hill: as if he expected something to happen. He was so preoccupied that he didn't seem to notice me at all. In fact, no one would have thought that we had only then broken off scuffling with each other.

Just then Alfie appeared at the top of the hill, riding Kappa's bicycle. Perhaps he was wondering what had become of Alfie, I thought, because

Alfie had told him that he wanted to reach home soon after dark. Anyway Alfie was coming, and my silent surmises must have been correct, because Kappa relaxed his watchful anticipation.

Alfie came down the hill gathering speed as he came. Since he had only one foot, and this was an all-pedal bike, he had taken that good foot off the pedal, letting the pedals swing to their own sweet tune: and the bike coursed down.

When he was about half-way down, he saw us and waved. He also saw the warning white rails of our cast-iron fence, and he immediately clutched nervously at the bicycle brakes, so he could slow himself for the sharp bend and so coast on, around, past us, on to his home. It was quite amusing to see how his smile at greeting shifted instantaneously to anxiety for his brakes.

But the brakes didn't work. It was getting quite dark now, but I could see that his face was registering the same surprise and fear I felt within me when I realized the danger. I could see his hands squeezing convulsively at the useless brakes. And all this helpless while, I was saying to myself, how strange, how strange; because this bike of Kappa's was a new one, and since our factory manufactured bicycles and nothing else, all of us were skilled mechanics and technicians in this trade if nothing else, and such a thing as faulty brakes was unheard of. Besides, I was sure that Kappa's cycle, until then, had been in perfect running order.

All this while Alfie was coming terribly towards us down the hill. I was too dazed to move. I felt I ought to act, to do something to avert his crash if I could, but only thoughts and pieces of hallucination flowed over me, soothing me, and carrying me down to dreams, like water.

And only after Alfie miraculously had jammed his only foot into the singing spokes of the front wheel of the careering cycle, and had given a cry of pain as the instep of his foot was broken, and the cycle wobbled but barely made the bend, just missing the railings, and went on, out of sight, on round the bed, did I then realize, from where I stood, that if he'd smashed, he would have crashed through me.

III

One evening soon after these events I arrived home to find old Ta Mega there. Mega was a pure gypsy, the only person not connected with the factory, though she spent most of her time in the camp. She was an ancient hag: so old and withered that she looked more like an old man than a woman. I suspect that under her faded yellow speckled bandana she was quite bald. She came around to our shack—and had been coming several months before my birth (my mother's adviser and midwife then)—once every month. There was a very real bond of affection and respect between herself and my mother: not only did Ta Mega depend on people such as my mother for her daily bread and butter (I don't think she had a place of her own; just moved from client to client: a visiting philosopher and prophet) but my mother was bound to her wisdom and her esoteric secrets. She knew how to drain fevers, how to revoke bad luck, and reflect misfortunes back on enemies. She could predict the future. And since the women of our world of mists and corrugated iron shacks were not blessed with the faculty of internal mirages and hallucinations (in the same way they were not cursed with our diseases and neuroses, though as I said before, they were carriers of them); they had resort to magic spells, potions, predictions and foretellings and secret hocus-pocus.

Ta Mega was high priestess of this cult; though, to predict the future she didn't have to resort to crystals as I've since seen gypsies at circuses do. She used the large domestic soup tureen, filled it with fresh boiled water, with a golden coin at the bottom, her honorarium. And, moreover, she could carry out this infallible procedure only when the moon was full.

That evening I came in very tired and nervous from the factory—I had been working overtime for a week: we were getting up a pension for Alfie. Ta Mega was sitting on a stool by the fire, combing at one of my sisters' hair. She didn't say anything to me when I entered, but I noticed that all through my meal—which I was eating very slowly, my appetite only half-attending—she had been carefully though surreptitiously watching me.

As soon as I was finished, she dispatched my sisters one and all to bed, despite the whining protestations of the eldest that her scalp had not been scraped and the hair combed.

"Let me see your hand!" she wheezed in her professional, old man's voice as soon as we were alone.

"Not *that* hand, dolt, your *heart* hand!"

Always I annoyed her with my disrespectful unco-operativeness, my heretical attitude to the ritual confessional.

Holding my left hand in hers, she long and carefully studied the lines; appearing uncertain of what she saw there; tracing her own index finger along the lines of my palm, like a blind woman tracing out in her mind a strange word on the embossed oblongs of her braille.

She appeared worried. She had never been worried about me before —not really. I had always held this good policy on her part; the careful professional tactic, keeping anxious *paying* mothers in good spirits. But this time she was worried, and genuinely so. She squeezed my hand so tightly against her large discoloured rings that she hurt my fingers.

"Open your shirt!" she commanded gruffly.

Now I was unfeignedly surprised. She wanted to chart my chest! And Ta Mega had resort to this supreme act of her necromancography only when she had intimations of catastrophe, only if I should have killed a man or was myself threatened, or perhaps if I were going to lose my job. But I was innocent of such dire possibilities. Besides, only three months ago, Mega had given me the quintennial 'check-up' my mother insisted upon. This business cost my mother three golden sovereigns, so I suppose that's why it wasn't annual. Since I was the sole breadwinner (the Factory Committee only employed women in exceptional circumstances), it was essential that my future be kept clear and open: a well-swept well-lighted passage down the years of my valuable virility. My sisters, poor non-essential darlings, had to be content with only two such expensive surveys of their future: they were 'charted' at seven years of age, and would be again at twenty-one —if they were safely married by then.

But, as I said, Mega's five-yearly arrangement with my mother had been successfully and uneventfully carried out only three months back; and here now was Ta Mega, without permission from my mother, on her own initiative, once again assembling the most precise machinery of her art.

My shirt was off, and with her blue mascara pencil which she kept in an empty snuff-box, at the bottom of her bundle, she had begun to draw the lines, the horoscope lines, on my chest. Starting from my shoulder-blades as base, she quickly constructed a rough rectangle, corresponding to the area of my chest: though the shape of the completed figure was also determined by the figure of my zodiac: Taurus, in my case. Lines were then drawn connecting the opposite corners of the rectangle (or rather, trapezium), and the forecast rested, it appears, on how near the tips of my breast were from these intersecting lines. Again, calculations varied with the individual and with his astrological birth, but the principle was simple enough: the state and well-being of your life was determined by the proximity of the human nipples to these artificial lines.

Ta Mega slowly drew these fatal lines. She did so slowly, anxiously, with less professional and far more personal concern than I had ever seen in her before. Her fears affected me. It was a serious matter. Her anxiety infected me like scarlet fever. I didn't have to see her frightened eyes to know that both those crossing lines had crossed across the nipples of my chest. I felt the pencil passing coldly over and across them like a curse.

Ta Mega trembled. Her fear was like a heavy stone dropped into silent water, and the concentric radiations reached over into me, one after one. She didn't speak. She hadn't said a word after she had told me to undo my shirt. And now she did speak: she spoke a gypsy tongue I could not understand.

Deep in the very underwaters of myself I trembled. It was as if my spirit was waking up in the middle of a very dark night; as if I were alone in a wood of presences and powers, vague potentialities I could not see or name. And beyond this wood, moving somewhere around and beyond, a moving gentleness, like the leaves of trees. But between this wind, this light, of outer gentleness, were these dark forms and presences. And when they seemed to move, they threw a shadow on my spirit, as a shadow passing over a wood darkens the faint trail.

My mother came in. In my coma I saw her as if from a great distance, or rather as through a separating medium, like a moving object seen through water. She was looking at me out of a tremendous silence. She seemed much less afraid than Ta Mega was.

They spoke together, looking at me as if I were some object in a pale aquarium, some object in a showcase to be looked at.

My mother left the room, my other, inner self still waking up to this new, unseen-peopled darkness, and she returned with something in her hand which looked to me; (my physical eyes still functioned, though turned around like looking through the wrong ends of a telescope) like a mathematical protractor, the celluloid half-circle I had used at school to measure angles. She handed this to Mega, who (yes) measured the angles of the mystical geometry she'd drawn upon my chest.

They were making quite sure.

Then my mother repeated the measurements, did it twice, making quite sure, and acting so impersonally now, as if they were grave-diggers, finishing off my already settled fate.

And for all I know my body might well have been in a grave. It felt inert and heavy, as if time had gone from it. But at the same time my inquiring consciousness explored the strange darkness like a green shoot.

And calling it onwards, outwards, towards the light and wind of the moving gentleness, beyond the wood of shapeless presences that threatened to envelop me, I heard a voice. And listened.

It spoke to me of Evil, and slowly the unseen people, the half-seen shapes, took form: they were being named at last.

These evil presences sought to find me out, the voice spoke on; they were investing me, snuffing out my light.

"I do not want to die," I heard my voice reply. "I do not want to die."

And the voice returned: "You must expel them then!"

At the word 'expel', I thought I saw a faint round glowing in the gentleness beyond the wood: as if a sun were out there shining, after all.

My voice replied: "How can I, when I don't know how? How can I when I don't know who or what thing to expel?"

And the voice replied: "I don't yet know the person or the presence either. But I can tell you how."

At the word 'how' a great gong sounded in my ears, as if some hand had struck the sun beyond with hope.

And the voice continued: "This is how: by an act of will, not power; remember, by an act of will!"

At the word 'will' the sun broke forth above the trees like a familiar echo. Hope struck again, and the sun broke forth in streams of light. The darkness of my eyes grew red with happiness; a noise filled up the tunnels of my ears like the roar of falling water.

IV

When I recovered consciousness it must have been the next day. It was late morning, a pale greenish springtime sun was shining; and it was time for work. No one was about in our shack. Ta Mega, of course, was gone. Daylight never seemed to agree with her, but there was no sign of my mother in the yard and my eldest sister who usually propped up her elbows on the table while I ate breakfast (it was one of the marks of respect shown to the breadwinning male that a female of his family attended him at meals, even if only perfunctorily, as my sister did), wasn't at her post either. I recalled the fantastic night, the seance, the dark consciousness of evil powers which were striving, unknown to me, for ascendancy over me. Because of this curse, it seems my family had avoided me. But they hadn't deserted me: they would not do that unless there was no hope; and Mega, in the seance, had opened up a chance. No, they had not deserted me: some oatmeal porridge had been left warming for me by the stove. This I shovelled and set out, almost late, for the factory.

I didn't speak to anyone that day, nor the next, neither at home, nor at work. I developed a headache, which the noise of machinery and the spell of the curse did everything to aggravate.

On the third day there was a fight at the factory. It was between Kappa and a thin nervous youngster called Delta.

I don't usually bother about other people's quarrels, but somehow I felt drawn to this one. I wanted to have a closer look at Kappa in action, remembering the unprecedented sensations I had had scuffling with him that evening by the bottom of the hill.

Delta didn't have a chance, really. It was a serious fight, both men were hot; but Kappa, working on interior lines, and keeping close and protected, as usual, by his Black Angel, beat Delta about the mouth and cheekbones until he got his head well-up (Delta was one of those people too nervous to turn up at Gamma's); and having got the lead on the boy's chin, simply went to work with his short lefts. He didn't seem to be hitting hard, just going at it regularly and firmly, but Delta began to whimper, not as if he were in physical pain (no man fighting would have made a noise like that), but as if some pressure were being exerted at the very roots of his living, and he was being made to groan like this against his will.

The memory of my own experience, these same groans, came back to me. Delta's intangible pain was within me reawakening like a whimpering echo. So it wasn't a hallucination after all. I thought, that evening by the railings, at the bottom of the hill.

After a time, under this punishment, Delta didn't fight back: he had tried some frantic sorties, swinging wild-fisted at Kappa's protected head, but after each one he weakened perceptively more and more. I wanted to shout (and that sun was shining inside me again: beginning to shine through the dark shapes in my aching head); I wanted to shout out to him: "Not force, man, *Will*, man, *Will!*" But I couldn't speak, I didn't speak. To my mind the words sounded sensible enough, but they would sound silly on my tongue, I knew; and neither Delta nor the men who watched the fight would understand. The sun went out and my head ached worse.

The fellows who were watching laughed when Delta fell. The strange thing was, they hadn't heard the noise. But this time I was sure: I had echoed Ta Mega's words in my mind. I was sure that Delta, when he fought, had had the same deep wrenching experience that I had had. And now I thought I knew what it meant, though even then I was not sure. As I said before, men in our condition, subject to neurosis and everyday hallucination, could be sure of little: divisions between reality and unreality had no definition here. We lived in a wood of dreams and twilight certainties.

But I was sure at this moment, with an unusual clarity, that the other men who had watched the fight had not heard Delta make those whimpering unbodily sounds, because they—all of them—not I—were suffering from hallucination. Looking back on it now, I find it strangely improbable, but I was unflinchingly convinced of it at that moment in the factory, with Delta lying there unconscious on the ground.

That evening, after my late-shift, I decided to walk around by Delta's place: to see how he was, have a chat, and try to confirm my hunch.

I knocked at his door and when there was no answer, I pushed open his dark-painted galvanized door and went in. Delta lived alone, and as a bachelor, he had only a bed-sitting room and a kitchen: the Factory Committee never allowed a single man more.

The room was untidy: pots, pans and greasy plates left dirty on the table: in fact, there was a considerable unfinished meal there. Delta was lying on his bunk, unconscious, his head twisted a little to one side, and his eyes open, showing the whites of them. He was wrapped in Kappa's Black Angel: it had been placed carefully around his shoulders and tucked in under his arms, like a blanket. There was a faint smell as of ammonia in the air.

I smiled. The generous Kappa, I thought, didn't let the fellow down.

Then suddenly I saw it: saw it again: clearly. The two empty sleeves of Kappa's leather jacket were gripped around Delta's body; the high, two-pointed collar, like two outrageous wings were fixed to Delta's neck. Perhaps all this was hallucination! the light from the fire threw shadows in the room, but it seemed to me, as it had seemed to me before, that Kappa's jacket was something living, a fabric inhabited by a dark presence, a living form: was something other than itself.

It was part of the same unseen evil power I had become aware of under Ta Mega's spell.

I rushed to the bed where Delta lay, tore the Black Angel from his throat, and lifting it up, and turning, threw it into the fire.

V

When I had held the jacket, and lifted it, it was very heavy and my whole self, physical and psychic, went dark as if I were being covered by a heavy shadow or a dark stone. But when I threw away the jacket, the stone was rolled away, and the great sun was shining in my now known wood like a great gong.

When I got home, Ta Mega was there. So were my sisters. Looking at my palm, Ta Mega laughed. My mother, coming through the door, brought chicken soup just as if it were Christmas Eve or Easter.

But high and low, although I looked, I couldn't find poor Kappa anywhere, to tell him what had happened to his jacket.

A. N. Forde (*Barbados*)

The Silk-Cotton Tree

R UPERT worshipped the silk-cotton tree.
 Since he could remember, it had stood towering over the house like a sentinel, its arms spread out and—when the wind fell—arrested as if in a gigantic act of prayer. Its trunk was big, bigger than a man's embrace, and its branches ran for the most part horizontal to the ground. From the distance, branches, leaves and trunk looked like a great umbrella-of-the-landscape.

The house was small, two-roomed, and had been left him by his mother. She had died five years ago, and, ever since, Rupert had lived alone, a man of thirty years' silence. He had no friends—unless you call old Brewster a friend. Brewster had a plot of land next to his and they occasionally exchanged words, chiefly on the subject of the silk-cotton tree. For Rupert had no other loves. At noonday, he basked in the tree's huge wing spread and at night its subtle leaf chirpings sent him off to sleep.

His half acre of land lay across the road. It ran down an incline and was tidily cut into beds, with well-kept drains that let off the water supply in rain. Since the last landslide which had taken away a sizeable bit of his hard work he was more careful to follow the agricultural officer's advice. So he kept his drains clean of sediment and weed. And now in the evening light he was finishing his chores, and in his heart pride bubbled at the healthy green ribbons of corn and the eccentric pumpkin vine and the firm tomatoes coming to view.

He stopped working and decided to pack up for the day. It was late, probably some minutes after six. He could still feel inside of him the regular vibration of the hoe striking and biting into the moist earth and hear its metal sound as it bruised an occasional rock couched in the soil.

Nearby a grasshopper scratched its high-pitched needle of sound on his ear-drum. That was something he liked: this hour of sound away from the human voice. The frog blowing his horn. The cricket pealing his shrill note. He adored the night with its wakeful animal and insect choirs.

And the tree, of course. How close to his home it was. Close to his heart. Even now as he crossed the road its dark-green lather of leaves seemed to beckon him invitingly. A sweet content nibbled at his breast.

The house was completely hidden by the tree—if you came by the path leading to it from the road—and was some twenty yards back from the road itself. It was on a slight eminence and was reached by crude ill-shaped steps which time and Rupert's foot-grips had forged in the earthy incline. As he passed under the tree now, he remembered the words of his dying mother:

"Rupert, not to cut down dat silk-cotton tree: leave it high where it is. Don' mind what nobody tell you."

And he had respected her words. He had known the tree from childhood. He would never cut it down. Couldn't bring himself to do it even if he wanted to. True, the roots were quite thick and of late seemed to be tampering with the foundations of the house. He had begun to see some slender cracks in the cement columns that supported the building. Of course the masons nowadays didn't produce as solid work as the oldtimers. Perhaps the cement mixture had been too weak.

He stopped and examined the roots bulging like veins out of the earth's skin. They disturbed the texture of the ground, and here and there lesions appeared on its surface. Cracks with water settled in them stretched wayward patterns around the big prickled trunk. The whole scarred surface seemed to be responding to some pressure from below.

Rupert recalled the many times Brewster had asked him:

"Why you keepin' dat silk-cotton tree. It isn' no use to you. All it doin' is encouragin' spirit. Dem tree does harbour devil."

True the tree wasn't of much material value. The wood wasn't good for building or for making coal. But if everything was judged on these grounds why should one, for instance, keep an old broken jar which couldn't hold water any more? Or keep old stained letters. No, he wasn't cutting down the tree. As for talk of spirits, that was all rubbish. Brewster didn't have to pass by the tree at night if he was afraid of devils. As a matter of fact he never came there at night. So why bother himself about the tree? It wasn't any trouble to him.

Rupert chuckled at the idea of devils 'confabbing' under the tree. What wouldn't people believe?

He entered the house, put the hoe, shovel and cutlass in a corner, lit a fire outside in a small enclosure at the back of the house and put on some sour-sop tea to boil. He was fond of sour-sop tea. It made him sleep soundly.

Meanwhile he sat under the tree and the lazy light of the sunset seeped through the leaves. But he couldn't see the sun: the tree always hid it from view.

A sharp mischievous breeze whipped up and he rose to see about the kettle and the fire. "It's going to be a windy night," he thought.

That night he went to bed to the sound of rain tickling the roof and wind teasing the tree. His bosom was warm with happiness at his cosy trinity of house and tree and land.

And he dreamt.

He dreamt that wool, white wool was falling out of the sky in fleecy downpours all around and about him and that he was lying on the ground in a green pasture feeling its soft touch as it landed on his passive body. He closed his eyes in an act of silent submission. Behind his eyelids he could see it piling up in great heaps all over the pasture. Then suddenly the gentle noiseless fall of the wool seemed to increase in weight and he could feel steady pummellings as it continued to fall on his body. He began to get panicky and he forced his eyes open, with difficulty. It wasn't wool! It was snow! That was why he felt so cold. He pulled himself together and awoke.

For a moment he couldn't quite catch his bearings. The steady beat went on above his head and something cold like water hit him in the face. He realized then that rain was falling and that he was getting wet. The wind squeezed through every crevice, whistling with every new spurt of its energy.

He pulled the coarse blanket up and over his head. It was always like this in bad weather: the rain banging away at the house and the wind helping it through every cranny. Tomorrow the wet patches would be visible on the floor.

He wrapped himself into a tight knot, and waited for the rain and wind to abate. Outside he could hear the tree lashing out and remonstrating against the onslaught of the storm.

And then, suddenly, it happened.

There was a splintering salvo of sound as of a hundred ropes straining to breaking-point and snapping in quick succession. An ear-splitting crash and a sea of crisp and rustling echoes. The house vibrated with a shock and a giant arm tugged at its foundation. It shook, like a startled animal.

Rupert made himself small on his small bed as the tremendous din subsided. Once again, after that awful parenthesis, he could hear the spitting rain slinging its spray through the holes in the house and feel the wind fitfully plucking at the blanket.

A vague nondescript terror chased through his brain-cells and Rupert knew fear.

The silk-cotton tree had fallen!

His mind quaked at the nearness of his escape. Suppose the tree had fallen on the house! He closed his eyes trying to shut out all reality, but reality pursued him.

He had better get up and see what was wrong. He threw one foot from under the blanket and was about to set it on the floor when he heard a noise, a steady trickling sound, outside the front door. What was it?

Fear clutched at the knob of his heart. He remembered the stories of the silk-cotton tree bleeding if you cut its trunk with a knife on Good Friday. Of the tree housing strange spirits at night. Did not some people call it the devil tree?

He remained petrified, his body half in, half out of the bed, not daring to move.

The trickling continued, an untidy scrawl upon his consciousness. Instead of the subdued sound it had been at first, it seemed now to defy the battery of the elements, so clear it was to his ear. He listened, strained his ear to . . .

But now it was changing, he thought. Sounded more like water, didn't it, water running down the muddy gutter that led to the road. Of course it was. What a fool he was, to let the fall of a tree knock his mind askew like that.

He scrambled back on to the bed, still not sure of himself, his eyes staring to catch an answer from the darkness.

But its only answer was the wild tattoo thumped out remorselessly by rain and wind.

When light came through the chinks in the hut, he got up. The early day seemed to sharpen the significance of every object he looked at, everything he touched. His clay pipe looked more dear than ever. His kettle no longer seemed too small for his use. He dressed quickly, untidily, and cautiously opened the door.

He had been visualizing this sight ever since the crash, but his imagination had not done it justice.

To see a tree alive and to see it cut off its legs were vastly different things.

The giant tree had been completely torn from its moorings and now lay across the road like a leviathan on some alien shore. What was once a tidal swirling of leaves and living branches was now a dead sea of foliage. The roots clung to the base of the trunk like twisted snakes caught in a magnificent contortion. The earth yawned around the house and the wooden steps to the front door were knocked askew. Some of the cement supports had been torn from their stance. A little more and the house would have gone!

For some minutes he tried to digest the magnitude of the night's event. This tree had been here since he could remember, had become part of him like a piece of his flesh. He had never imagined life without it no more than you imagine life without your middle finger. But now it was a mere swollen log of wood, and he would have to do without it whether he liked or no. Well, nothing was indispensable. You could always get over its loss. This great wound which the fall of the tree had left gaping in the earth would heal, and time would smooth its skin till you couldn't tell a tree had been there. The wind itself would find another haunt for hide-and-seek. And now that it had gone, strangely enough, he felt something of relief, as if he could breathe a little more freely. Perhaps the tree had kept him too close. Now there would be no more talk of spirits. The tree had done its worst already.

He looked down on it and his thoughts crept back to the past; to the days of its yearly bloom when the wind would pluck its feathery down from the split pods and waft it sailingly away; or when the whole ground beneath it would be strewn with white silk-cotton that had fallen like wool from the branches above. The cotton would make a carpet for feet and he would bundle it up in bags and stuff pillows with it and perhaps sell some cheaply. Now the tree was gone, its majesty reduced to the substance of a corpse.

He raised his eyes from the fallen giant and a distant gleam caught his glance. It was the morning light brightening the sea. He felt a queer compensatory thrill. He had never seen the sea from his little perch of a hut before. The tree had always blotted it out. Now there was a soft sheen lightly spread over the water. A fisherman's boat crossed into view and as slowly went out of sight. He watched it all, feeling an inward stir, as if something was awakening in his breast. I have not lost everything he thought. There is my land, house, unstable now, but I can fix it again.

And there is the sunset which I shall sit and watch this evening; the rain would not have troubled it.

Cecil Gray (*Trinidad*)

Set Down This

Two men climbed the stairs leading up to the restaurant and stood together on the landing looking around. It was peak time they saw, and almost every table was occupied. Lee Yun Kow was hustling his diminutive self from place to place in a flutter of self-importance and the waitresses threw languid, insolent looks at him when he upbraided them for slow movement and not noticing when a customer wanted something.

"Oh, Kow!"

The tall man called peremptorily and some of the people eating raised their heads to look at him. He had a paunch that fitted well with his height and he carried his head tilted slightly backwards. He was dark brown in colour, almost black. The suit he was wearing was well-tailored, grey, and buttoned over his egg-shaped belly. He wore a maroon bow tie.

"Meester Monteil!"

Kow came hurrying up, his face beaming with a professional smile of welcome. He seemed constantly in danger of tripping up over his stumpy legs and falling on his flat, round face. He was in his shirt and pants and had his arms thrown open as he approached.

"Meester Monteil," he said joyfully, "so glad to see you. How you keepin?"

"Kow, I want you to meet a friend of mine," Monteil said with a proud air, as if he were presenting a king. "He's an American. Just come from the States for our famous Trinidad Carnival. Heard so much about it."

Kow bowed and grinned. "Happy to know you," he said. "Always glad when strangers come—specially American. Please to meet you." He kept on grinning broadly and held out his hand with the five, thick fingers pointing in five different directions. The American took the fingers and squeezed them together and Kow chortled in an ecstasy of satisfaction.

"Name's Robinson," the American intoned. "Glad to have met you." He was a little over five feet and very thin. When he smiled, you saw he had a lot of rotten teeth in his mouth. His complexion was a washed-out yellow and his hair woolly. He wore a multi-coloured shirt hanging out of his pants and he had a large signet ring on his right index finger.

"I want you to give us a real good meal," Monteil said. "I've told my friend here all about your little place. Giving him a touch of our local colour. Don't let me down now." Monteil laughed and Kow laughed with him. The American stood by, smiling benignantly.

"You come bad time," Kow said, throwing his eyes around. "Too much clowd."

"What about the room in the corner that I always use?" Monteil asked. "My room—can't we use there?"

Kow's face fell sharply. "Lil bit too late," he mourned apologetically. "Room all full up. Plenty people this time now. Only two table." He pointed. He waited sadly, humbly, while Monteil looked about the place to confirm what he had said.

Monteil was disappointed. He wanted privacy. Kow should know that, he thought. He didn't like this eating out in the open like that—so —so undignified. Especially as he was entertaining a visitor to the island. True, his thoughts ran on, it was only one of those cheap Chinese restaurants on the east side of the city where, as he had already warned Robinson, standards were low wherever you went; still . . . He looked at the American.

"Oh, well," Robison put in, with affable superiority, "if it's all right by you it's all right by me. Anything goes, far as I'm concerned. I'm not fussy. Besides, it gives me more of the local atmosphere—the reel Port-of-Spain. See what I mean?" He chuckled richly.

"Come this way, please." Kow led the way quickly to a table in the middle of the congested floor. Cases of beer and aerated drinks were stacked against the counter and the side of the dirty wall. A loudspeaker emitted harsh jazz music interspersed with commercial announcements in superlative language from a voice with a synthetic foreign accent. Prints of Japanese-looking women hung about the place between advertising posters and calendars. A Chinese cook, clad only in a vest and short khaki pants, crossed before them as they weaved through to the table. Kow said something sharply to him in Chinese. The cook muttered a surly reply and went on, unimpressed.

The table Kow took them to had just been used. Dishes and plates still littered the top. Kow made them sit and went to call one of the girls to attend to them. She was light brown in colour, with fine, bony limbs as if she were underfed. But her breasts were full and pulled up high under her chin and she had crimson lipstick smeared over her lips. As she cleared the table she looked at both of them covertly, measuring their pockets. All around, the voices of the customers rose in loud staccato conversation against the background of the radio programme and the traffic down in the street outside. From one of the cubicles louder noises spilled over as several men speaking together, waged an argument about calypsoes and the year's pick of calypsonians.

The girl cleared the table silently, unhurriedly. Kow had already put in an order for the two men. A spoon fell. And as the girl bent to pick it up Monteil looked deep down into her bosom. He winked at his companion and gave a low whistle of acclamation. The girl glanced at him and when she straightened up he looked straight at her and smiled. She smiled back apathetically, her eyes brightening up a little with the prospect of the heavy tip his smile offered. Kow didn't pay her enough to live on. They all had to rely on tips.

"Nice headlamps you got there," Monteil said and he reached out to hold her hand. The girl laughed indecisively. "What's the charge to use the battery?" Monteil went on. The girl laughed lightly again as if she knew it was expected of her.

"No charge, mister." she said. "Strictly N.F.S." She drew her hand away from his and picked up the tray with the things she was clearing.

"N.F.S.?" Monteil said. "What's that?"

"Not for sale," the girl answered. And she moved away to get the order Kow had put in for them. The form of her body showed clearly beneath the soft dress she was wearing. Robinson and Monteil watched with fixed eyes the play of her hips under the cloth.

"You sure have nice women in this country of yours, Monty," Robinson said laughing. "They got something you don't find up my part of the world."

"Oh, well," Monteil said, becoming serious, "they do have a certain physical attractiveness I admit. But it's their morals that let you down, man. Our local people are too immoral, man. They seem to think only of sex and more sex."

Robinson guffawed. "Can't say as I blame them, boy."

"Take that one, for instance," Monteil went on explaining. "She's not at all above having a little fun, you know. If you bring yourself down to her level. Quite amenable to a suggestion, if you see what I mean. But you've got to keep these local girls in their places. I make a little joke sometimes, I admit, but I never let them get out of hand. They forget themselves. You take it from me, eh. I speak from experience."

Robinson nodded understandingly. "Yeah," he said. "Yeah, I see your point."

The girl came back. Her manner was changed now. She was more frigid. She wasn't smiling any more. It was as if she was advised about something. Her face had taken on the sulky and bored expression characteristic of shop assistants, waitresses and Civil Service clerks. She began to lay the table. Monteil and Robinson watched her arrange the pieces, keeping their eyes fixed on her movements and saying nothing, trying to make her look at them again. They watched her steadily, with unmistakable lust in their eyes. She didn't look up. She kept her mind on what she was doing. When she had finished and was turning to go, Monteil spoke. "Bring the food hot," he said. "Don't let it get cold; I like hot things. How about you?"

She looked down at him coldly. He was smiling blankly up at her. He expected her to giggle a reply. "You look as if you like hot things," he said.

"Anything else?" she said, hardening her lips forward and looking towards the ceiling.

"What about a drink, Monty?" Robinson said. "I could go for a drink before the chow comes."

"Good idea," Monteil said. "How about a Scotch and soda, eh?"

"What's wrong with rum, boy?" Robinson said.

"Oh rum, well to tell you the truth, Robbie, I don't go much for this rum business, especially the local rums we've got here. Give me a Scotch and soda any time." The girl turned her lips up scornfully.

"Well, I ain't got nothing against rum," Robinson retorted. "You can have your whisky. Make mine a rum and ginger. Best drink in the world."

Monteil ordered two rums and ginger and the girl turned abruptly and walked off.

"Just like Trinidad," Monteil commented. "These damn bitches so blasted stupid they don't know when you're trying to be nice to them.

Everywhere it's the same thing. The lower classes are a hostile, resentful lot. You just can' tell how to deal with them."

"We've got the same type back home. It's just a matter of technique. You gotta know how to take them. Never rush things. She don't mean nothing, putting on them airs. She's just as willing as anybody else, believe you me."

Monteil laughed feebly. "I suppose you're right," he said. "It's just that I'm not accustomed to being treated like that—by any of her kind."

They sat waiting for a long time for the food to come. They saw the girl passing up and down attending to other people, but when Robinson asked her about their meal she answered curtly that it wasn't ready. Twice afterwards they asked her to bring drinks and they sat there drinking and talking until the food came.

Robinson was enthusiastic about Wan Tung soup and the fried rice, but he didn't like the Chop Suey half as much as he said. It was too slimy. Monteil asked him whether he had eaten callaloo. He said he didn't know what the hell that was. And they laughed and went on talking about Carnival and the calypso tent, the steel band and the girls you can get at the night clubs on Wrightson Road. Robinson wanted a cigarette. He had run out of weeds he said. And Monteil called out to the girl to bring a pack of American cigarettes.

"What kind you got?" Robinson asked him.

"Oh, what I have on me is something they make here, local stuff," Monteil answered. "I don't suppose you'll like it. It can't be compared with your American cigarettes."

Robinson sniggered a denial.

"You Americans are tops in everything boy," Monteil said, "No foolin'."

Robinson laughed and took one of the cigarettes Monteil had.

The girl came up with the cigarettes and when Monteil told her that he didn't want them any more she sucked her teeth loudly and muttered something under her breath.

"Don't take it so hard, Cutie," Robinson said reaching over and passing his hand along her arm.

"My name isn't Cutie," she said, and she moved his hand away from caressing her arm.

"Then what is your name?" Monteil directed at her leaning back in his chair and surveying her body like a slave dealer. He looked haughty and offensive.

"That is my business," she snapped at him quietly. "You better don't ask me anyting. You is one o' those who feel they white, you know. If you was even an American like this gentleman here it wouldn't be so bad. But you is a Trinidadian just like me an' you blacker than me, so what you playin'?"

Monteil was upset. He didn't lean back any more. He groped for a rebuttal but the attack was too unexpected. He didn't know what to say. He knew he had to say something.

"Come on, come on," Robinson admonished, forcing a placating smile to lessen the embarrassment. He smiled, and smiled, showing the girl all his decaying teeth. "That's no way to behave."

"I can't say that I like the tone of your remarks," Monteil managed to bring out. "I don't like it at all."

The girl gave a mocking laugh. It was a laugh of one who was fed up and didn't care any more. "Do what you like," she said. "All you could do is make me lose the job. But the job ain' so rosy, so what. Is only a stinkin' ten shillin' a week they payin' to run up and down here whole day."

"I think you're definitely getting out of line," Monteil said, feeling his way and trying to avoid another onslaught.

"If you don't want me to get out of line you stay in line yourself," was her rejoinder, but she nearly said it pleasantly. Robinson gave her a quick look.

"Look, let's stop all this line business," he said. "What the heck is this place anyway, a telephone exchange?"

Monteil simpered at the strained joke. The girl laughed openly as if nothing had happened. A waitress over at the kitchen window bawled, "Marjorie!" The girl turned and screamed in answer, "Uh comin'!" Then she turned to the two men and said easily she'd bring the bill in a while if they didn't want anything else. She went over to the kitchen entrance.

"I don't know how to take her," Monteil said in a baffled tone. "I just can't understand it."

"She likes you, Monty," Robinson said. "That girl sure likes you."

"Ah, go on, Robbie. Stop pulling my legs," Monteil said, searching Robinson's countenance. He wasn't sure Robinson meant to be taken seriously.

"I mean it," Robinson said. "I really do. I've seen women blaze up like that before and I know what it means. It means you haven't been paying her sufficient attention. She feels like a woman scorned."

"You think so?" Monteil said, grasping quickly at the relief.

"I'm absolutely certain, my boy."

"But, she hasn't been here long, I'm sure. I think I've seen her somewhere else before," Monteil said.

"You have?" Robinson drawled.

"Yeah, I'm almost certain . . . somewhere . . . could be one of the clubs," Monteil tried to remember.

"You mean she's a prostitute or . . . or . . . something like that? Trying to go straight? They never succeed. They always go back." Robinson dismissed the idea with a wave of his hand.

"The fact is I never really noticed her. I just knew she was there," Monteil explained.

"That's just it, man. You probably looked through her without seeing her. A woman can't stand that no time. Worse luck if it's a man she wants to notice her."

"I'm not so sure you know, Bob, but you may be right. In fact, that will explain the whole damn unpleasant business."

The girl returned. She put the bill down on the table between them and held the metal tray in front of her respectfully. Monteil was digging into his pocket for the money.

"I have a feeling you really like this guy," Robinson addressed her.

"Who? Me? Never happen," she answered. "Where you get that idea from?"

"Oh, let's say I got it from experience. I know women," Robinson said with good-humoured confidence.

Monteil put the money with the bill on the table and the girl took them up and put them into the tray she was holding. "You only think you know women," she said to Robinson, moving off to go to the cashier to discharge the bill.

"No doubt about it," Robinson declared to Monteil when she left. "You could see it in her face. She wouldn't look at you at all. And you heard how she answered?"

Monteil laughed with quick elation. He laughed a light bubbly laugh as if someone were tickling him. He was very flattered.

"I guess there must be something in what you say," he said securely. "I have an idea. I think I'll put your theory to the test when she comes back with the change." He was leaning back again. The girl was approaching.

"Don't be too rash now," Robinson said, but Monteil didn't hear. He was looking at the girl walking between the tables towards them. He looked at the swing of her hips with a sly smile playing around his mouth.

She put down the tray with the change flat on the table and remained holding it with a bored air, waiting. Monteil leaned over slowly and picked up the coins one by one. "Have this for yourself," he said, putting a shilling on the table on the side away from the girl. He pretended he had done it absent-mindedly. He was over the table with his elbows far forward on it. Displeased but grateful, the girl stretched over the table for the coin, and Monteil brought up his hand and brushed her bosom as she bent over. The girl stiffened and looked at him to see whether it was an accident. Monteil had a conceited smirk spread all over his face. "No hard feelings," he said, looking directly at her, his fingers drumming a tattoo on the tablecloth.

The girl slammed the tin tray down hard on the table. "Cut that damn stupidness out!" she cried hotly and loudly. "Don't play the fool wid me, you hear!"

Monteil lost colour beneath his dark skin. He looked hastily around. The restaurant was almost empty now. He was glad about that but the few eaters and two of the waitresses were looking in his direction. The girl was going on loudly.

"What the hell you come touching me up for? What you take me for? I ain' no prostitute, nuh. Because you see me working here now you think you could play monkey wid me? I don' stand no blasted nonsense. My days for that done. So you better know yuh place." Robinson had risen. "Look, look, calm down now, calm down," he said. "You don't do nobody no good by blowing off the top. My buddy was only making a little joke, only tryin' to be friendly like. No reason to make a scene. Be a good girl now. Forget it."

Kow came hustling up looking alarmed. "What happen Meester Monteil? What happen this girl?"

Monteil rose. He drew himself up like one affronted. He threw his head back further than usual. "These uncouth niggers you employ here, Kow. I've told you already if you want to keep your good customers you must not employ these impudent girls. You can't expect people to come to your place to be disrespected, and with a visitor too, besides. It just isn't done, Kow. You'll have to do better than that."

Kow gabbled how sorry he was. He promised it would never happen again. The girl made an attempt to butt in. "The man insult me first," she said. Kow shut her up.

"You fire," he said to her. "I pay you now and you go. You fire. An' you no get no work any more restaurant at all. I tell all 'bout you. You fire. Go!"

The girl screamed a filthy word at Monteil, swung her chin in an arch away from them and walked off, tugging at the apron tied around her. "Better I go back right where I come from," she said. "No man ain' go insult me and get away with it."

Kow went on apologizing while Monteil and Robinson made their way like monarchs to the head of the stairway, Monteil accepting Kow's assurances and revealing by his manner that he had forgiven him. Kow was pleased. Monteil was pleased. Robinson was very pleased.

When they returned to the sunshine and the smelly street, Robinson chided Monteil that he ought not to have taken a chance like that; that he was too rash. Monteil dismissed all blame. "Black people are all alike," he said. "You give them an inch, they take an ell. Forget that, Robbie. That's all past and dead as far as I am concerned. Let's talk about the future. Tonight we take in the calypso tent. Is that down on the programme?"

"Okay," Robinson said. "Okay. Fine."

And as they wound their way between the shifting pedestrians along the narrow pavement, Monteil was carrying his head held high and tilted slightly backwards.

BIOGRAPHICAL NOTES

V. S. NAIPAUL
 TRINIDAD (1932). Educated at Queen's Royal College, Trinidad, and at University
 College, Oxford.
 Novels: *The Mystic Masseur; The Suffrage of Elvira; Miguel Street* (Collected Short
 Stories); *A House for Mr. Biswas; Mr. Stone and The Knights Companion*
 Non-Fiction: *The Middle Passage; An Area of Darkness*
 Prizes and Awards: John Llewellyn Rhys Memorial Prize; Trinidad Fellowship; Somerset
 Maugham Award; Phoenix Trust Award; Hawthornden Prize

SAMUEL SELVON
 TRINIDAD (1923). Educated in Trinidad.
 Novels: *A Brighter Sun; An Island is a World; The Lonely Londoners; Turn Again, Tiger;
 I hear Thunder; The Housing Lark* (Coming)
 Short Stories: *Ways of Sunlight*
 Awards: Guggenhem Fellowship; Society of Authors Travelling Award; Trinidad
 Fellowship

R. O. ROBINSON
 JAMAICA (1930). Educated at Calabar College, Jamaica, and at Trinity College, Cam-
 bridge. Professor of Mathematics, University of Ife, Nigeria.
 Short Stories: Broadcast on the B.B.C.

DONALD HINDS
 JAMAICA (1934). Educated in Jamaica.
 Short Stories: Broadcast on the B.B.C.
 Articles: *The Observer*

H. ORLANDO PATTERSON
 JAMAICA (1940) Educated at Kingston College, Jamaica, University College of the
 West Indies, and London School of Economics.
 Novel: *The Children of Sisyphus*

MICHAEL ANTHONY
 TRINIDAD (1932) Educated in Trinidad.
 Novels: *The Games Were Coming; The Year in San Fernando* (Coming)

C. L. R. JAMES
 TRINIDAD (1901). Educated at Queen's Royal College, Trinidad.
 Novel: *Minty Alley*
 Non-Fiction: *The Life of Captain Cipriani; The Case for West Indian Self-Government;
 World Revolution: the Rise and Fall of the Communist International; The Black Jacobins;
 The History of Negro Revolt; Mariners, Renegades and Castaways; Party Politics in the
 West Indies; Beyond a Boundary*
 A Play: *Toussaint L'Ouverture*

JOHN HEARNE
 JAMAICA (Born in Canada, 1926). Educated at Jamaica College, Edinburgh University,
 and London University.
 Novels: *Voices Under the Window; Stranger at the Gate; The Faces of Love; The Autumn
 Equinox; Land of the Living*
 Non-Fiction: *Contrasts* (with Rex Nettleford)
 Prize: John Llewellyn Rhys Memorial Prize

GEORGE LAMMING

BARBADOS (1927). Educated in Barbados.
Poetry: *Swans* (P.E.N. *New Poems*, 1952)
Novels: *In the Castle of My Skin; The Emigrants; Of Age and Innocence; Season of Adventure*
Non-Fiction: *The Pleasures of Exile*
Awards: Guggenheim Fellowship; Somerset Maugham Award; Canada Council Fellowship

JAN CAREW

BRITISH GUIANA (1922). Educated at Berbice High School, British Guiana, Howard University and Prague University.
Novels: *Black Midas; The Wild Coast; The Last Barbarian*
Non-Fiction: *Moscow is not my Mecca*

CLAUDE THOMPSON

JAMAICA (1907). Educated at Wolmers School, Jamaica.
Short Stories: *These My People*
Non-Fiction: *A Foot in Jamaica* (in preparation)

EDGAR MITTELHOLZER

BRITISH GUIANA (1909). Educated at Berbice High School, British Guiana, and privately.
Novels: *Corentyne Thunder; A Morning at the Office; Shadows Move Among Them; Children of Kaywana; The Weather at Middenshot; The Life and Death of Sylvia; The Harrowing of Hubertus; The Adding Machine; My Bones and My Flute; Of Trees and the Sea; A Tale of Three Places; Kaywana Blood; The Weather Family; A Tinkling in the Twilight; Latticed Echoes; Eltonsbrody; Thunder Returning; The Mad MacMullochs; The Piling of Clouds; The Wounded and the Worried; Uncle Paul*
Non-Fiction: *With A Carib Eye* (Travel); *A Swarthy Boy* (Autobiography)
Award: Guggenheim Fellowship

DENIS WILLIAMS

BRITISH GUIANA (1923). Educated in British Guiana and England. Novelist and Painter. Former Lecturer at the Central School of Art, Holborn, Visiting Tutor at the Slade School of Fine Art, and Former Lecturer in Fine Art, Khartoum Technical Institute. Now Research Fellow at the Institute of African Studies, University of Ife, Nigeria.
Novel: *Other Leopards*

O. R. DATHORNE

BRITISH GUIANA (1934). Educated in British Guiana, at Sheffield University and London University. Now Lecturer in English and African Literature at Ibadan University, Nigeria.
Novels: *Dumplings in the Soup; The Scholar-man; One Iota of Difference* (Coming)
Non-Fiction: *An Anthology of West Indian Prose* (Coming); *A Comparative Study of West Indian and West African Writing* (Coming)

EDWARD BRAITHWAITE

BARBADOS (1930). Educated in Barbados and at Pembroke College, Cambridge. Lecturer in History at the University of the West Indies.
Short Stories: Broadcast on the B.B.C.
Poetry: Broadcast on the B.B.C.

A. N. FORDE

BARBADOS (1923). Educated in Barbados and at London University. Former Grammar School Master in Tobago and Grenada. Now Permanent Secretary in the Ministry of Education, Barbados.
Short Stories: Broadcast on the B.B.C.

CECIL GRAY

TRINIDAD (1923). Lecturer in Education at The University of the West Indies.
Short Stories: Broadcast on the B.B.C.